IMAGES
of America

MAHANOY AREA REVISITED

ON THE COVER: SCHUYLKILL COUNTY FIREMEN'S CONVENTION. Seen here is the Schuylkill County Firemen's Convention held in Mahanoy City on October 7–8, 1960. The downtown section of Mahanoy City used to be bustling with activity. Numerous stores, restaurants, and businesses could be found up and down Centre Street. Cars lined the blocks as families went about doing their shopping. It was not necessary to leave town since everything needed could be found right here. (Tim Zoba.)

IMAGES
of America

MAHANOY AREA REVISITED

Mahanoy Area Historical Society

ARCADIA
PUBLISHING

ISBN 978-0-7385-9904-5

Published by Arcadia Publishing
Charleston, South Carolina

Printed in the United States of America

Library of Congress Control Number: 2012951109

For all general information contact Arcadia Publishing at:
Telephone 843-853-2070
Fax 843-853-0044
E-mail sales@arcadiapublishing.com
For customer service and orders:
Toll-Free 1-888-313-2665

Visit us on the Internet at www.arcadiapublishing.com

CONTENTS

ACKNOWLEDGMENTS

The Mahanoy Area Historical Society MHS has flourished since its inception in 1998. As the town approached its 150th anniversary, the historical society took on the task of writing a sequel to our history, Images of America: *Mahanoy Area*. To gather original photographs for the Images of America series was a task only accomplished by scores of people hunting in closets and boxes. Their effort mandated that we thank them individually as follows: Diane Ambrose (DA) Andrea Schlosser Bashore (ASB), Marle Becker (MB), Carol Koval Blue (CKB), Ken and Michelle Boyle (KMB), Francis Brennan (FB), the Brill family (BF), Patricia Brown (PB), Melina Capitanio (MC), Monica M. Capone (MMC), Francis Chesko (FC) Nancy Truskowsky Cohn (NTC), Don Coombe (DC), Paul Coombe (PC), Barbara Nolter Dereskavich (BND), Kathleen McGroarty Erbe (KME), Ann Marie Kaczmarczyk Evans (AKE), Joseph Swing Flamini (JSF), Marjorie Fletcher (MF), Rose Durkin Fletcher (RDF), Dr. Joseph Glaudel (DJG), Joan Goodman (JG), Betty Goodolf (BG), Janet Klees Gore (JKG), Peg Grigalonis (PGG), Marylou Henninger (MLH), Cheryl Herring (CH), Antoinette Wufsus Houser (AWH), Joseph Jordan (JJ), Michael Kaczmarczyk (MK), Dennis Kinsinger (DK), Janet Schock Kline (JSK), Dr. John Kubert (DJK), Frank Lashinsky (FL), Alvin Luschas (AL), Elaine Mack Luschas (EML), Mahanoy Area Historical Society (MHS), Mahanoy City Public Library (MCPL) Anna G. Markey (AGM), Virginia Mammarella Martin (VMM), Joseph Matalavage (JMA), John McCloskey (JMcC), Arlene Murphy (AM), John Murtin (JM), Maria Luschas Oien (MLO), Order of St. Francis (OSF), Mary Ellen Roberts Peel (MERP), Shirley Thomas Ryan (STR), St. Paul's Church (SPC) Cynthia Beynon Sakshaug (CBS), Frank A. Selgrath (FAS), Frank Senglar (FS), James Setcavage (JS), James Shaup (JSH), the Skeath family (SK), Mary Ellen Koval-Steeves (MEKS), Stony Brook University Special Collections Libraries, (SBU-SCL) Edward Surfield (ES), Elsie Tolan (ET), Joe Buddy Tomko (JBT), Thomas Ward Sr. (TW), Florence Wellington (FW), Ruth Hart Wildoner (RHW), Thomas Whalen (TWH), Jeanne Burke Woody (JBW), and Tim Zoba (TZ.).

Special thanks go to caption writers Peg Guinan Grigalonis, Paul Coombe, Alvin Luschas, Elaine (Mack) Luschas, and Marylou (Wellington) Henninger; Frank Selgrath, chief research assistant and photograph resource; Shirley Ryan and Peg Coombe, editors and photograph resource; Alvin Luschas, legal consultant; Janet Klees Gore, for her donation of the Maurice Pedriani Photography Collection to the Mahanoy Area Historical Society; Mary Ambrose, Mahanoy City Photo Studio; Janet Schock Kline, Bill Miles Collection; and Charlie Palulis.

INTRODUCTION

By 1913, as our story begins, Mahanoy City was a bustling town filled with immigrants escaping poverty or persecution. Merchants, professionals, and accomplished craftsmen came to embark on business ventures in this newest boomtown. A coal-mining town was built, like most cities, beginning from the middle business district out to the surrounding residential areas. Space to build on was scarce because valuable coal was in veins underground in the surrounding mountains.

In Mahanoy City, the downtown area was eight blocks from east to west and two blocks from north to south. Properties in the business district were constructed side by side, at least three stories high. Most buildings, even in the business district, were wooden, with high ceilings with accompanying high steps. In this section of town were many retail stores, professional offices, theaters, hotels, and most of the churches. Every space on every floor was occupied. Retail space was on ground level, and professional offices were located one or two floors above. A trip to the dentist was a climb up narrow, dark steps, which only added anxiety to the dreaded appointment. The business owners and professionals tended to live in this part of town. Their homes were the earliest to sit on paved streets and to include indoor plumbing and centralized heat powered by automatic stokers.

Surrounding the business area were the neighborhoods of wooden structures. With land becoming scarce, almost all residence lots were 12.5 feet wide. Homes were two or three rooms deep and three stories high. Most did not have running water and were heated with a bucket-a-day or a Heatrola. Heat rose to the bedrooms through open vents in the floors. Gradually, by the 1950s, most homes had indoor plumbing and central heat.

Although homes had more land, patch life was more difficult. Construction was wooden double side-by-side homes where two families lived. Small yards surrounded the double homes, and in the rear were outhouses. Many homes were company homes, and the tenants paid rent. Trains, trolleys, buses, or factory trucks provided transportation to employment for those not working in the nearby mines.

Along with merchants, professionals, and craftsmen came musicians and writers. There were men and women who sang and wrote about their pasts, their futures, and their town. Augusta Dillman Thomas, daughter of early settlers, wrote the history of Mahanoy City. Arthur Lewis wrote fact and fiction, both based on his hometown region and the history contained in its newspaper pages. Composing Oscar-winning music (for best score) was Victor Schertzinger, a Mahanoy City native. Michael Slowitzky, another Mahanoy City native, wrote the No. 1 Billboard hit "Once in a While." Our high schools had accomplished bands, vocalists, and thespians performing under the watchful eyes of teachers devoted to the arts. Bill O'Brien and John "Puck" Sullivan wrote stories and sang songs in the best tradition of Irish storytellers.

As we gathered our photographs for this book, we found that we told the story in words that we had discovered in our fantastic pictures. For a moment, let Puck Sullivan, Mahanoy's "Memory Man," take you back to his younger days at about the age that our story begins.

In Reminiscing with Puck, our thoughts go to the lost landmarks of youth including the train stations of both the Reading and Lehigh Railroads. The trains were the main means of getting around both far and near. Folks could board the trains to head to the big cities of Philadelphia or New York. The tunnel was part of the trip if you were headed to Lakewood or Lakeside. As Puck describes it, "A minute or two of pitch black darkness that seemed an hour while your nostrils stung from the sulfurous black engine smoke." At the end of the Mahanoy Tunnel, however, one was rewarded with a joyful time at the lake. We swam, picnicked, and met with friends to ride the rides as well as watch numerous plays and musicals at the Lakewood Playhouse. The Lakewood Ballroom was home to many famous entertainers, some of whom are featured in this publication. In addition, fond thoughts of prom night at the Lakewood Ballroom cannot be erased from our memories.

Our town and surrounding communities or patches were blessed with competitive and talented athletes. The town celebrated as the 1922 Mahanoy City High School basketball team won the state high school championship. We celebrated also with the success of such athletes as George Senesky, Jack McCloskey, John Sluzevich, Joe Matalavage, Joe Boley, Joe Dugan, and Jack Picus Quinn. Celebrate their accomplishments as you read and look at their photographs.

Who could forget hanging out "over town, downtown, or uptown" depending on where in Mahanoy City you resided? Remember George's, Gus's Embassy Grill, the Mansion Coffee Shop, Woolworth's, Newberry's, Timm's Drugstore, Guinan's, and countless other stores and restaurants too numerous to mention? Remember going into various stores on Saturday to pay the clubs or play the "pools" hoping for a win? Let this book take you back to those long-past days of joy in our beloved town.

It was not all fun. Young citizens in our town and nearby patches went to war, and many were lost. In this book, we have attempted to show respect and gratitude for the sacrifices made during those years. Women contributed to the home front effort during World War I. They came together to become surgical dressing workers as well as members of the American Red Cross. They raised money and helped outfit our soldiers by using their sewing skills. One of our native sons, Sgt. Harold Messerschmidt of Grier City, gave his life and was awarded the Congressional Medal of Honor for his heroic actions during World War II. Our town celebrated the return of Stephen Gavula when the prisoner of war returned home from Korea to his family.

Our churches and synagogue were gathering places for families and friends. Many of them have long since closed, and the buildings stand empty in tribute to a time when they brought solace and fellowship to many.

An integral part of any community is its schools. Numerous schools contributed to the education of the youth of our area. Public schools were found both in Mahanoy City and the surrounding patches. Mahanoy Township High School operated from 1918 to 1959. Mahanoy City High School existed from 1864 to 1959. In 1960, a consolidation of the local high schools resulted in the current Mahanoy Area High School. In addition to the public school systems, the Catholic churches in the area also had schools associated with them. The ethnic schools were begun by German, Irish, Lithuanian, Polish, and Slovak descendants and took a burden off the public schools.

Our book committee has compiled a photographic history of our area covering the years 1913–1963. We hope that you find it interesting and that it brings back memories of a time gone by. We are grateful to all of the friends of the historical society who shared their photographs and memories with us throughout the writing of this book.

One

EAST SIDE, WEST SIDE

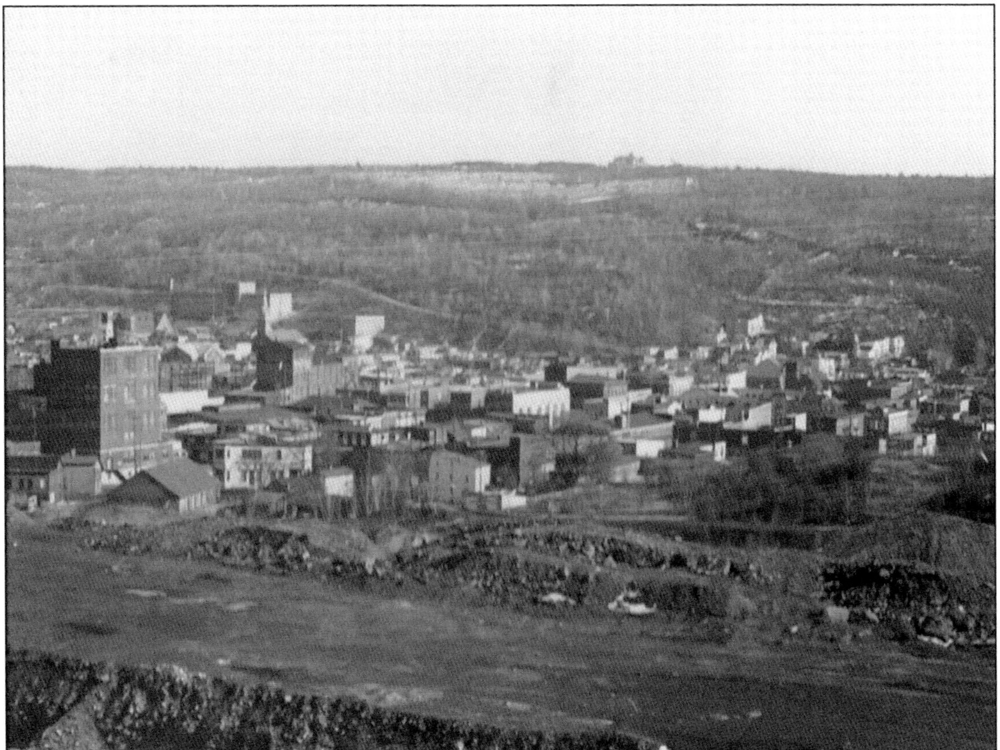

MAHANOY CITY VIEW. Mahanoy City is one mile long, divided into east and west by Main Street, and bordered by coal banks on both sides. By 1913, the east end was home to immigrants from the British Isles and Germany. The west end housed Eastern Europeans, who settled around their churches. (JKG.)

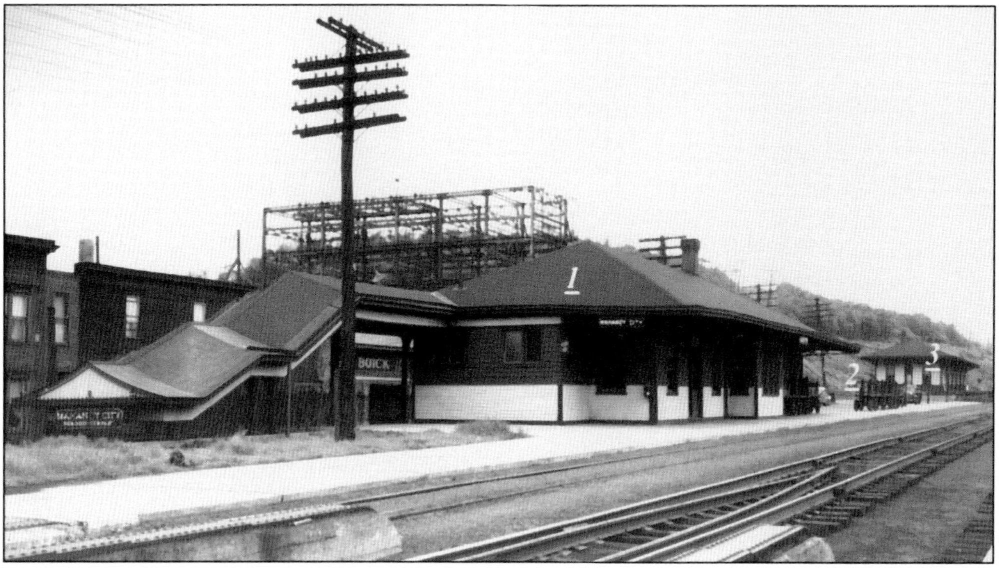

Reading Railroad Station. The railroad serving Mahanoy City was completed to and through the Mahanoy Tunnel in 1863. The impetus for the railroad was to carry coal from the anthracite mountains to the industrial centers. This photograph was taken in the 1940s and shows, in numerical order, the passenger station, the carts for luggage, and the freight station. The last passenger train came to Mahanoy City in 1963, some 100 years after the first. (JKG.)

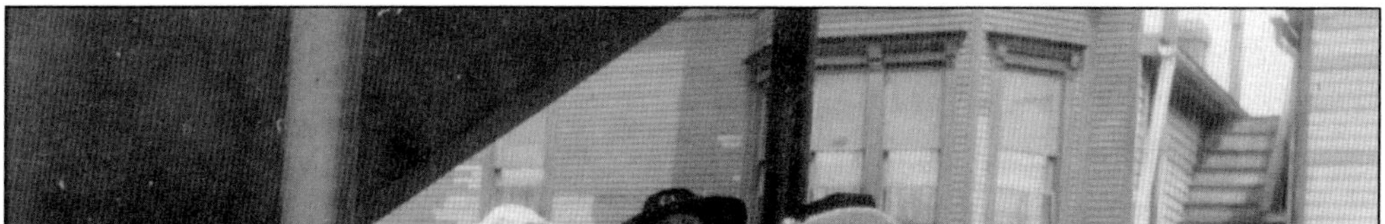

Reading Station, 1916. Three stylish McCarthy sisters wait with their leather cases for the train to New York. The coal regions had excellent train service to and from the big cities. Victor Herbert and John Philip Sousa came by train to perform at Kaier Opera House and the Victoria Theater. Piano teachers from Philadelphia traveled to town weekly. European-born and -trained musicians, craftsmen, and professionals lived in the community with struggling miners. (JBW.)

VISITING NURSE ASSOCIATION. By 1914, a group of medical professionals and interested citizens formed the Visiting Nurse Association, with the following motto: "No one in Mahanoy City should die neglected." A tag drive raised enough money to hire one nurse. In the first year, almost 2,000 visits were made to 250 patients. Pictured are Pauline Kistler Reed (right), a visiting nurse in Mahanoy City from 1923 until her retirement, and her mother-in-law, Julia Reed, a member of Mahanoy City Borough Council. (FAS.)

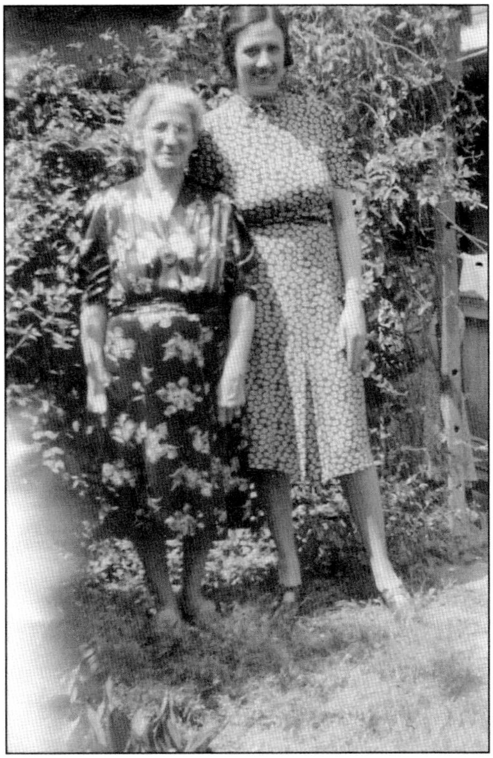

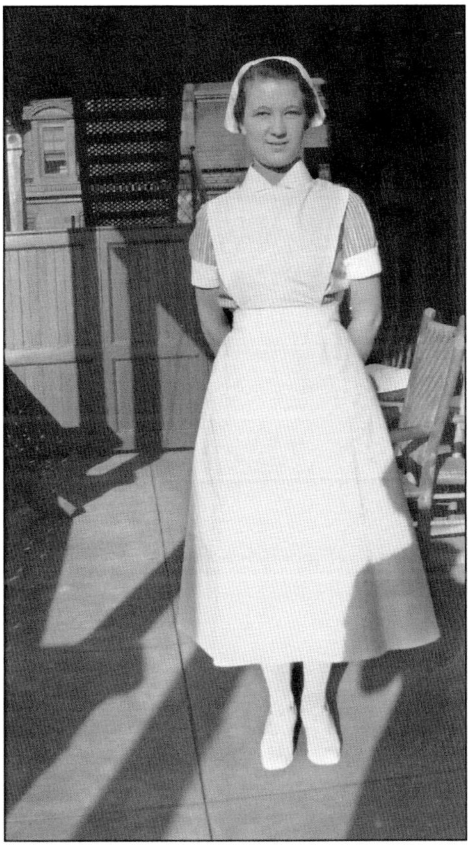

VISITING NURSE. In addition to home visits and insurance checkups, the Visiting Nurse Association ran baby clinics, educated young mothers, and administered antitoxins against diphtheria beginning in 1923. Elizabeth Fox (pictured) graduated from nursing school in 1938 and began her service as a visiting nurse soon afterwards. (CH.)

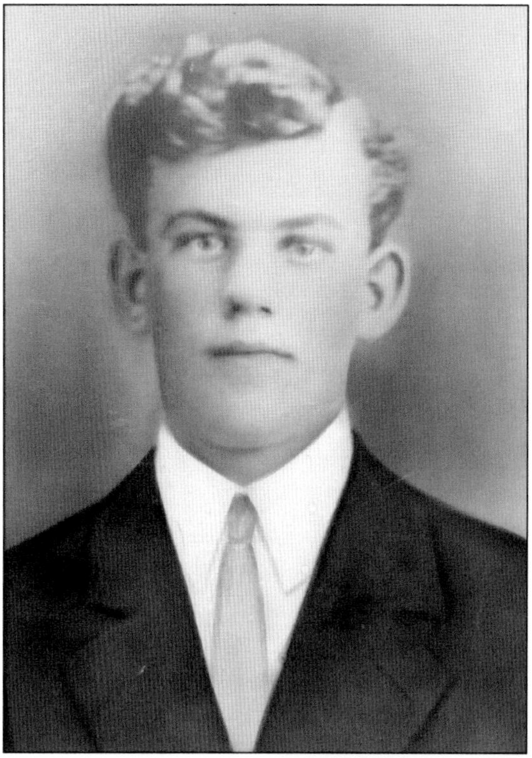

INFLUENZA EPIDEMIC. The Spanish flu struck Mahanoy City swiftly in 1918. Healthy young men, like 20-year-old John Turik (pictured) died, as well as hundreds more. The recently organized American Red Cross, joined by the Boy Scouts, town doctors, and railroad and school personnel, cared for the hundreds of critically ill; public buildings including churches were closed; the high school became the hospital, and the junior high school became the morgue. (AL.)

GEORGE'S CONFECTIONERY. This popular handmade-candy and soda shop was in operation from 1902 to the 1960s. For as long as it existed, teens, entitled to sit there with the purchase of a 10¢ soda, hung out in the booths. The real fame of the shop was its assortment of candies. At Easter, children in town received a coconut or buttercream egg covered in dark chocolate with the child's name written with icing on top. (MHS.)

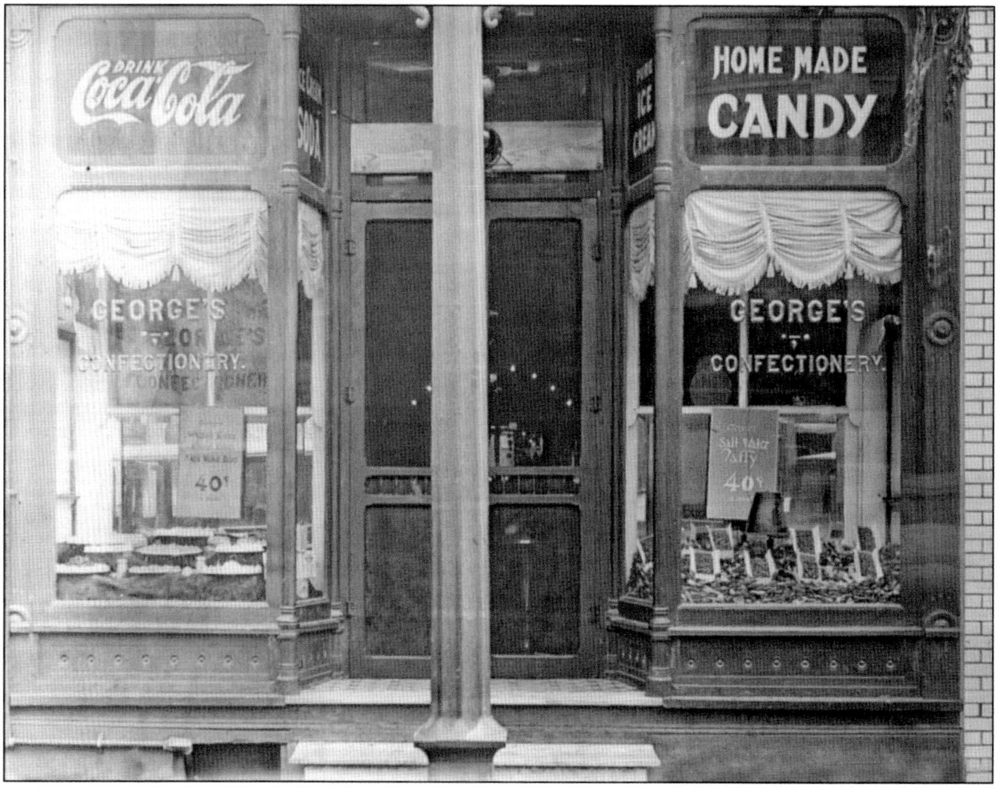

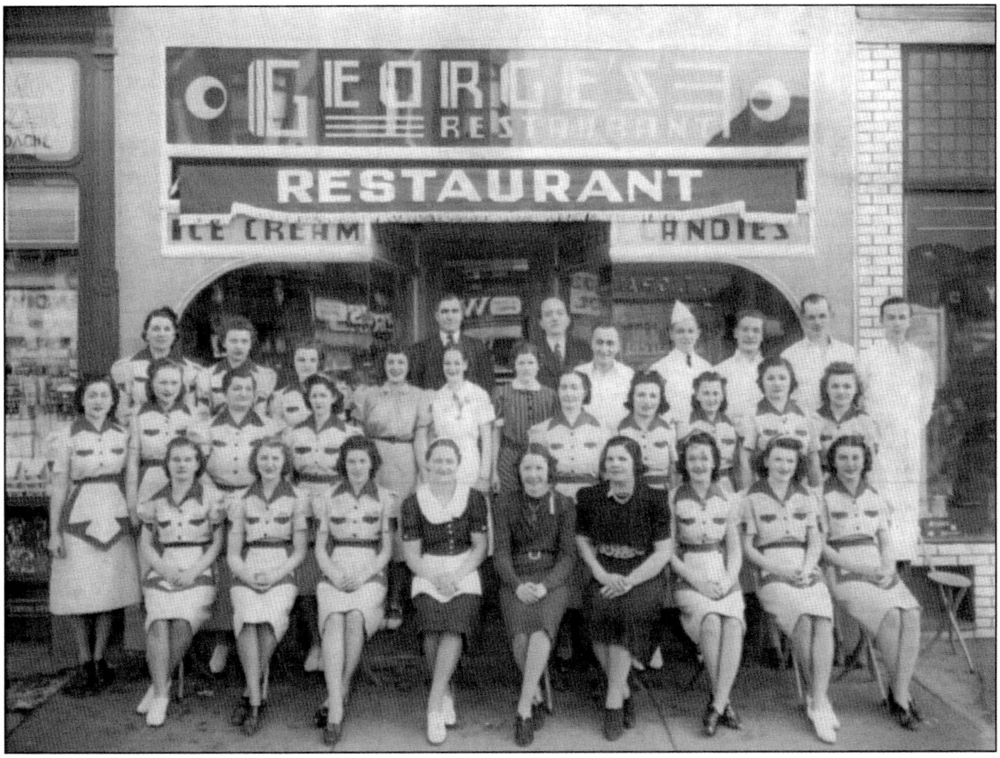

GEORGE'S CONFECTIONERY. The 30-plus uniformed employees worked at making candy, serving at the counter, or waiting on booth customers. In this 15-foot-wide store, there was a soda fountain counter with short stools on the west side, large glass-enclosed cabinets filled with candy on the east side, seasonal candy down the center aisle cases, and four rows of wooden booths across the back. (MHS.)

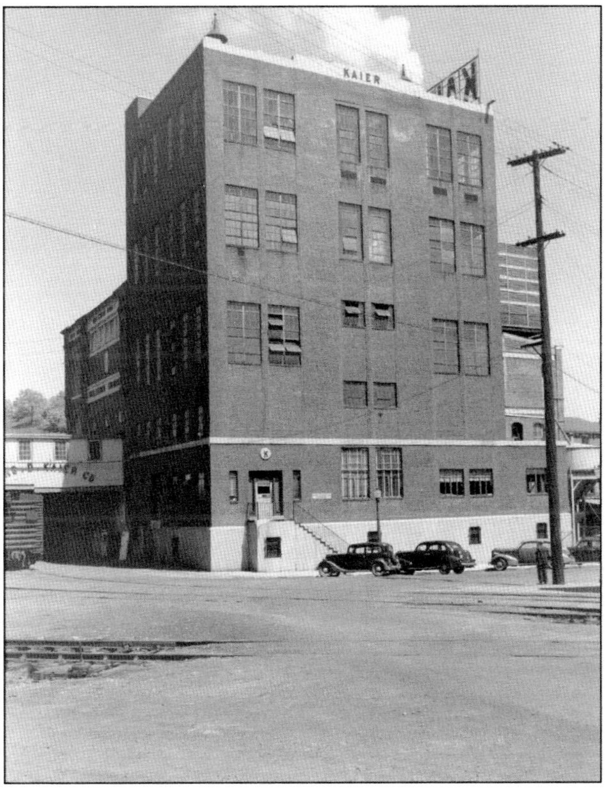

KAIER BREWERY. The Chas. D. Kaier Company was founded in 1862 and continued in operation for over 100 years. The first Kaier Brewery was built in 1880 and expanded in 1892. The building pictured was dedicated in 1937. At its peak in the late 1940s, Kaier Brewery produced over 200,000 barrels of beer annually. The company was sold to Ortlieb's Brewery in 1966. (JKG.)

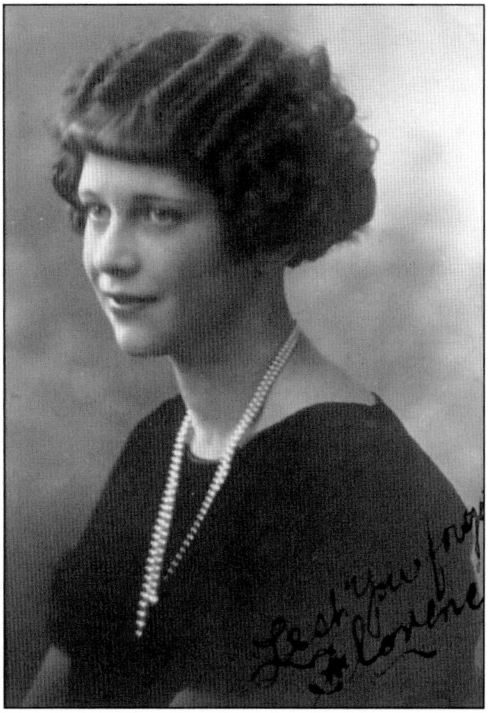

Florence (née Sullivan) Kubert, 1929. The war was over, and women were buoyed by the passage of the women's right-to-vote amendment. Skirts were shorter, and so were the hairstyles. Pictured is Florence Sullivan, voted Miss Mahanoy City by the Personality Boys in St. Fidelis Hall in 1929. The future Mrs. Kubert, mother of Jack, makes quite an impression in her marcel wave, or finger wave, hair. (DJK.)

Union National Bank. Founded in 1889, the Union National Bank erected this building in 1930 on the corner of Main and Centre Streets in Mahanoy City. Through the bank crisis of the 1930s and beyond, the Union retained its name until 1964, when it became the Pennsylvania National Bank. A bank is still located there today, but now under the name M&T; it is the only bank in Mahanoy City. (MCPL.)

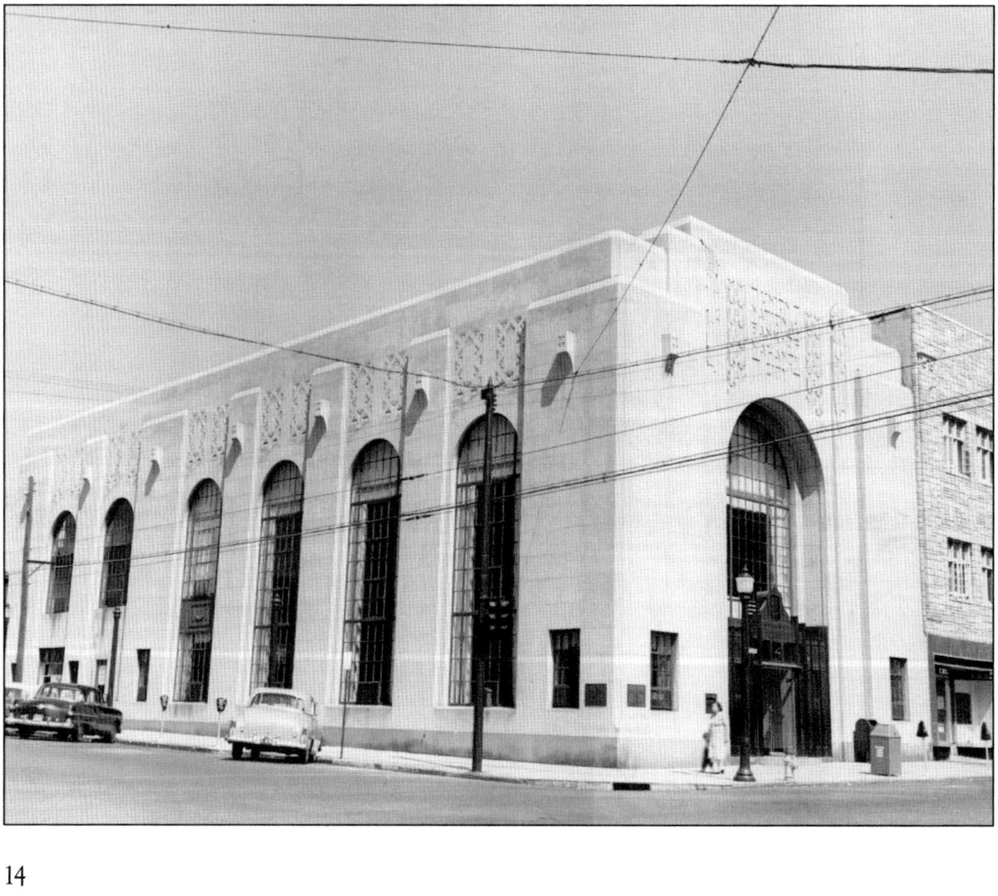

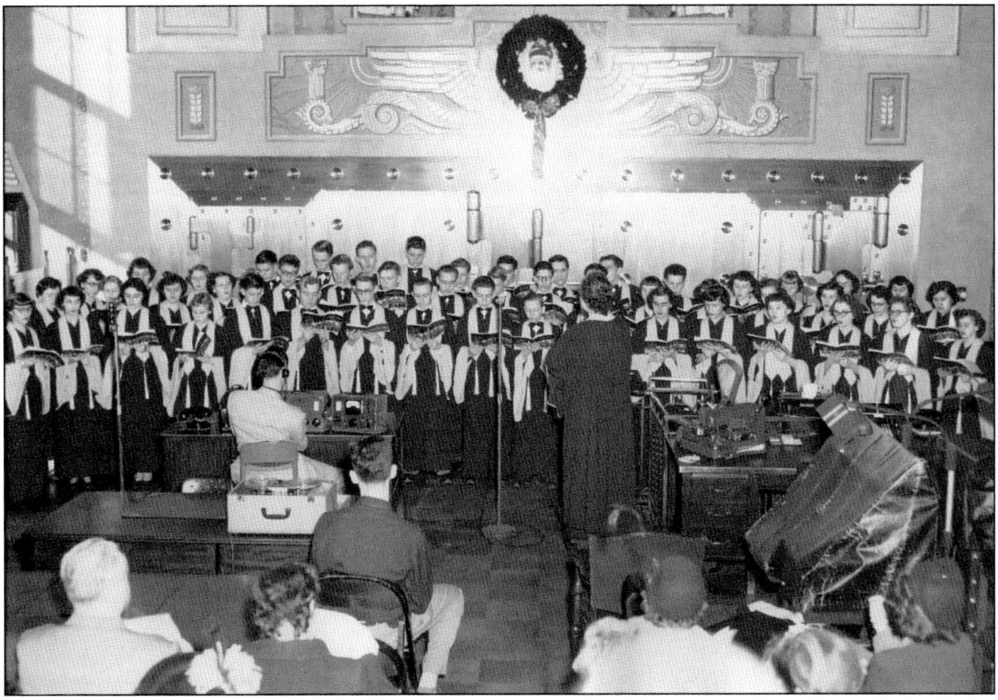

CHRISTMAS CONCERT. Each year, under the direction of Estella M. Barnhart, the Mahanoy City High School choir performed at the Union National Bank and was broadcast on local radio. For their efforts, the choir members were given a crisp $1 bill. Pictured here is the choir of 1950 with the broadcasting equipment and audience in the foreground. (MHS.)

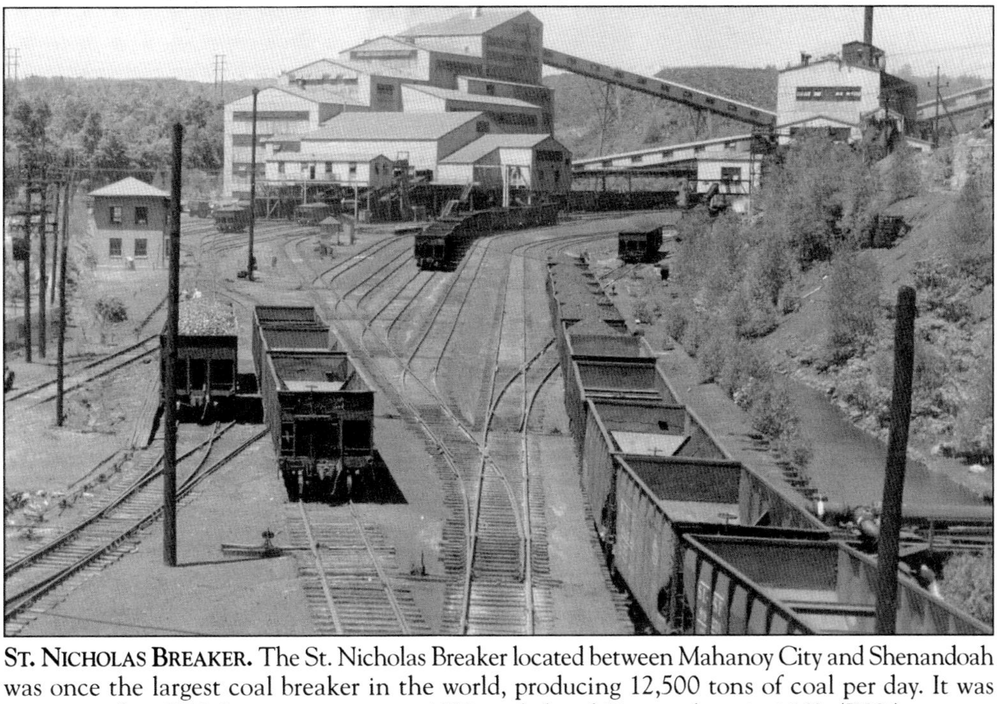

ST. NICHOLAS BREAKER. The St. Nicholas Breaker located between Mahanoy City and Shenandoah was once the largest coal breaker in the world, producing 12,500 tons of coal per day. It was constructed in 1930, began operating in 1932, and closed 31 years later in 1963. (JKG.)

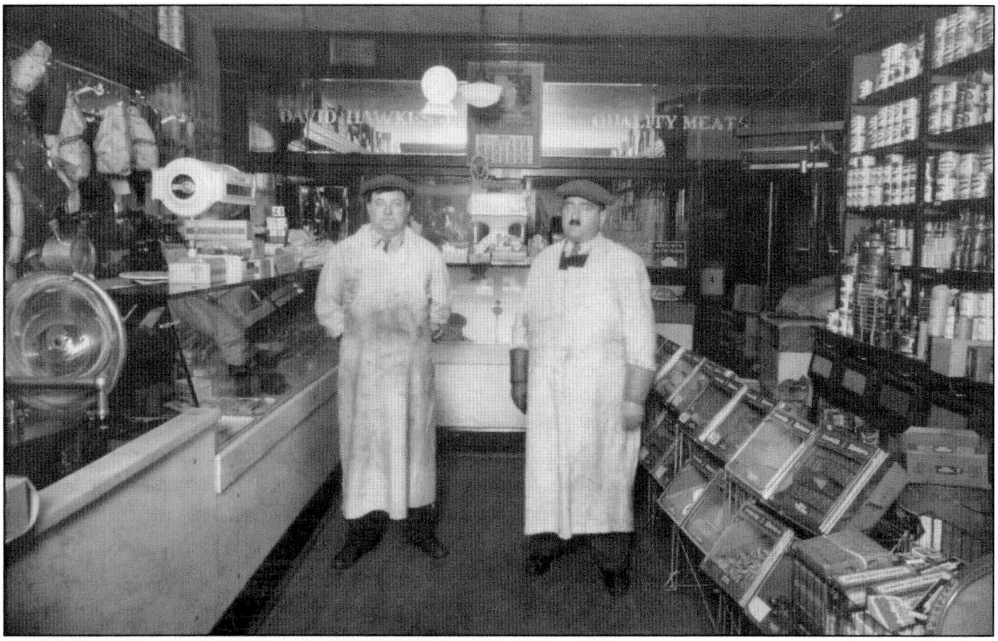

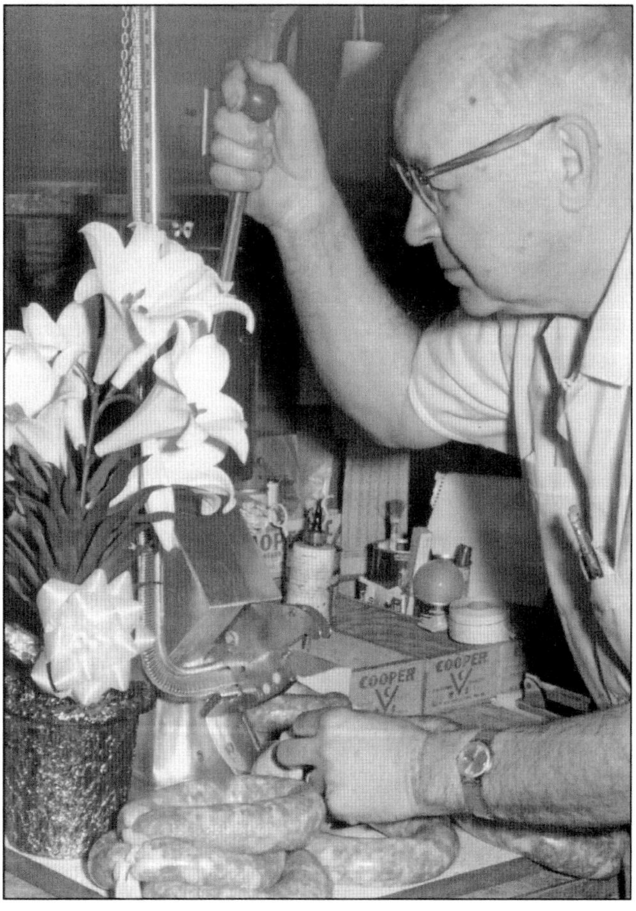

BUTCHER SHOP, 1930. Neighborhood butcher shops were a common convenience in town. Pictured is the shop opened by Leon Eckert at 301 East Pine Street, Mahanoy City. After his death, his apprentice David Hawkes Jr., on the right, continued to operate the shop. In recent years, the store was owned and operated by the Huebners, descendants of the Eckerts. (PGG.)

JOHN KUBERT. Butcher/grocer John Kubert, husband of Florence (née Sullivan) Kubert, is shown here making kielbasa for the Easter season as his father did before him. John owned three stores in Mahanoy City and was in business for over 50 years in both the east and west ends of town. (DJK.)

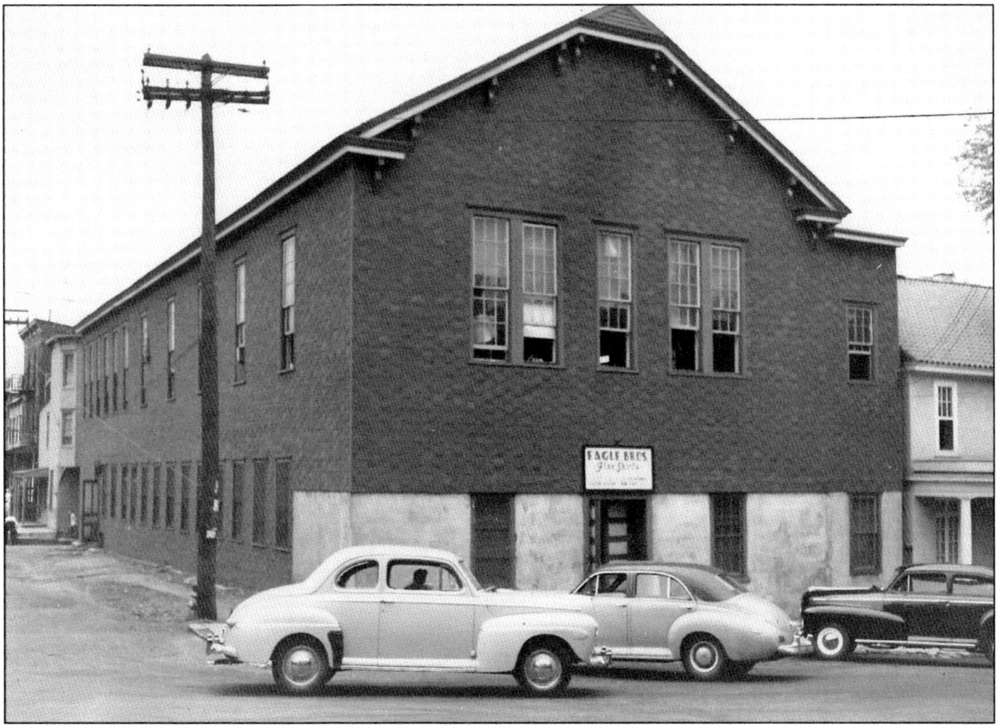

EAGLE BROTHERS. This former church on the corner of South Main and West Maple Streets, Mahanoy City, was operated for a time by Eagle Bros. until a new plant in the west end was built in 1948. According to Susan Shanfield, Irving Shanfield, her father, owned and operated a factory in this building, under the name Mahanoy City Sportswear, from the mid-1940s until closing in 1960–1961. (JKG.)

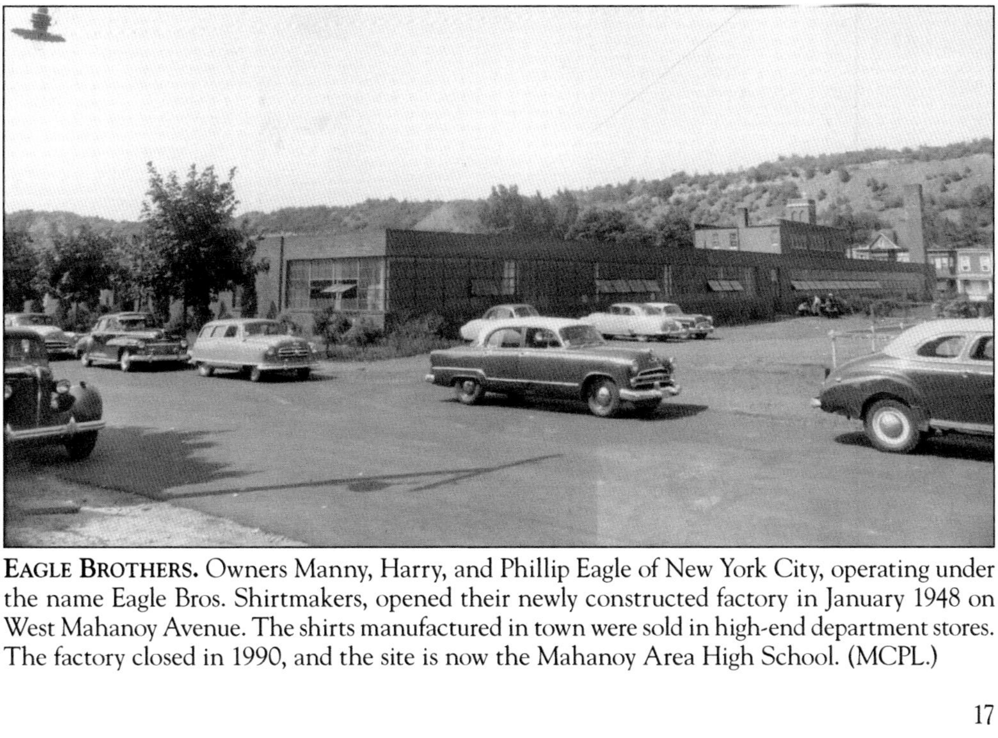

EAGLE BROTHERS. Owners Manny, Harry, and Phillip Eagle of New York City, operating under the name Eagle Bros. Shirtmakers, opened their newly constructed factory in January 1948 on West Mahanoy Avenue. The shirts manufactured in town were sold in high-end department stores. The factory closed in 1990, and the site is now the Mahanoy Area High School. (MCPL.)

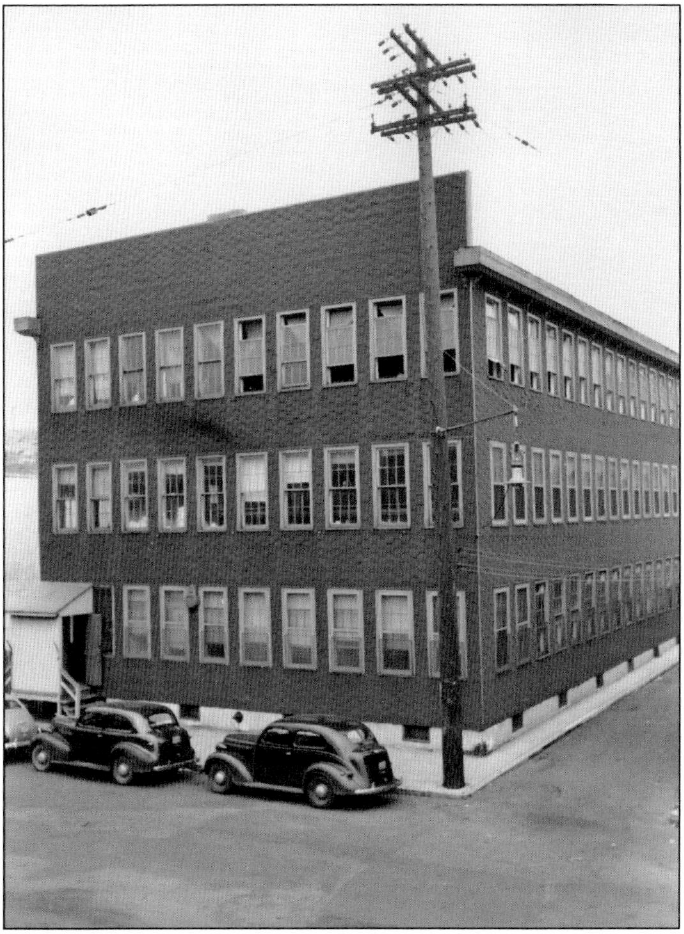

CITY SHIRT BUILDING. In 1939, Sidney Shanfield and Mark Janov purchased the City Shirt factory at 19–21 West Vine Street and eventually expanded it to employ 500 women by 1963. Students often waved to their mothers at work as they passed on their way home from school to signal that they had arrived home safely. (JKG.)

FACTORY WORKERS. This photograph shows Margaret (left) and Mary Curtis at their place of employment, City Shirt. The Curtis girls lived in Buck Mountain, a patch about two miles outside of Mahanoy City. Each day, the sisters, as well as about 24 other workers, climbed into a factory truck with two bench-style seats for the ride to and from work. (JBW.)

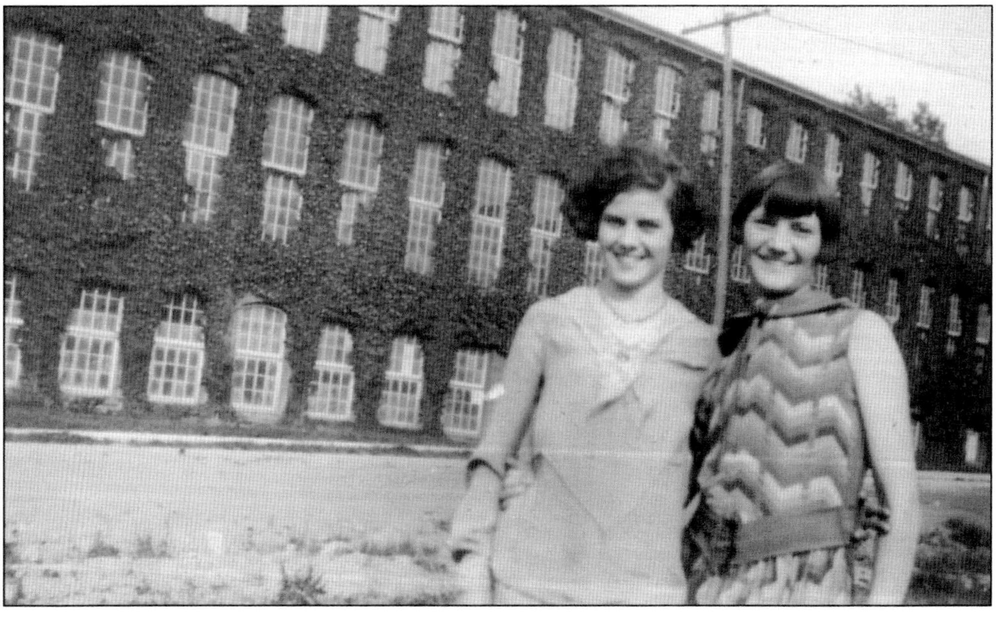

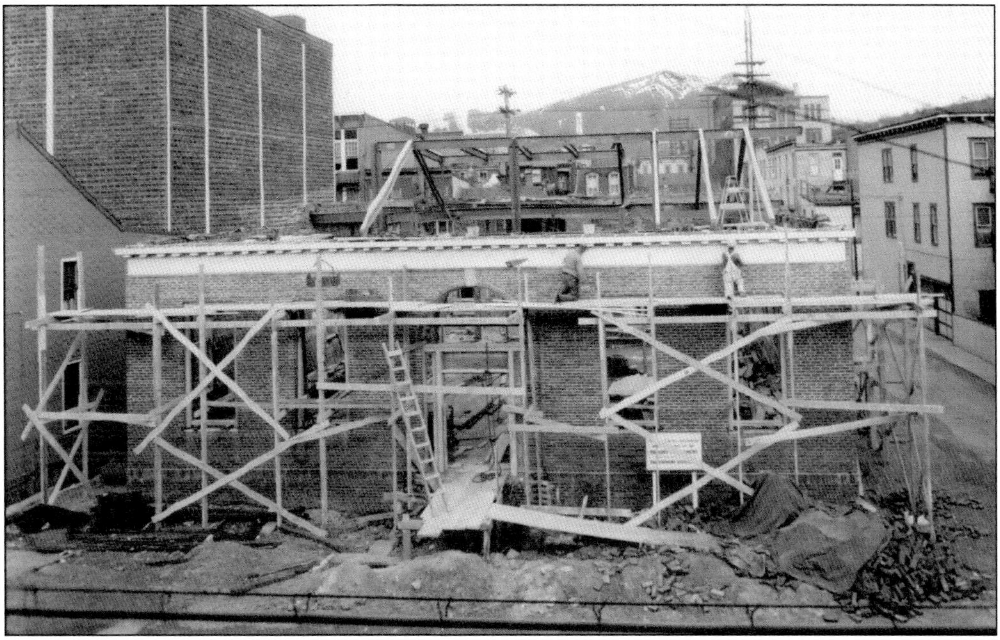

CONSTRUCTION, 1937–1938. In 1935, Pres. Franklin Roosevelt and the US Congress created the Works Progress Administration (WPA). During its eight years, it employed eight million people on 1.5 million projects. One of those projects was the Mahanoy City Post Office, seen under construction here. In the distance, the Kaier tower is visible, and the back of the Victoria Theater is on the left. (MHS.)

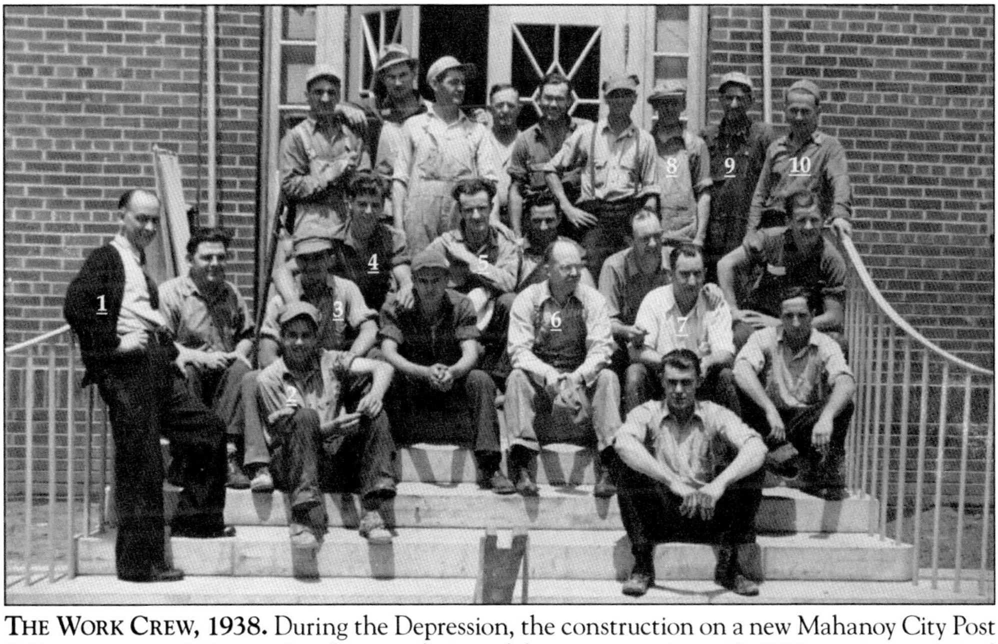

THE WORK CREW, 1938. During the Depression, the construction on a new Mahanoy City Post Office was started. Pictured at the completion of the project on June 15, 1938, are, in numerical order, John Morgan, assistant postmaster; Robert Heckman; Frank Selgrath; James Post, who was killed in action in France; Bill Coombe; John J. Murray, building inspector; William Rambo, construction superintendent; Frank Holzenthaler; Frank Techentin; and Larry Ryan. (PC.)

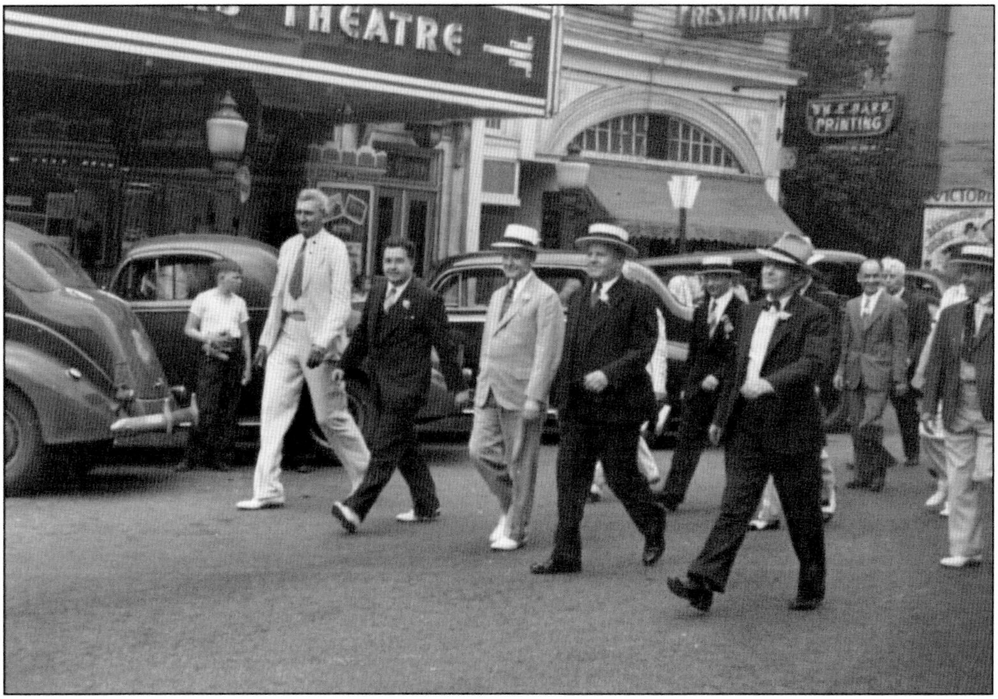

PARADE, JUNE 25, 1938. A short street parade of local civic, business, and fraternal organizations commences the dedication the new post office. Postmaster Daniel F. Guinan II, wearing a dark suit but without a hat, is seen leading the parade. (PGG.)

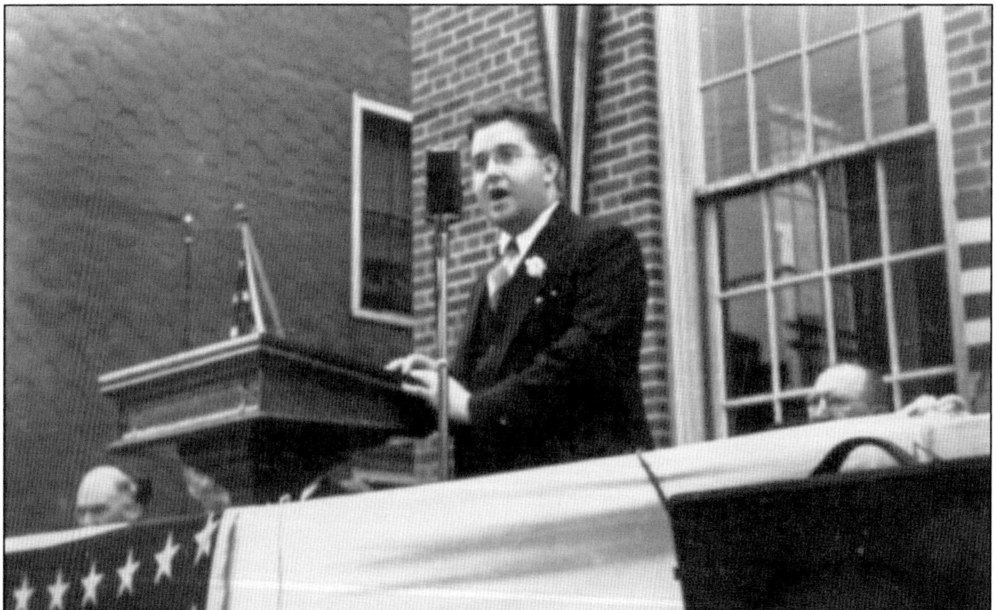

1938 DEDICATION. Daniel F. Guinan II, postmaster of Mahanoy City Post Office, addresses the crowd gathered to dedicate the new building. Dignitaries in attendance were United States assistant postmaster general Ramsey Black; Congressman Dan Gildae of Coaldale; and US marshal Joseph Reing of Mahanoy City. (PGG.)

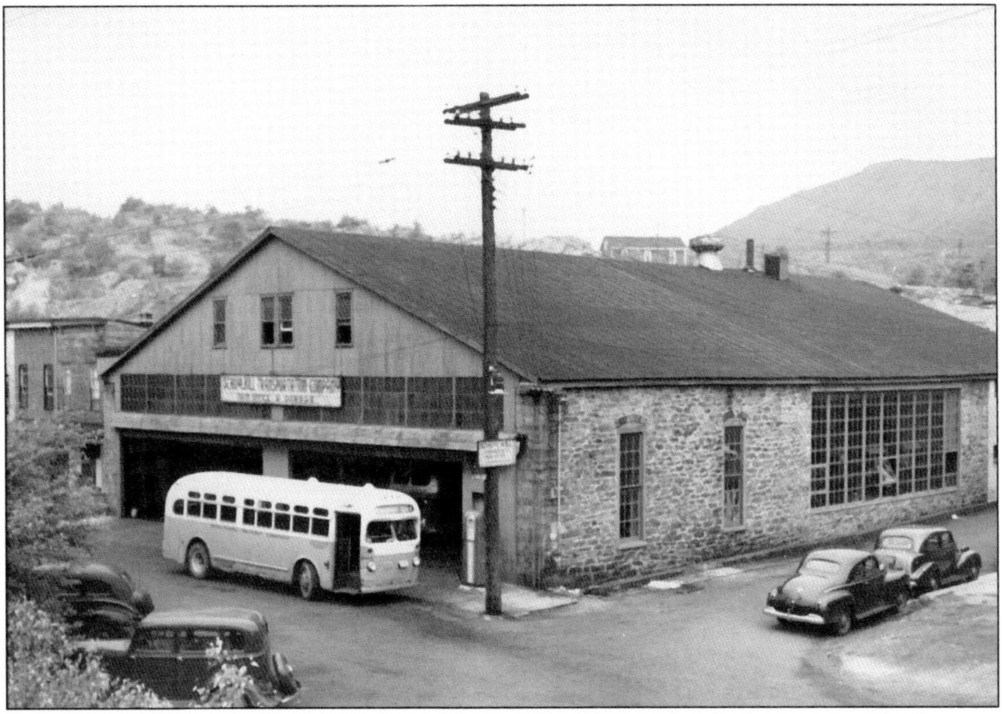

SCHUYLKILL TRANSPORTATION COMPANY, 1938. It did not take very many years for buses to take over the routes of the trolleys. The Mahanoy City–based Schuylkill Transportation operated school and commercial routes from the 1930s until the 1950s, when East Penn Bus Company took over the routes. (JKG.)

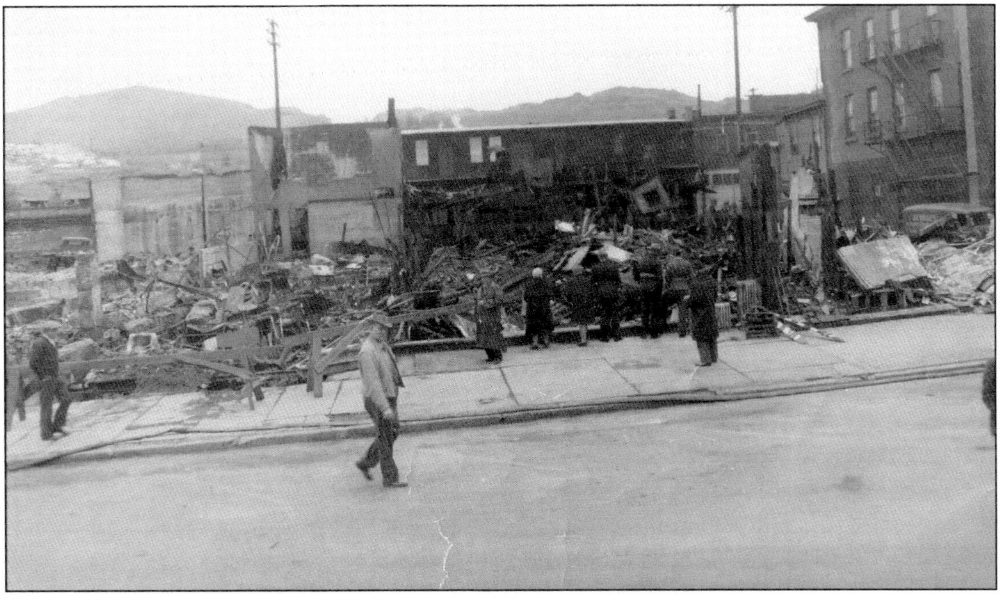

MEMORIAL DAY FIRE, 1945. Postwar Mahanoy City was prosperous. Centre Street from Catawissa Street to Fourth Street was lined with businesses. On May 30, 1945, Anna George discovered a fire as she walked across Centre Street to her apartment from George's Confectionery. In the end, nothing was left on the block but George's business truck, seen at the far right. (DA.)

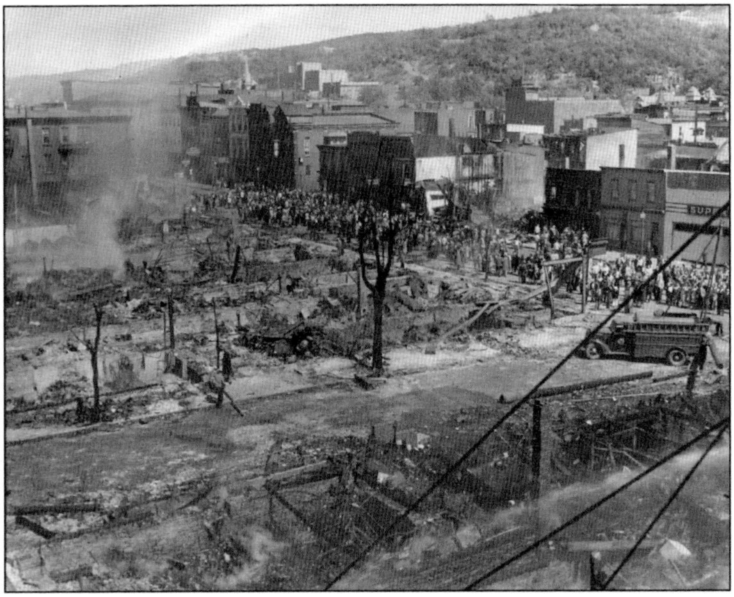

1945 FIRE, LOOKING EAST. Anna George warned her neighbors and fed firemen and victims through the night. A contingent of firemen fought winds for hours, but the fire continued to move east. Suddenly, the wind shifted, and the fire crossed two streets. Only a brick wall stopped the spread past Guinan's and the A&P. Residents who witnessed it thought that their whole town would burn. (JKG.)

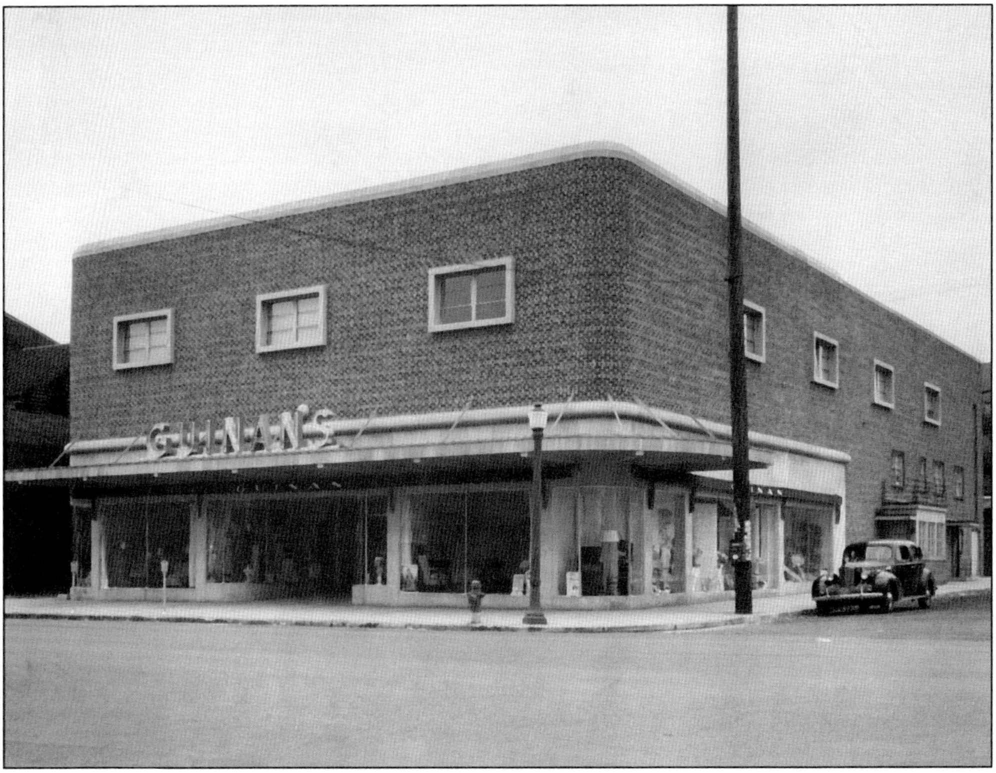

GUINAN'S DEPARTMENT STORE. Julia Guinan, store owner, was a recent widow with no home, no business, and no insurance. After offering aid to all the victims, she went to church. Within hours, business competitors offered her space to sell merchandise. The next day, the people of Mahanoy City stood in line two blocks long to "pay their clubs" to a store that did not exist. This loyalty and friendship motivated the Guinan family to rebuild. Guinan's Department Store opened one year later. (MCPL.)

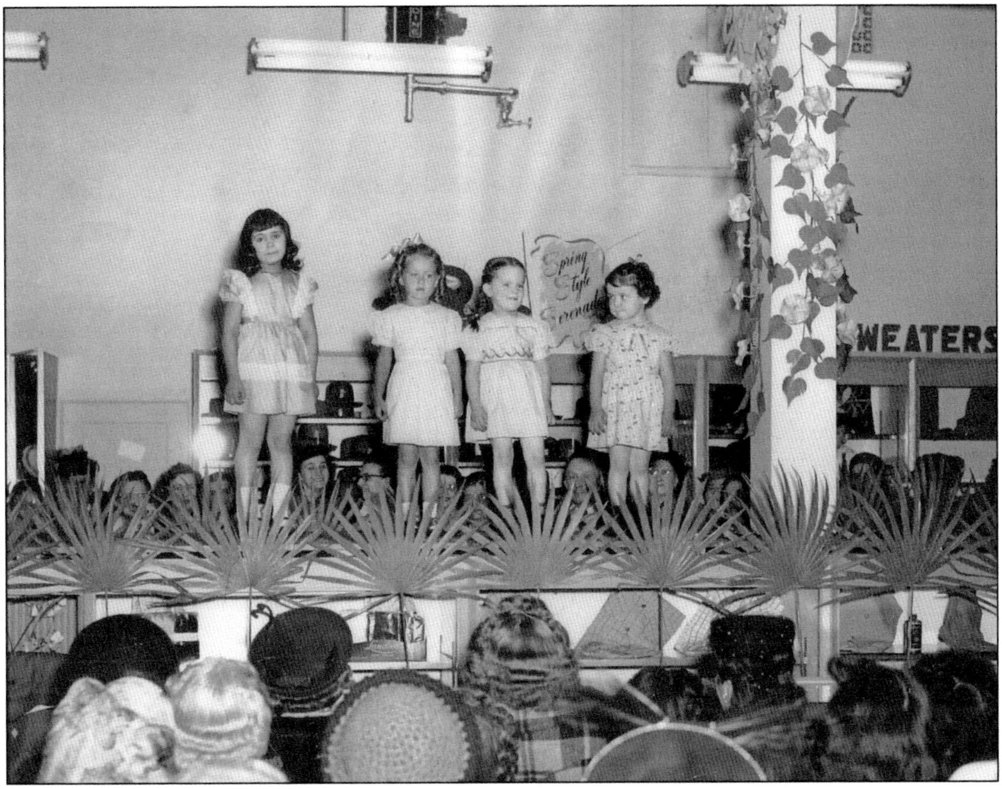

GUINAN'S FASHION SHOW. Guinan's was always on the cutting edge of fashion. In 1946, a fashion show titled "Spring Fashion Serenade" opened the new store. Featuring local talent, the show included these four young girls in updated style for children of the day. (PGG.)

CABLE TELEVISION, 1948. Congress and the National Cable Television Association recognize John Walson Sr. as the inventor of cable television. Its beginning was in the spring of 1948. He was a 1933 graduate of Mahanoy Township High School, and his family was from Patriotic Hill. Service Electric Company provides cable television to customers in Pennsylvania and northwestern New Jersey; Walson's descendants run the company today. (MHS.)

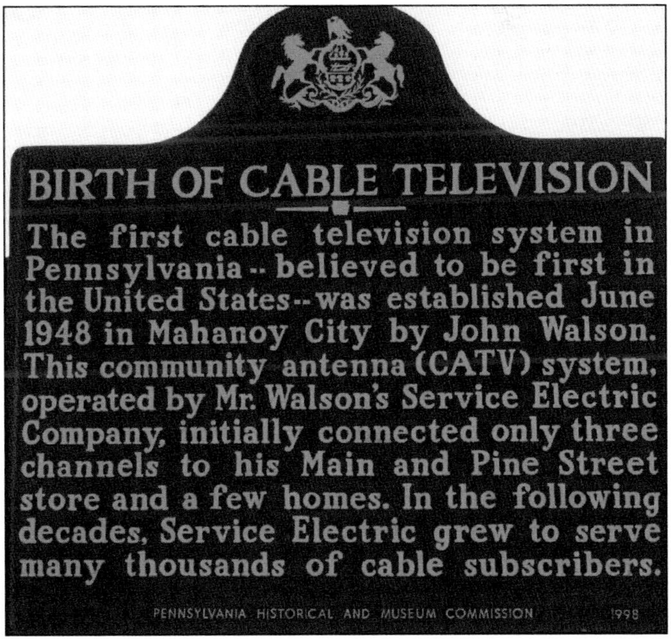

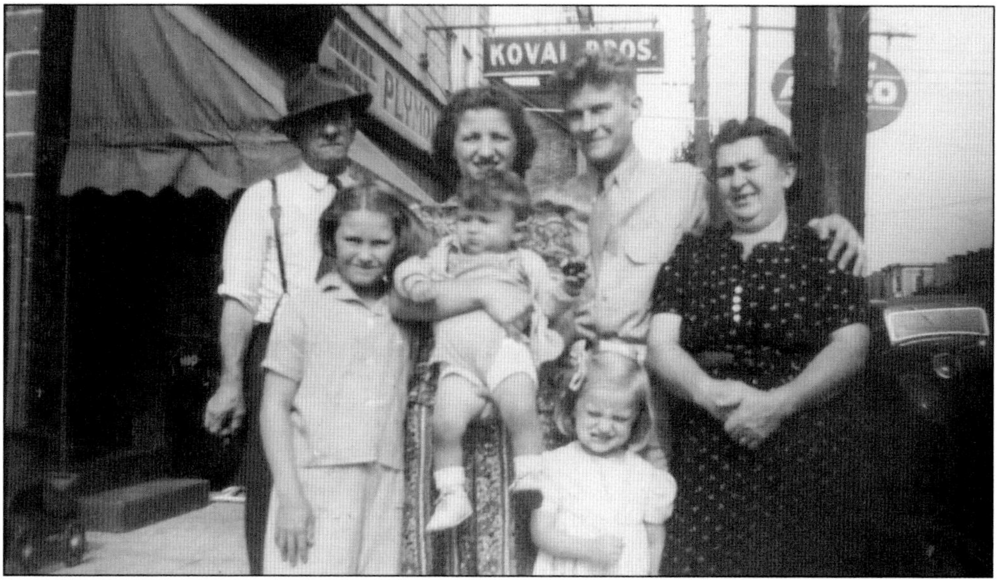

KOVAL BROTHERS, 1942. If one were to mention the first ward in Mahanoy City in the 1940s and 1950s, the name Koval would have come to mind. There was the Koval Flower Shop, Koval Brothers Plymouth-Dodge-DeSoto (above), and Stephen and George Koval's Oldsmobile car dealership. Pictured are, from left to right, (first row) children Theresa and George Koval and Julie Nepywoda; (second row) Stephen Koval, owner of Koval Brothers; Marie and husband, George Koval; and Mary Koval, the wife of Stephen. (CKB.)

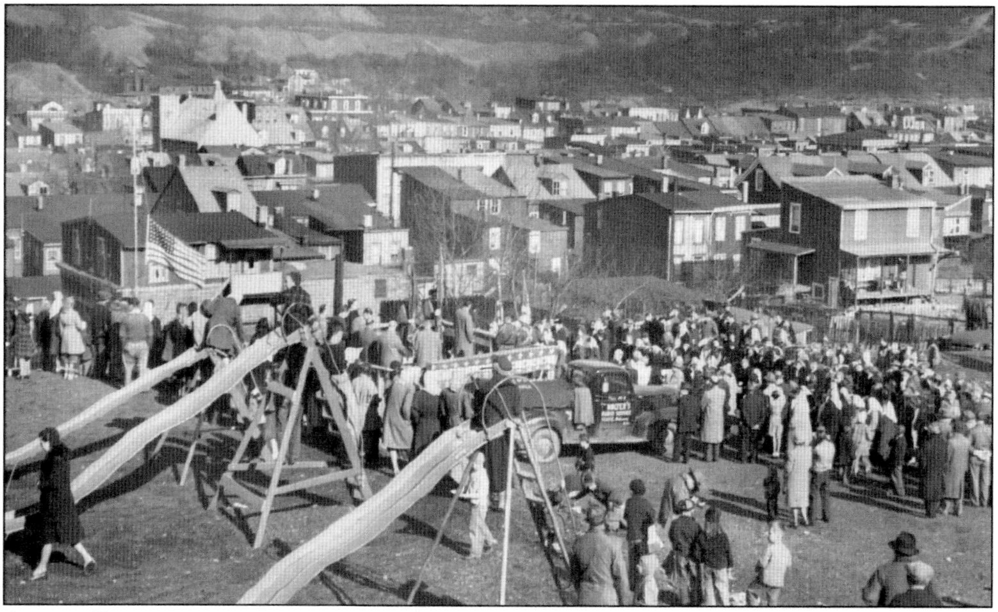

AMVETS PLAYGROUND, 1948. Sponsored by the Mahanoy City Lions Club, the Amvet's Memorial Playground at Sixth Street was dedicated on November 11, 1948, Armistice Day. That day was chosen so the citizens of Mahanoy City could always remember the date that ended World War I. Clyde Holman served as dedication chair, a bouquet was donated by Luke's Floral Shop, and the monument was made by Everett Monument Company, a town business for over 100 years. (MHS.)

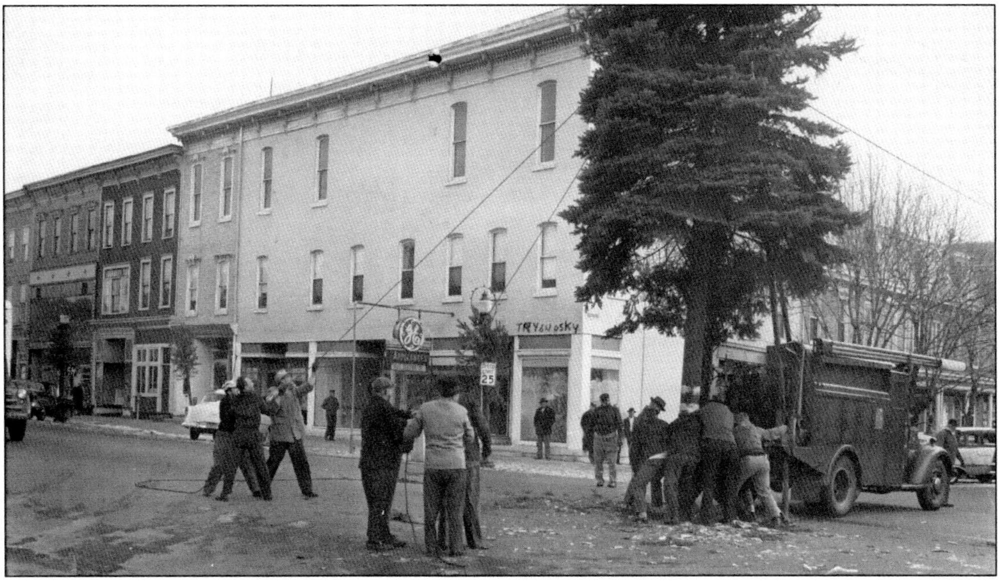

Town Christmas Tree. In this photograph are members of the Mahanoy Area Social Club erecting the Christmas tree at Centre and Catawissa Streets. This was only one of the club's many activities throughout town. The social club was established in 1934 and was started as a result of Boley Sadusky's love for baseball. The club quickly grew to include a variety of community and charitable services. Serving as its first president was Joseph Murtin. (MHS.)

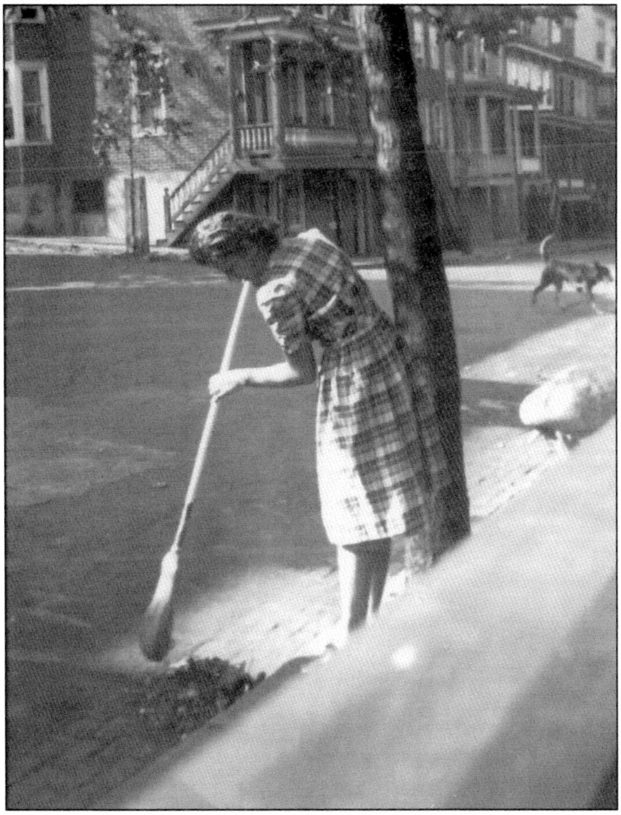

1950 Cleanliness. Taken on West Spruce Street in Mahanoy City, this scene of a woman sweeping the street could have been taken anywhere in town. The weekly housekeeping ritual, along with spring, fall, and holiday cleaning, was washing down the front porch and sweeping the pavements and street. (JKG.)

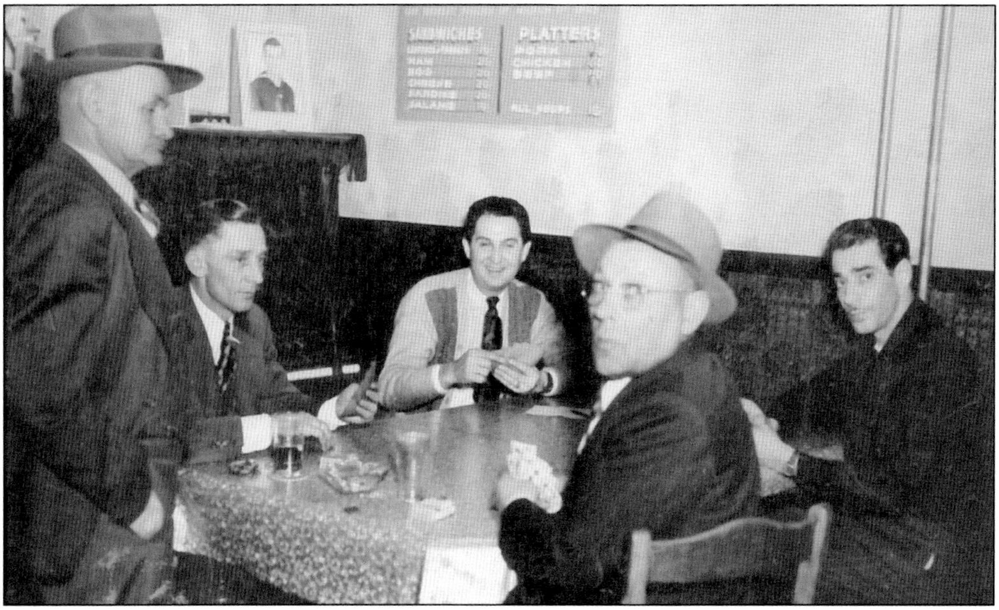

AMBROSE CAFÉ. In the ethnic neighborhoods, each block had its own favorite barroom/saloon. The Ambrose Café (pictured) in the Lithuanian section of town was a daily stop for some and weekly for many. Along with a beer, there were simple meals, also known as "platters." Friday night was fish night, with deviled crabs a specialty. After the meal, the regulars met at the bar for darts or a card game, called Hausey. (DA.)

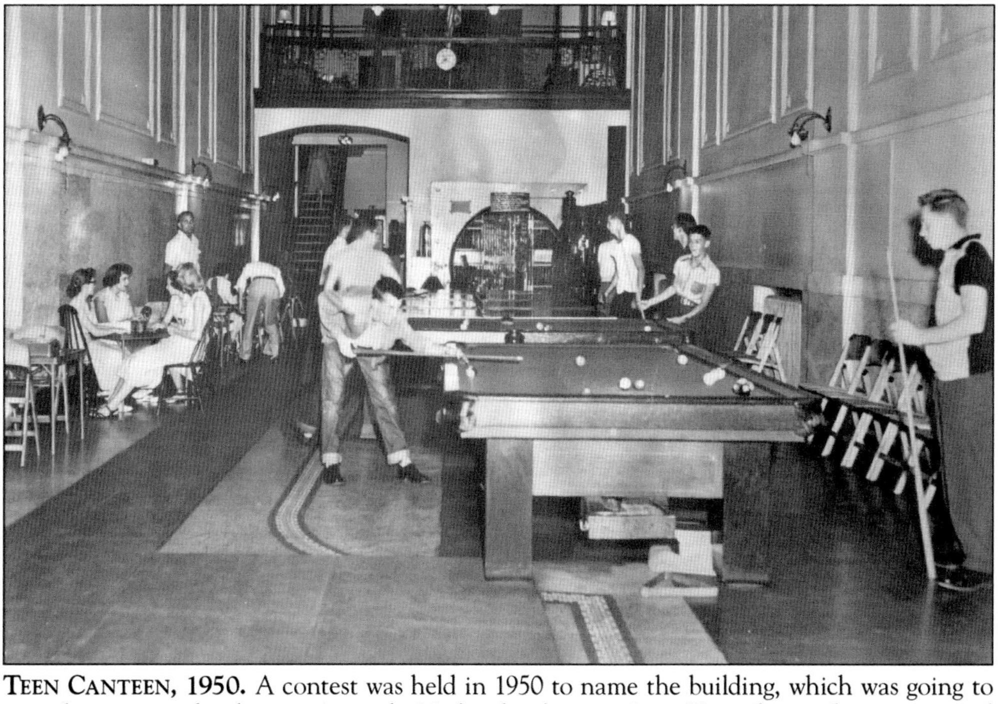

TEEN CANTEEN, 1950. A contest was held in 1950 to name the building, which was going to provide activities for the town's youth. High school senior Joan Havard won the contest and named the establishment the Teen Canteen. There, students played board games, shot pool, played volleyball, and honed their dance skills on the upper level. (MHS.)

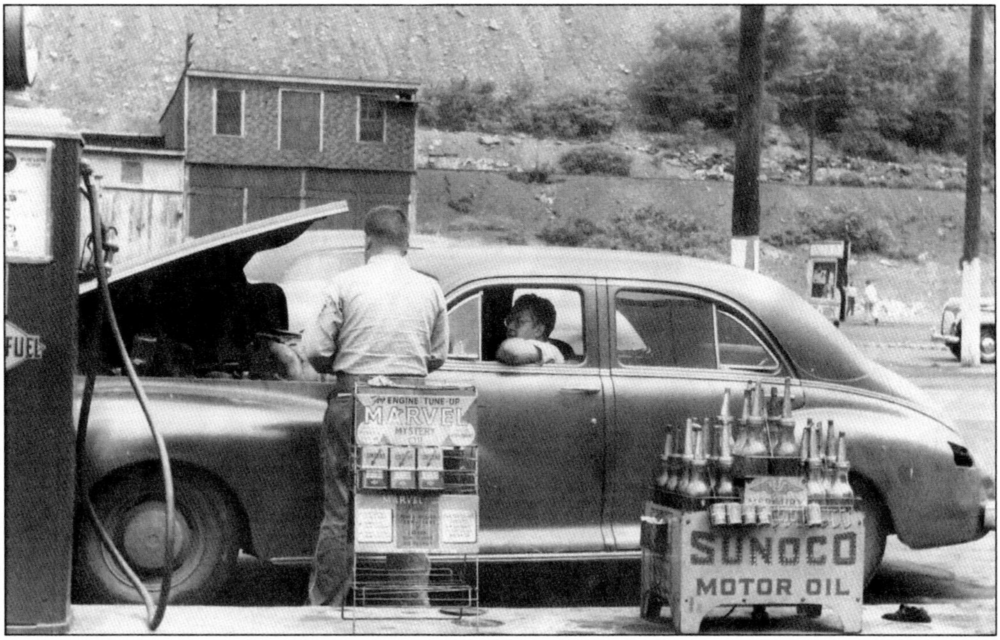

JOHN KLINE ATTENDING TO A CUSTOMER, 1950. The family of John Kline Sr. of Cole's Patch had a major impact on the business growth in the Mahanoy area. The eldest son, John, maintained a Sunoco garage on West Centre Street, adding a Ford Dealership in the 1950s. John is pictured with his back to the camera. (PGG.)

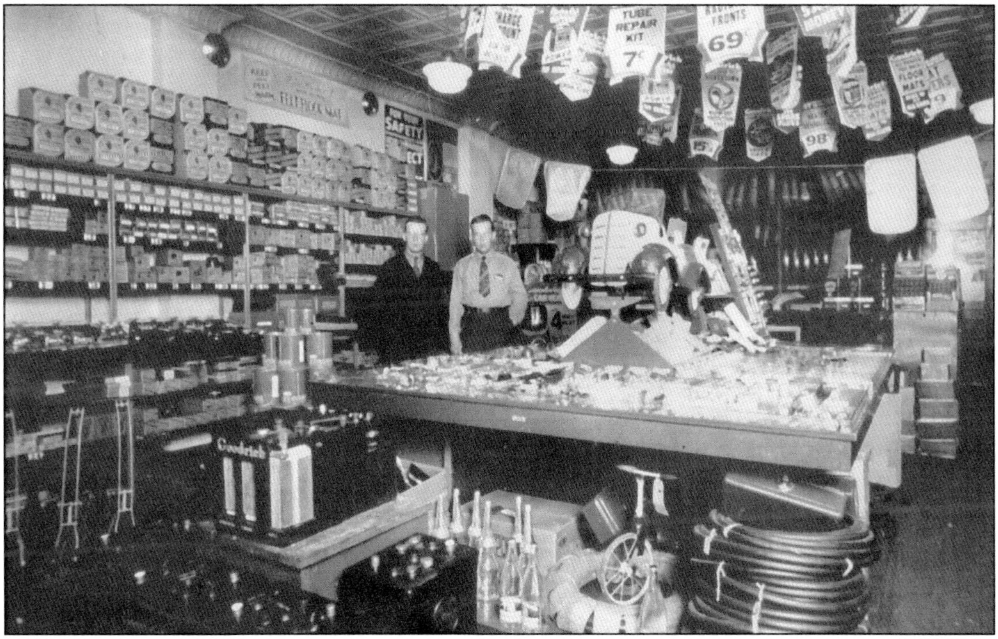

KLINE AUTO PARTS, 1950S. Twins Frank and Robert Kline stand in their newly opened auto parts store on the south side of Centre Street across from Foundry Row. The brothers began in partnership with a gas station on the first block of South Main Street. Working seven days a week, they expanded in the mid-1950s into the auto parts business, eventually owning stores in Mahanoy City, Shenandoah, and Tamaqua. (PGG.)

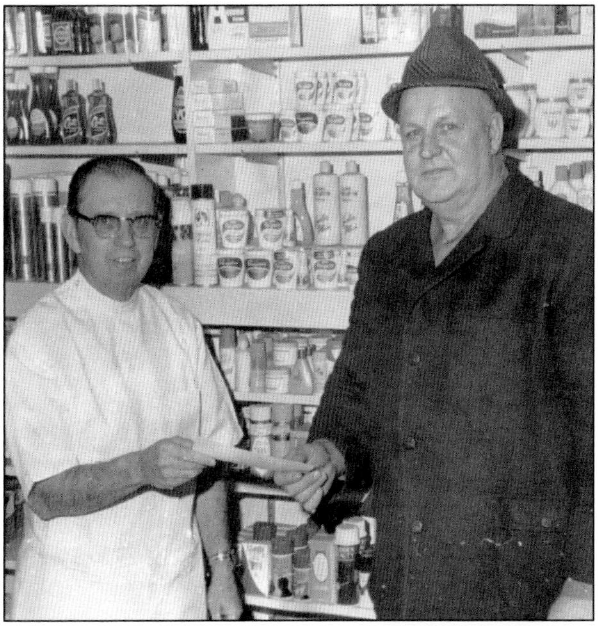

MICHAEL KACZMARCZYK. From 1867 until its closing in 1995, a drugstore was located at this West Centre location in Mahanoy City. The pharmacy was established by George Kennedy, continued by Adolf Timm, and, in 1929, acquired by Michael Kaczmarczyk, then a pharmacist at Timm's. In the 1920s, pharmacists mixed their own medicines and filled capsules individually, often without a prescription. Here, in 1973, Kaczmarczyk is dispensing his millionth prescription. (MK.)

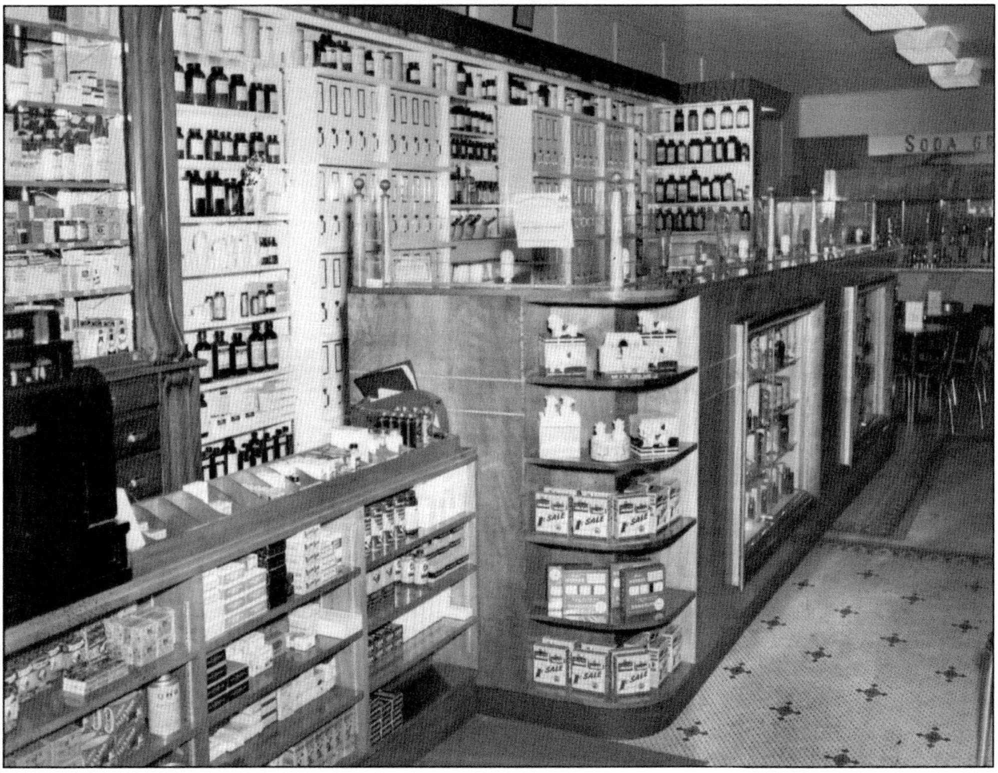

TIMM'S DRUGSTORE AND SODA FOUNTAIN. Large bottles of medications filled the shelves on the west wall and behind the counter where the pharmacist filled prescriptions. Front counters were stocked with medicines and supplies. The beautiful tile floor led to the back where, in the tradition of the earliest drugstores, there was a soda fountain and ice cream shop where customers came for a CMP (chocolate, marshmallow, peanut) or banana split sundae. (MK.)

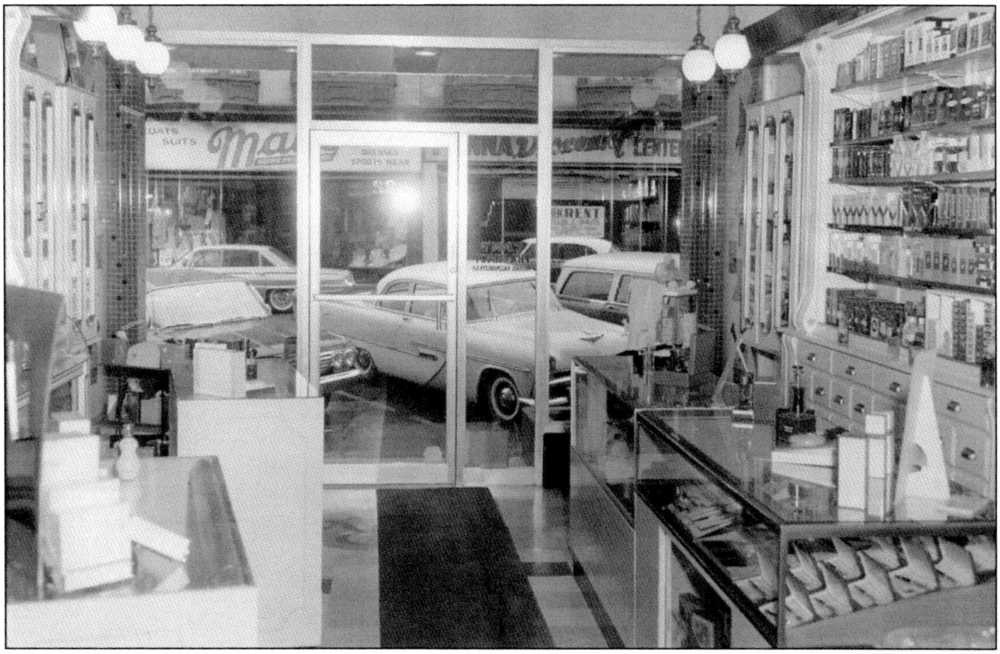

VIEW OF CENTRE STREET. As they left Timm's, patrons were tempted by the display cases filled with fine perfumes and chocolates. Looking out through the sparkling windows, one could see the busy downtown business district. Following his father's death, Michael Kaczmarcyzk Jr. operated Timm's until 1995. (MK.)

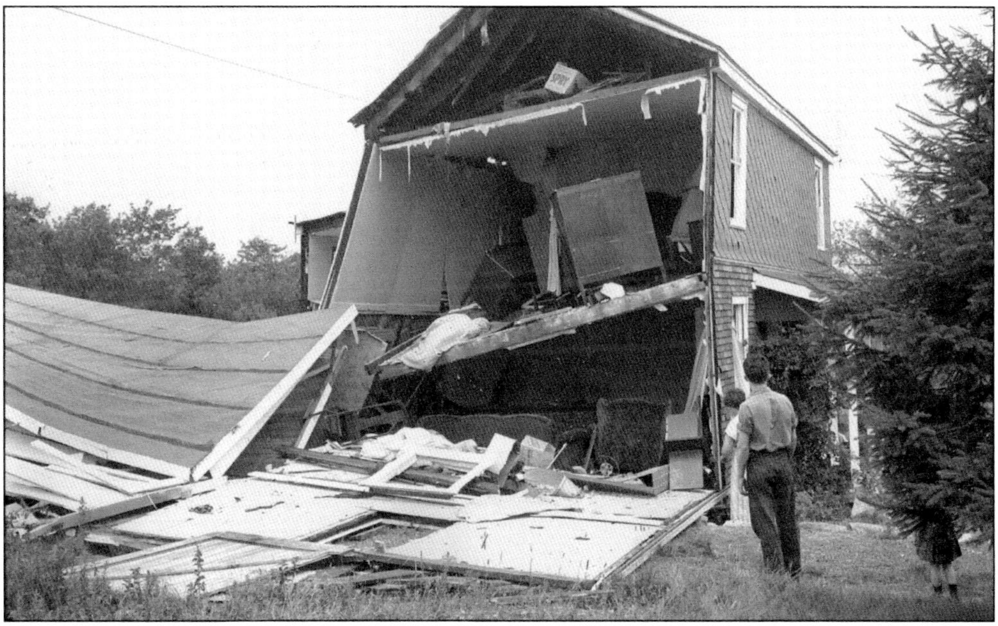

CRAIG'S PATCH. On August 5, 1952, a truck belonging to a West Pittston firm exploded on the road near Craig's Patch. According to the *Record American* newspaper, the driver saw smoke and jumped out of his truck in time to escape the explosion. All of the homes in Craig's Patch were damaged, and a young boy was hospitalized with injuries. The blast knocked 14 windows out of a home in Robinson's Patch, located five miles away. (JKG.)

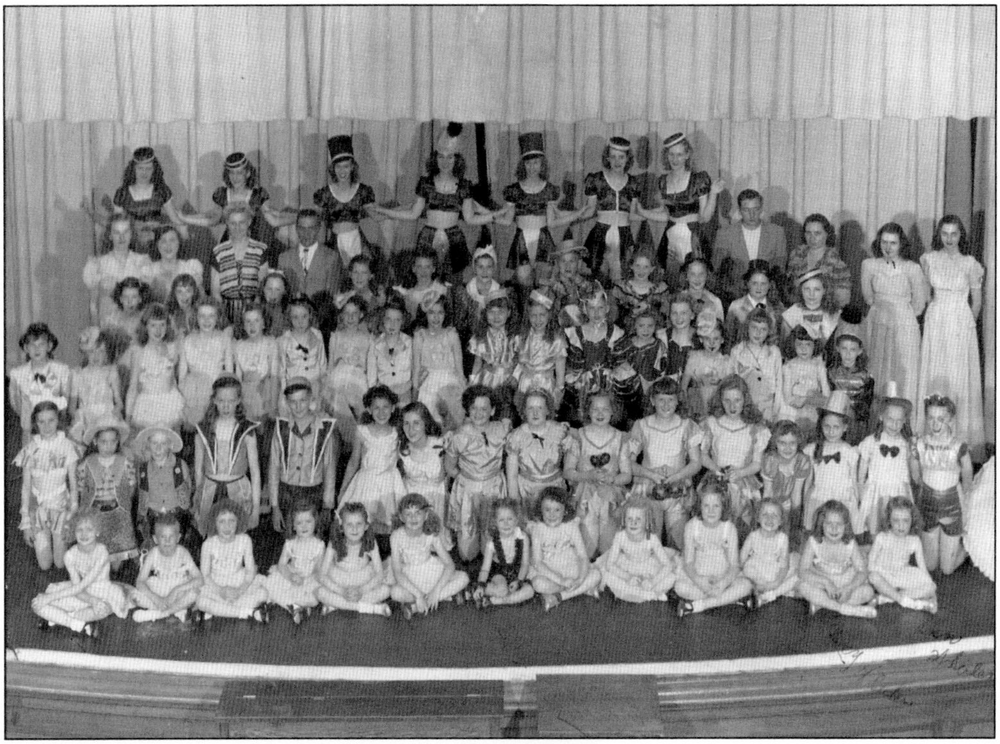

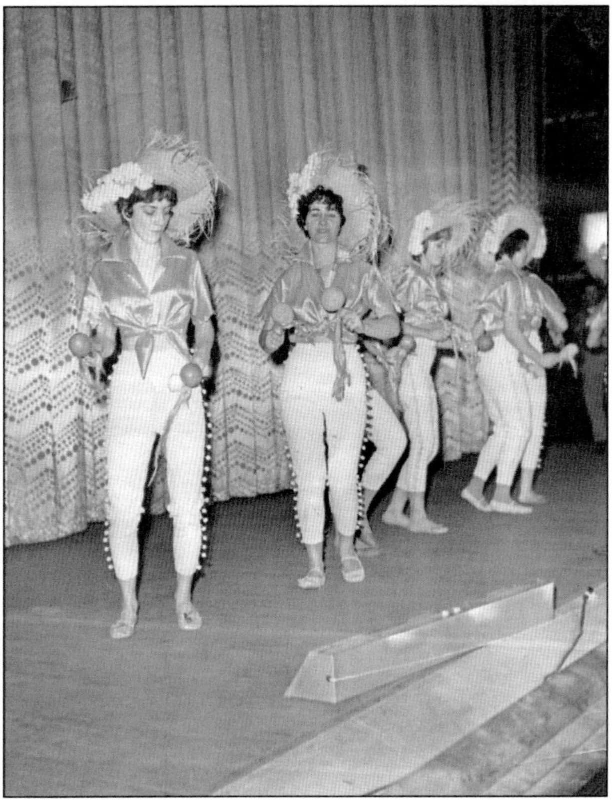

JEAN DIXON. Jean T. Dixon operated dance studios in Mahanoy City, Shenandoah, and Tamaqua. The studio in Mahanoy City operated at several locations throughout the town. Yearly dance recitals were held. Pictured is the troupe from 1946. In the center of the photograph is Peggy Guinan, age four, who did a solo Hawaiian number to rousing applause from the audience. (PGG.)

JEAN DIXON. A performer and dancer herself, Jean Dixon was a talented woman who was responsible for introducing dance to many children. Here, she (second from the left) is performing with some of her teachers and students in a lively salsa number. (JBT.)

DAVID BLIGHT DANCE STUDIO. Dancer David Blight had a satellite studio in Mahanoy City during the early 1960s. Lucky dancers were selected to appear on his television show, which aired each Sunday afternoon. Pictured are Marylou Wellington (left) and her unidentified partner preparing for an appearance on the show. (FW.)

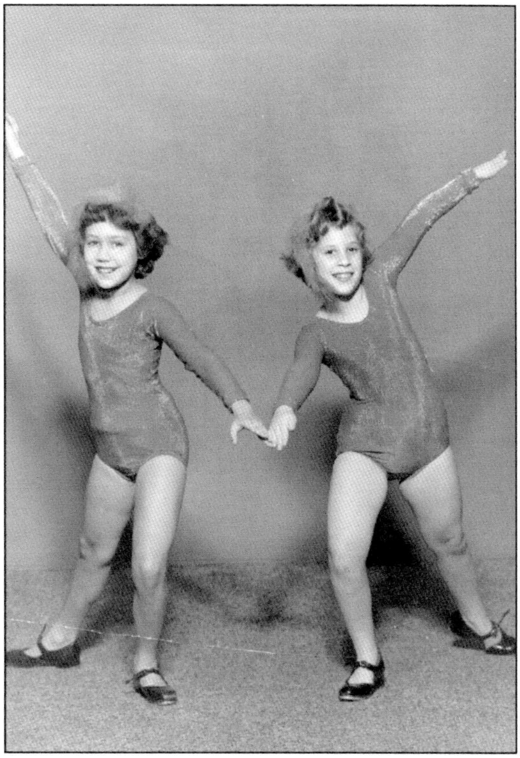

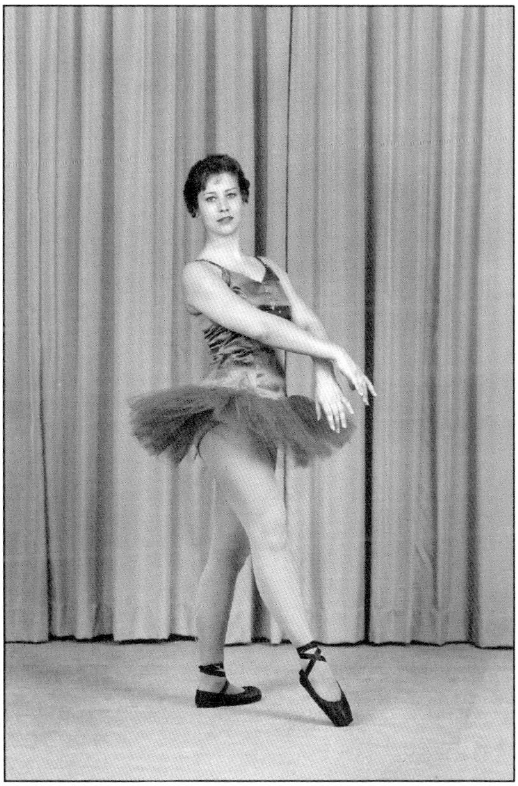

DIXON ASSISTANTS. The Jean Dixon Studio grew quickly. Successful teachers, like Jean, trained their older students to teach the younger ones, strengthening everyone's performance. Nancy Truskowsky (pictured) was one of those students who took her dance studies seriously and enjoyed teaching. To further enhance her skills, Nancy studied dance at the Ballet and Repertory School in New York City. (NTC.)

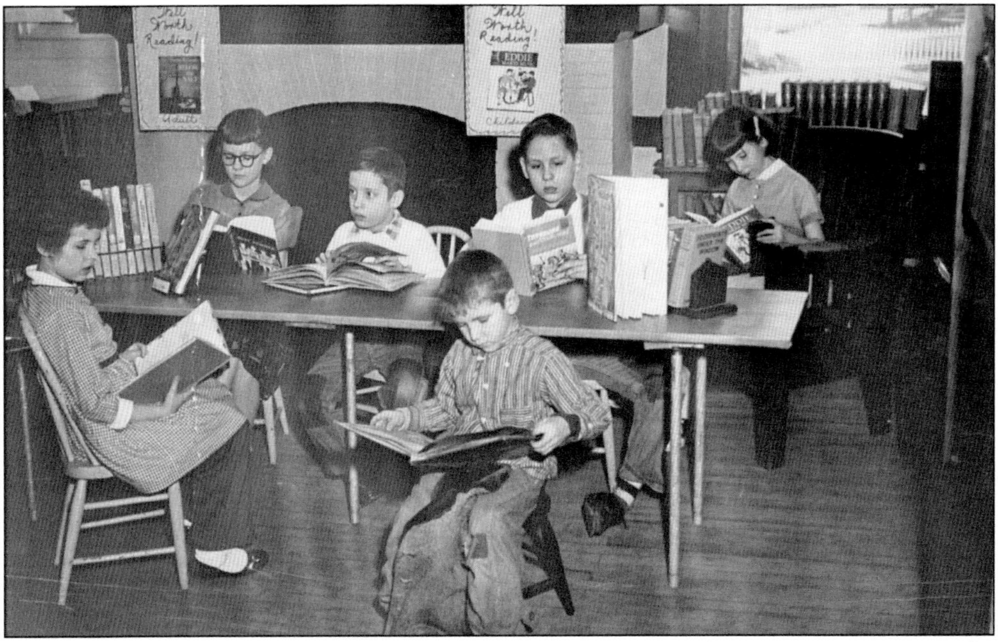

THE LIBRARY. Always a meeting place for children and adults, the library continues to serve the citizens of the town. Pictured here in the 1950s, a group of children gathers to read the latest publications. They are, from left to right, (first row) Nancy Lou Krolick and Robert Wargo; (second row) Betty Ann Kieres, brothers Jerry and George Medwick, and Cindy Shuey. (MCPL.)

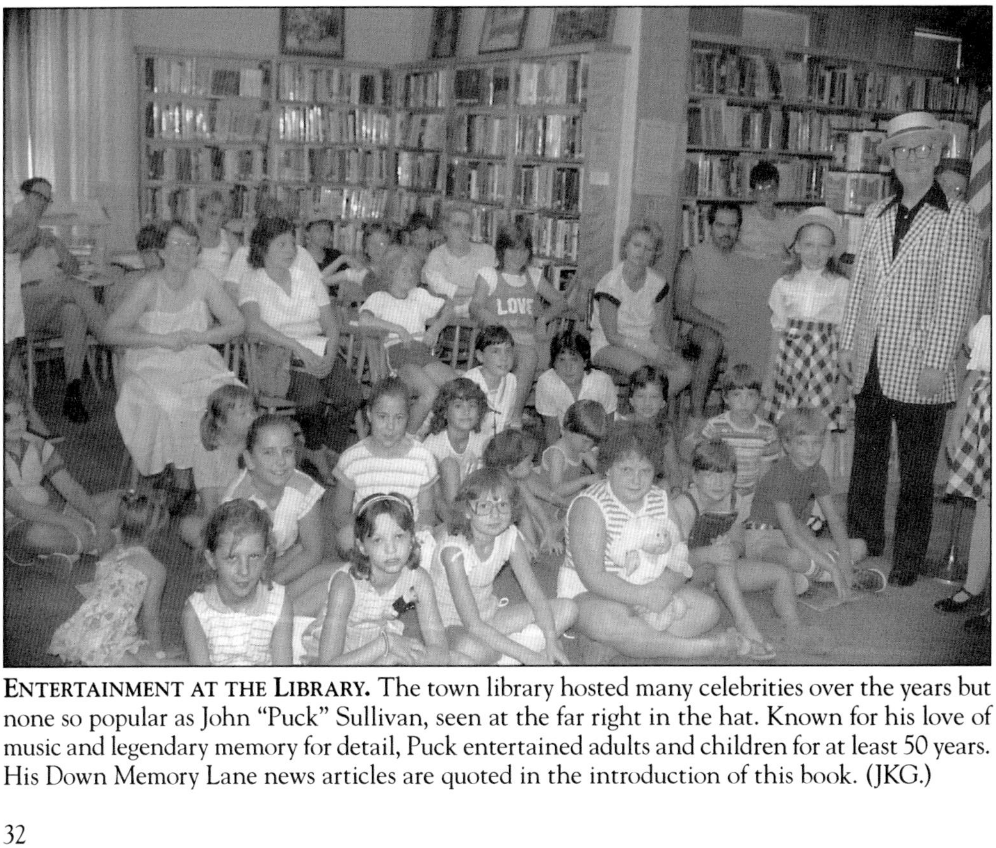

ENTERTAINMENT AT THE LIBRARY. The town library hosted many celebrities over the years but none so popular as John "Puck" Sullivan, seen at the far right in the hat. Known for his love of music and legendary memory for detail, Puck entertained adults and children for at least 50 years. His Down Memory Lane news articles are quoted in the introduction of this book. (JKG.)

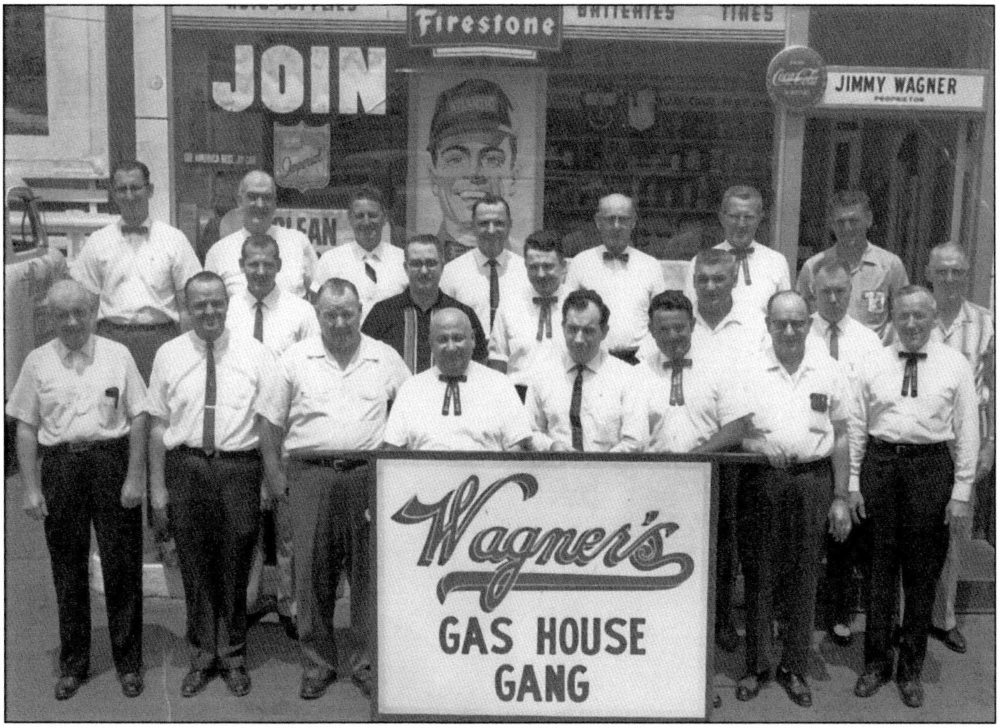

GAS HOUSE GANG. Established in 1958, the Gas House Gang began with 27 members. By 1963, the group had grown to 58. The organization's purpose was simple—"There is no greater thrill in life than that of having served a youth." The group sponsored an all-sports banquet, the Mardi Gras dance for all high school seniors, and the yearly arrival of Santa Claus to town. Pictured is the group as it existed in 1963. (MCPL.)

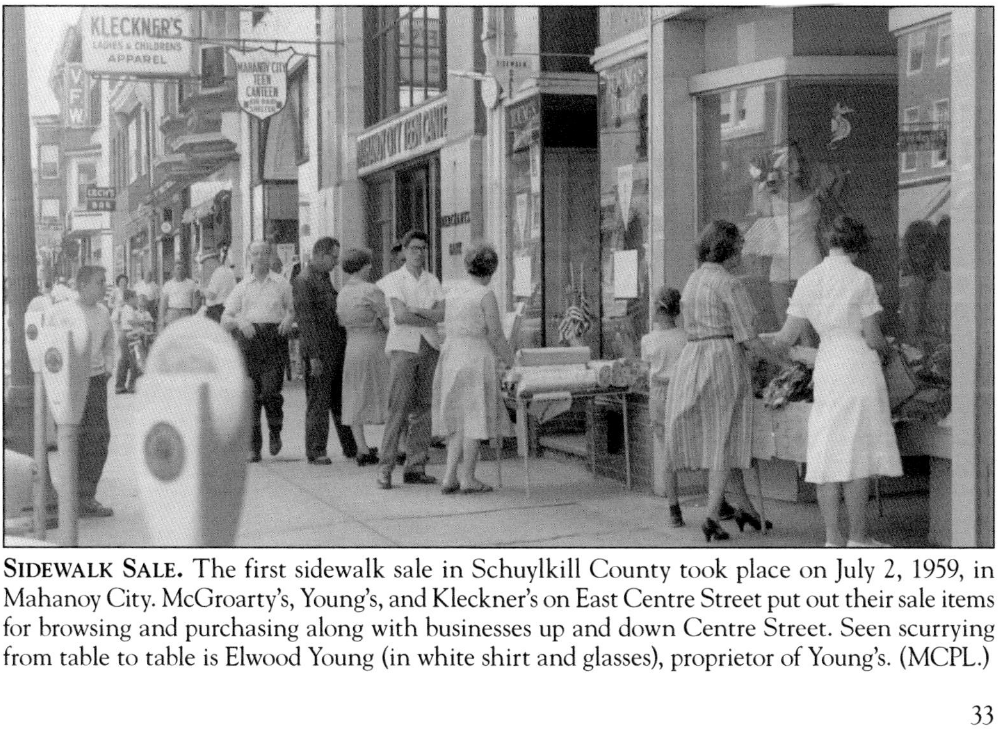

SIDEWALK SALE. The first sidewalk sale in Schuylkill County took place on July 2, 1959, in Mahanoy City. McGroarty's, Young's, and Kleckner's on East Centre Street put out their sale items for browsing and purchasing along with businesses up and down Centre Street. Seen scurrying from table to table is Elwood Young (in white shirt and glasses), proprietor of Young's. (MCPL.)

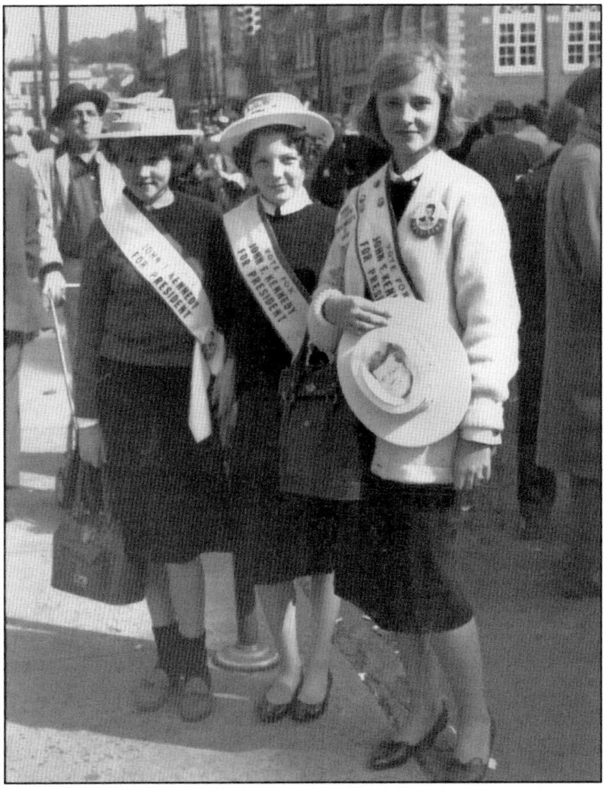

KENNEDY. When John F. Kennedy arrived in Pottsville in 1959 to speak to the good people of Schuylkill County, three Mahanoy City girls were there to help greet him. Showing off their "Vote for John F. Kennedy for President" political hats and banners are, from left to right, Kathy Whitaker, Adele Pace, and Diane Ambrose. (DA.)

***BANDSTAND* PICTURE.** Hosted by Bob Horn, Dick Clark's predecessor, the Philadelphia-based television show *Bandstand* was so popular in town that Tony Maff, owner of the London Shop, sponsored Philadelphia trips for Mahanoy City's students to an annual *Bandstand* picnic. Teens enjoyed dancing and mingling with the stars they watched daily on television. Attending this picnic were fans of the show from all over the area. (TWH.)

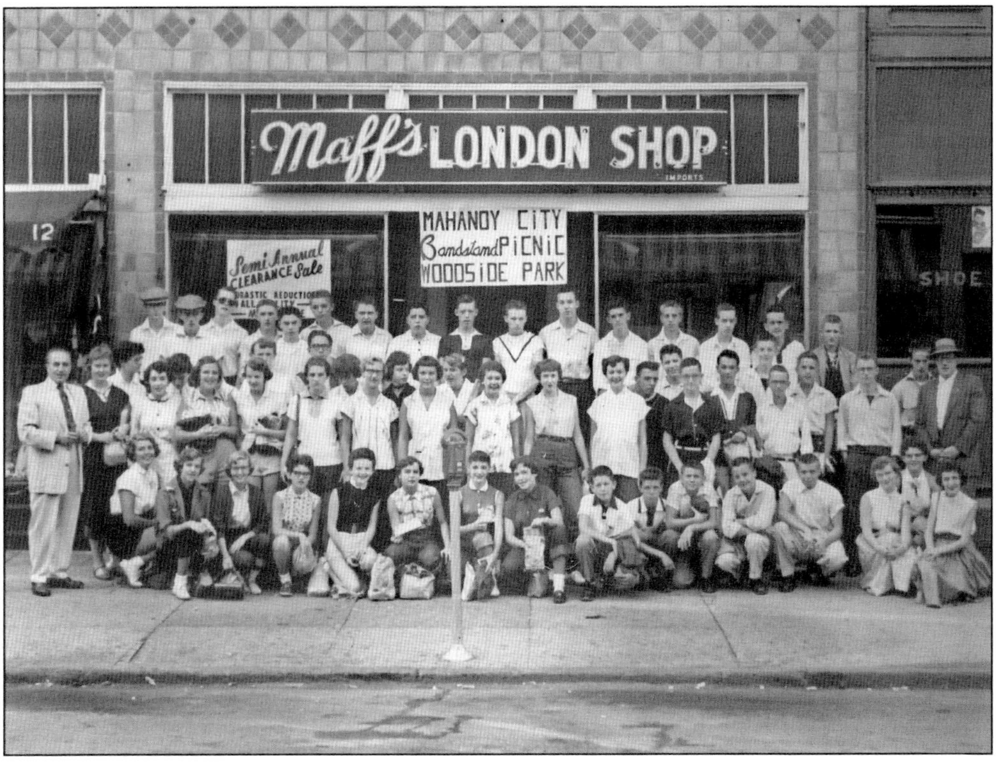

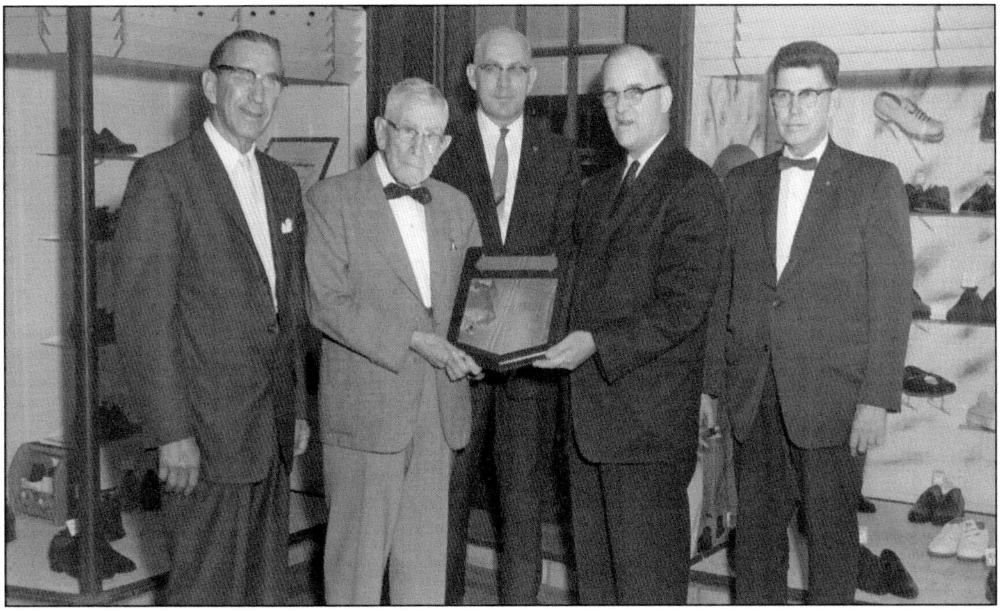

PLAQUE TO THOMAS E. TREGELLAS. In honor of his 95th birthday and celebrating his 75th year in business, Thomas E. Tregellas was presented a plaque by the Merchants Association on September 23, 1961. Pictured, from left to right, are Louis Liachowitz, Tregellas, Edward R. Shomgard, Elwood M. Young, and Tregellas's son Paul E. Tregellas. (MCPL.)

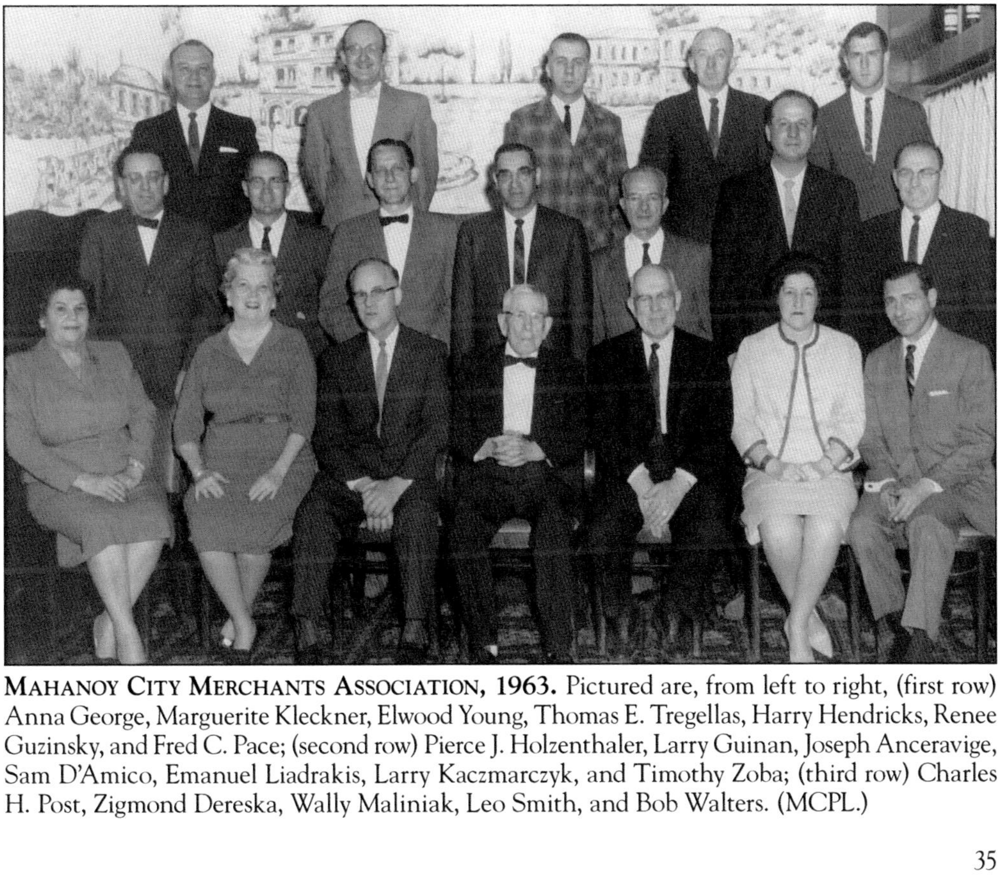

MAHANOY CITY MERCHANTS ASSOCIATION, 1963. Pictured are, from left to right, (first row) Anna George, Marguerite Kleckner, Elwood Young, Thomas E. Tregellas, Harry Hendricks, Renee Guzinsky, and Fred C. Pace; (second row) Pierce J. Holzenthaler, Larry Guinan, Joseph Anceravige, Sam D'Amico, Emanuel Liadrakis, Larry Kaczmarczyk, and Timothy Zoba; (third row) Charles H. Post, Zigmond Dereska, Wally Maliniak, Leo Smith, and Bob Walters. (MCPL.)

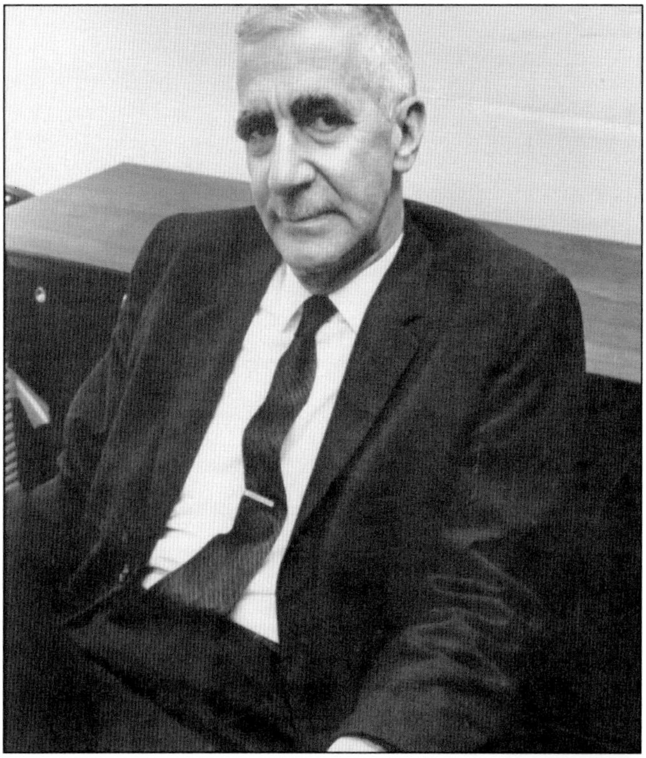

Arthur Lewis. Arthur Lewis (1906–1995) was a 1923 graduate of Mahanoy City High School. Lewis was a journalist, college professor, and best-selling author of seven books, including *Lament for the Molly Maguires*, *Carnival*, and *Hex*. When the *New York Times* asked Lewis about career highlights, he stated, "Nothing comes close to the happiness I felt when my hometown library gave a lunch in my honor." (MHS.)

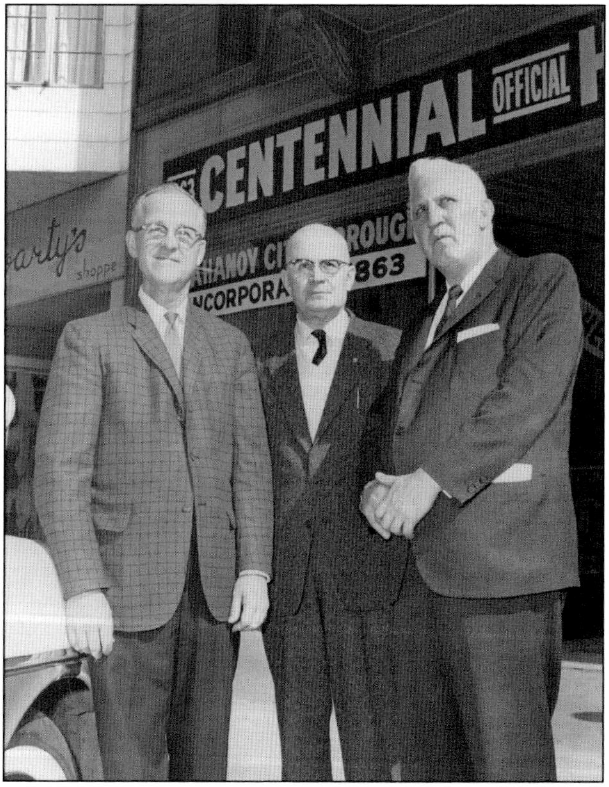

Historians. Every town has individuals who either by avocation or chance become the keepers of the community's history. Three of them are pictured together here. They are from left to right, Elwood Young, Joseph Davies, and Charlie Engle; the three compiled the history of Mahanoy City for the centennial celebration in 1963. (MCPL.)

Two

And the Band Played On

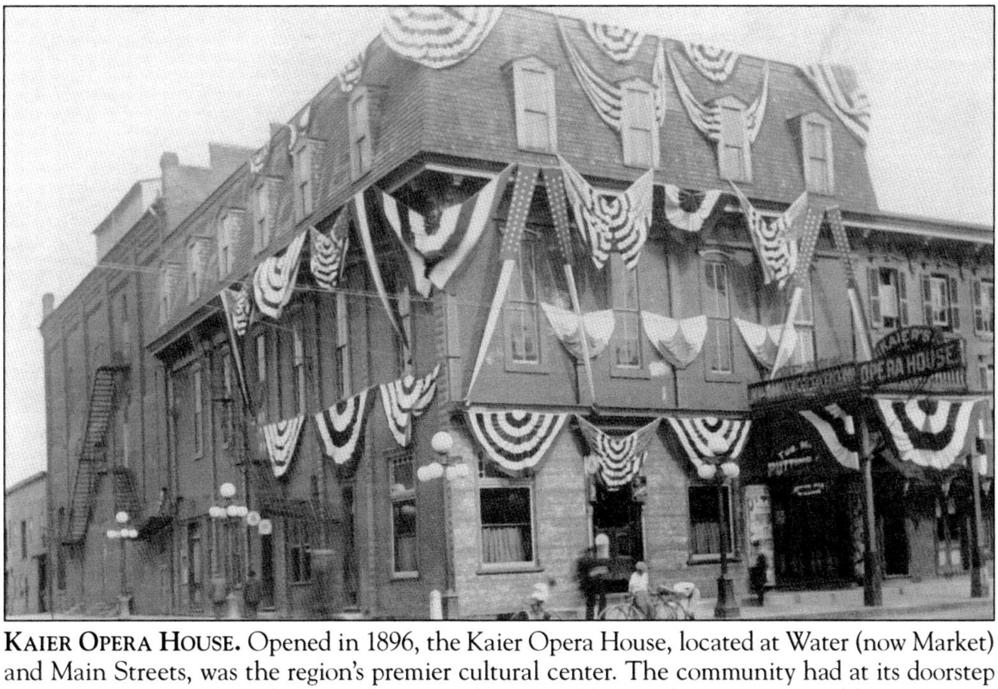

Kaier Opera House. Opened in 1896, the Kaier Opera House, located at Water (now Market) and Main Streets, was the region's premier cultural center. The community had at its doorstep a musical venue with high standards. This chapter celebrates the area's musical heritage, as it existed like a thread in Mahanoy City's daily life. (MHS.)

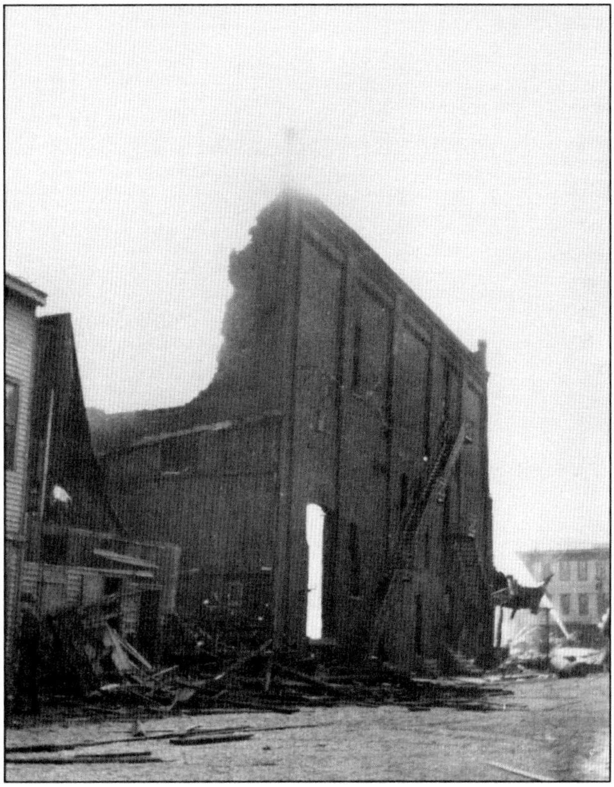

OPERA HOUSE FIRE, 1913. The diverse immigrants of the coal regions brought a love of music with them. Music, as varied as classical, choral, folk, and popular, was heard in many languages and in most homes. Many were inspired to make music an important part of their school, social, and family lives. When the opera house was destroyed by fire, residents felt the loss but were encouraged by Margaret (née Curry) Kaier's promise to rebuild. (MCPL.)

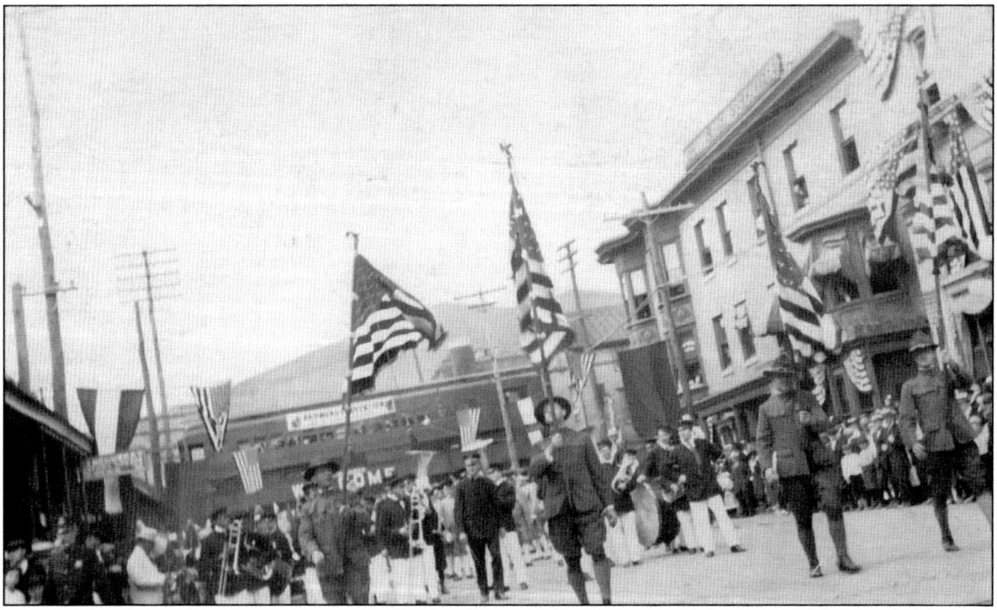

REDMEN CONVENTION, 1917. Just as the opera house was held in high esteem in Mahanoy City, so were parades with bands of paramount importance. Learning to play an instrument was a normal part of growing up. Most civic groups had organized bands with uniforms. Pictured is the Mahanoy City Tribe of Redmen, a national patriotic organization modeled after Indian tribes. The group convened in Mahanoy City as America was entering World War I. (PGG.)

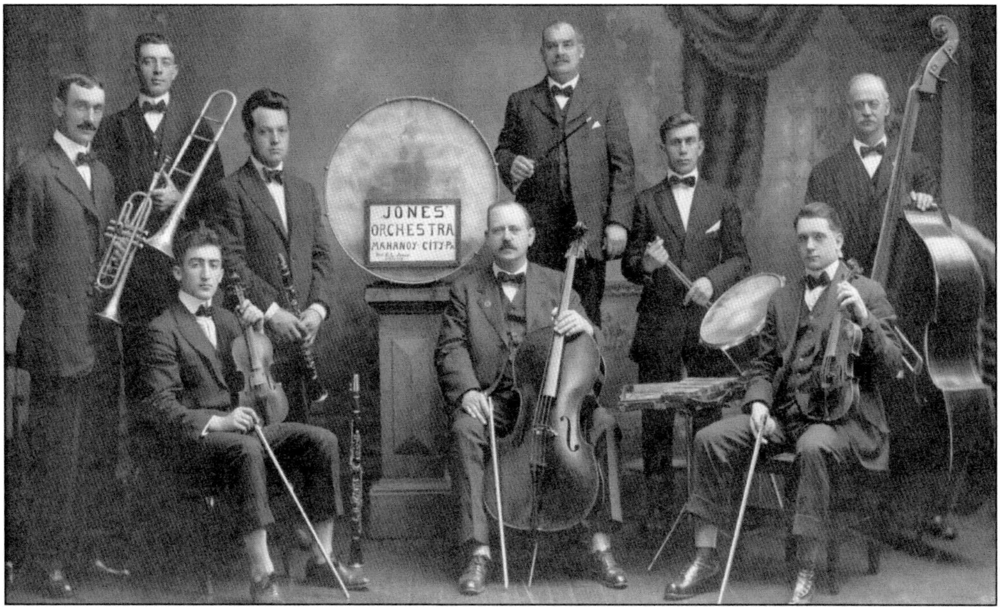

JONES ORCHESTRA. One of the most popular attractions in the many halls and social clubs of Mahanoy City and surrounding towns in the 1920s was the Prof. E.L. Jones Orchestra. On February 4, 1920, on the way back from an engagement in McAdoo, the orchestra was stranded in a snowstorm in Delano. Throughout the night, the band played every song in its repertoire to keep from freezing. (JG.)

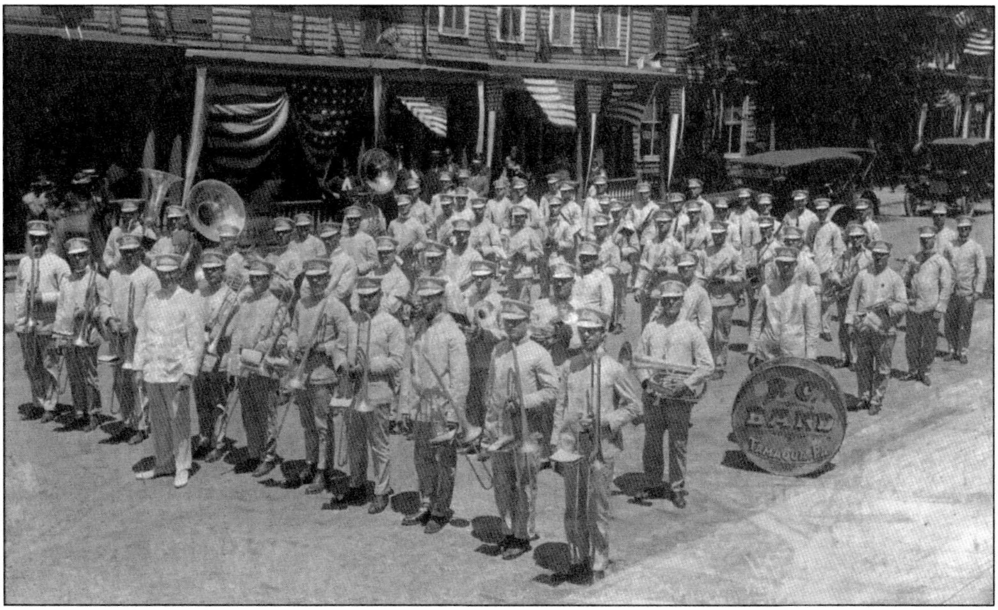

PROFESSOR DORSEY, 1921. For major events, towns combined marching bands and traveled by train to surrounding counties. For the June 21, 1921, Shriners parade, pictured here, Professor Dorsey, storied father of Tommy and Jimmy, brought his band from Tamaqua to Mahanoy City. Thousands of Shriners, dressed in their fezzes, traveled with their drum and bugle corps and caged animals to the Rajah Temple in Reading, 60 miles away. (PGG.)

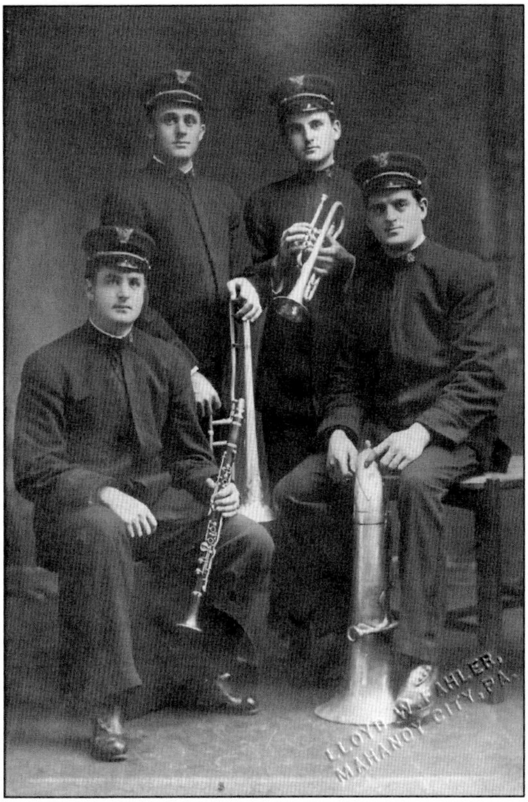

UNSINN BROTHERS, 1919. Music was so important to the Unsinn family that a photographer was hired to take the brothers' picture dressed in Eagles Club Band uniforms. They are, from left to right, (sitting) Charles, bandleader with the P.C. Band of Tamaqua, and John, leader of Eagles Club Band and Minstrel of Mahanoy City for nearly 30 years; (standing) Joseph, a member of the Navy Band during World War I, and George, a featured cornet soloist in Mahanoy City. (PC.)

VICTORIA THEATER, 1925. Sadly, Margaret (née Curry) Kaier died two months after the 1913 opera house fire, and it was not until 1924 that the Chamberlain Amusement Company purchased the land and built the magnificent Victoria Theater. Finally, the region had a first-class musical entertainment facility, with its own orchestra able to accommodate vocalists and instrumental soloists. March 9, 1925 was opening night. (MEKS.)

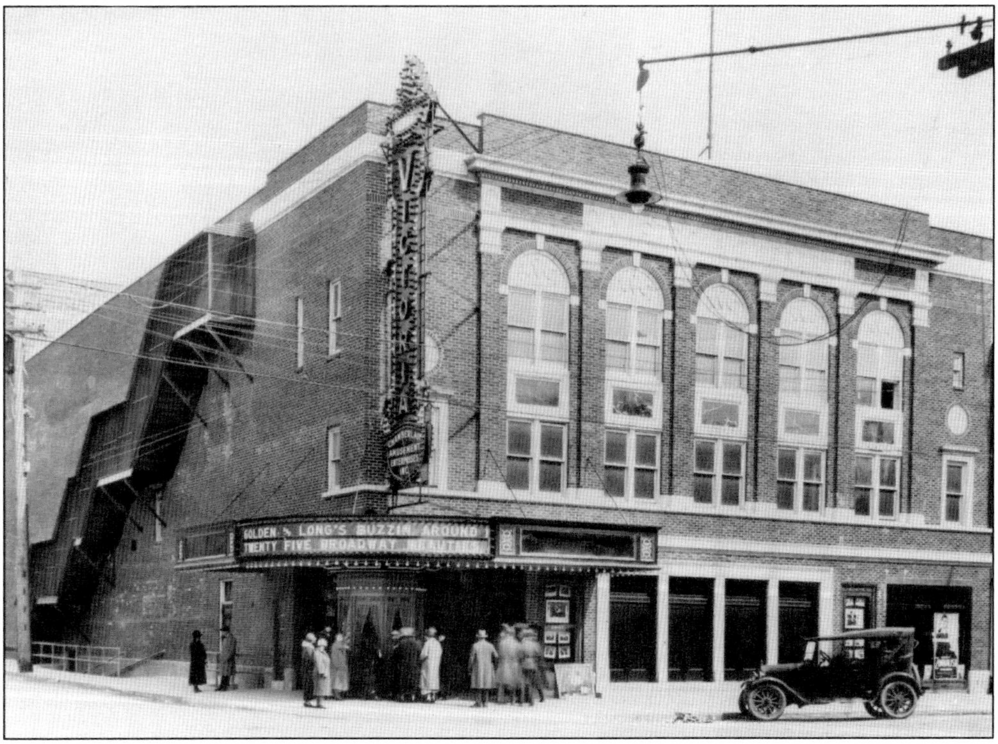

MICHAEL SLOWITZKY/SLOWITSKY EDWARDS. In the rich atmosphere of Mahanoy City, at least two musical geniuses of national fame were nurtured and educated within a few years of each other. Taught by his father, Michael Slowitzky/Slowitsky performed on the violin at the Kaier Opera House as a young boy. Slowitzky is described in the *Record American* newspaper as "having inherited the talents of his ancestors and has attained an unusual standing in the musical world." (SBU-SCL.)

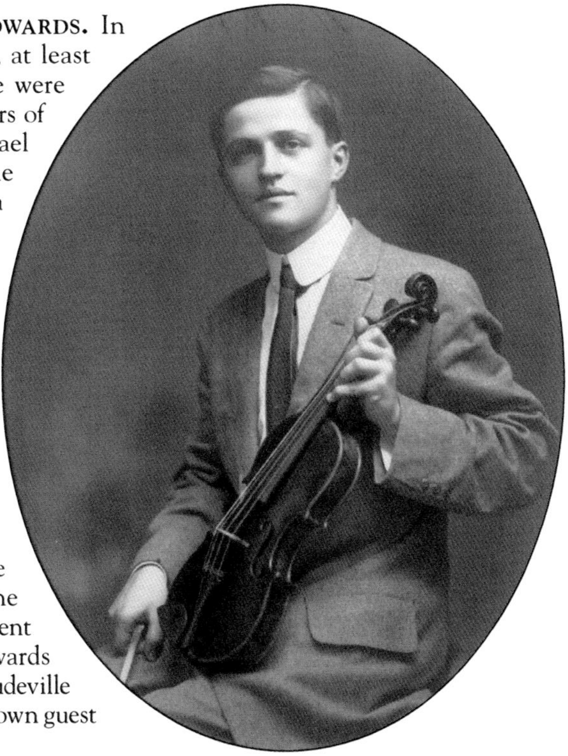

MICHAEL SLOWITZKY EDWARDS, ORGANIST. In 1926 at age 33, Michael was selected as organist and musical director of the Victoria Theater, where he performed with his orchestra. The Moller concert organ, as described in the opening night program, was one of the largest in the musical world and equivalent to a 130-piece orchestra. Slowitzky Edwards played the organ to accompany movies, vaudeville acts, musical comedies, and nationally known guest artists. (SBU-SCL.)

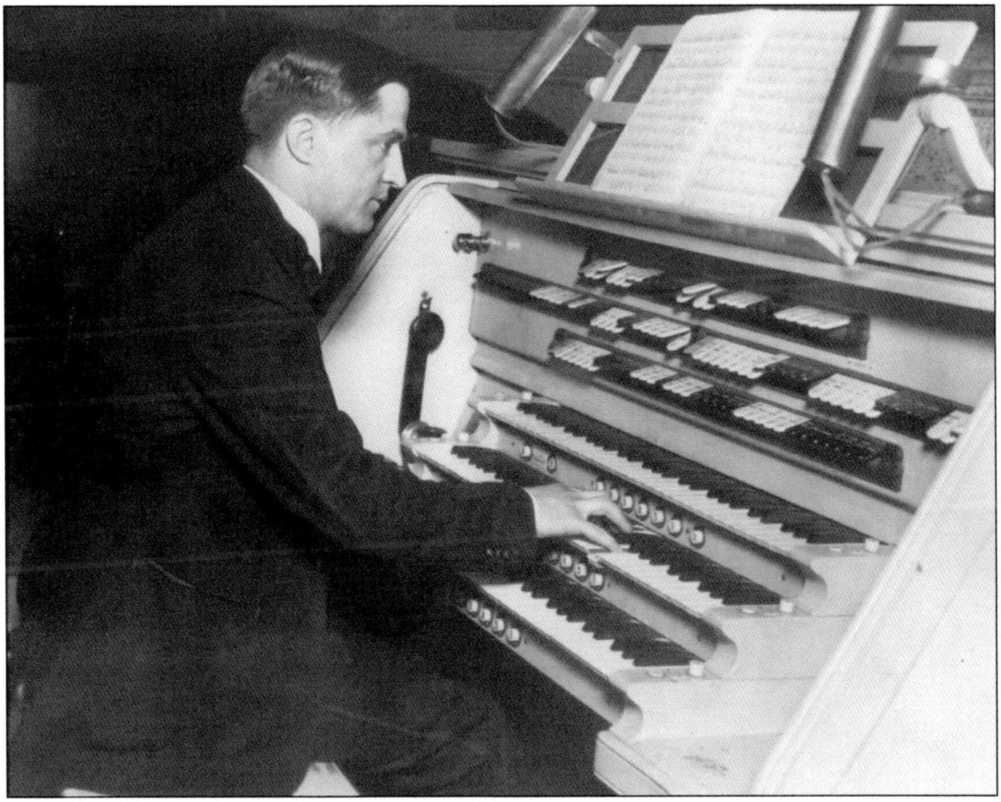

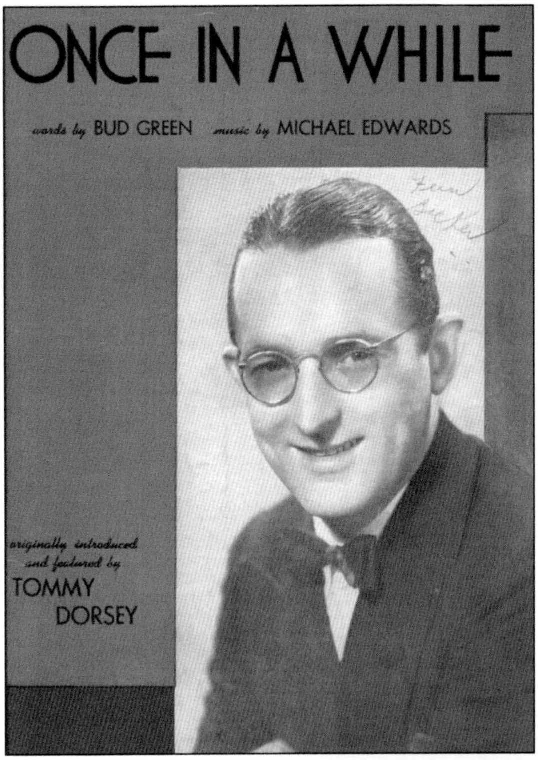

"ONCE IN A WHILE." Leaving the "Vic" in 1928, Slowitzky went to Philadelphia, where his career flourished as composer, songwriter, conductor, violinist, organist, and arranger. His jazz standard "Once in a While," recorded by the Tommy Dorsey Orchestra, gained No. 1 status in *Billboard* magazine in 1937. His "Tell Me Why" (1940s) is a standard learned by thousands of Girl Scouts. During his long career, Slowitzky arranged music for Leroy Anderson's "Sleigh Ride." (MHS.)

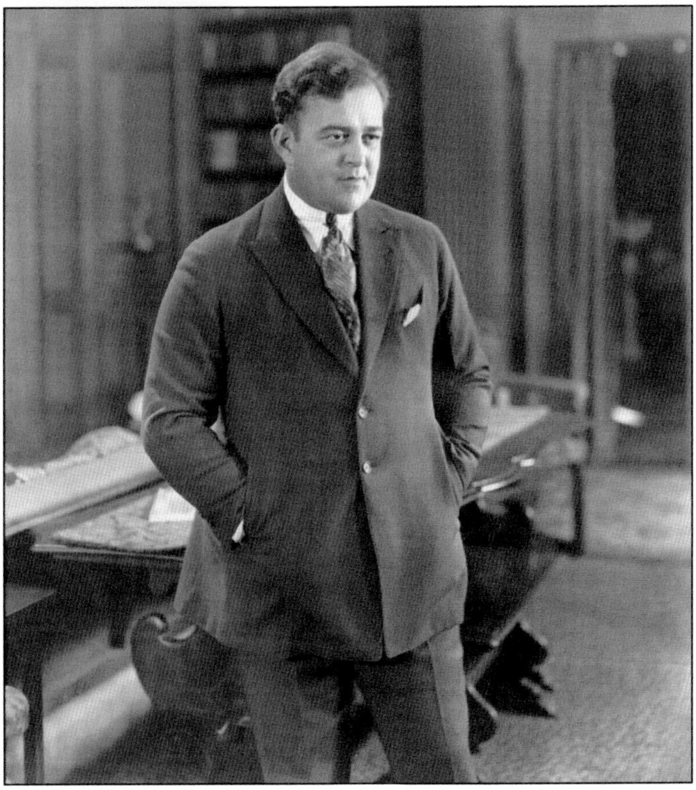

VICTOR SCHERTZINGER. The second musical genius of the Kaier/Victoria era was Victor Schertzinger, a film director and composer. Born in Mahanoy City, he was taught the violin by his mother, an internationally applauded musician, and by Prof. John Jones, director of the Mahanoy Township High School band. Victor performed at the Kaier Opera House with his parents before going on a world tour. At age eight, he was called "the Greatest Boy Violinist in the World." (MHS.)

"MARCHETA." To further his career interests, the Schertzinger family moved to California where Victor immediately found success as a songwriter and conductor. "Marcheta," written by Schertzinger in 1913, sold four million copies on the pop market. By 1915, Schertzinger had caught the attention of movie producers who hired him to compose film scores. (MHS.)

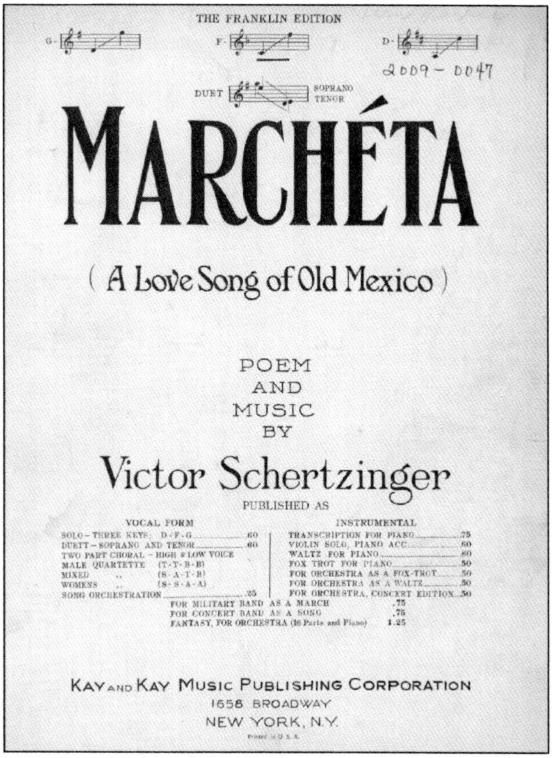

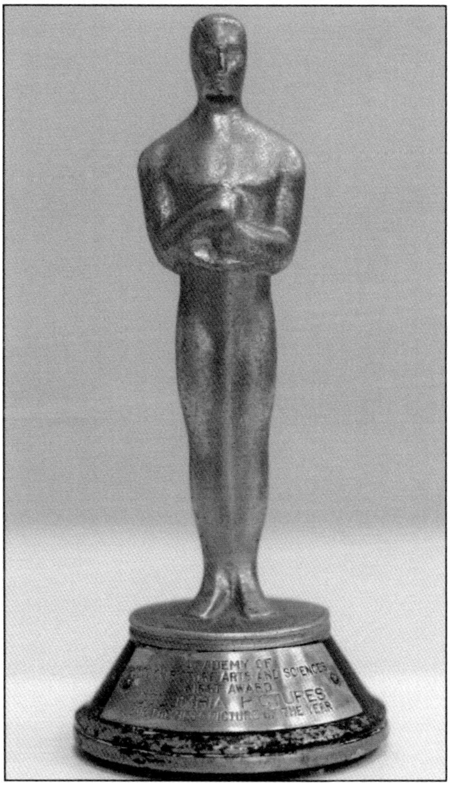

THE OSCAR. Schertzinger pioneered the use of original music for film, produced the first Technicolor movies, and composed many songs for the Ziegfeld Follies. In 1935, his music for *One Night of Love*, cowritten with Gus Kahn, won the Music (Scoring) Oscar. Schertzinger went on to direct the first two movies of the Road series starring Bob Hope and Bing Crosby and has a star on the Hollywood Walk of Fame. (MHS.)

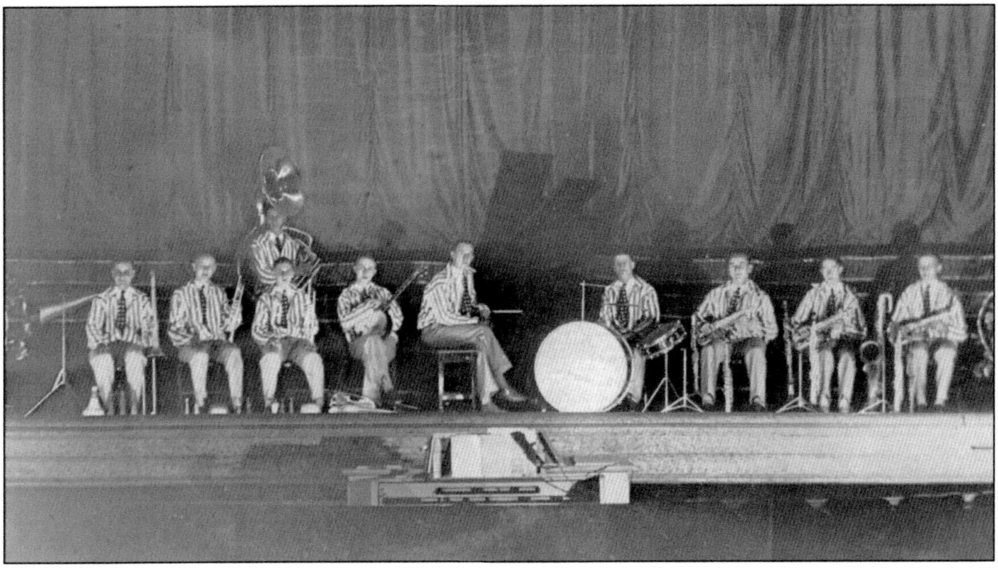

VICTORIA BAND, 1920S. Typically, the Victoria featured a short (20-minute) movie, a big-name entertainer/musician, and a "house band" to accompany the traveling acts. Pictured are musicians referred to as the "Vic Band." Playing tuba is Thomas A. Ward and at piano Harold Williams. Ward, with a background of piano lessons, taught himself to play the bass horn (tuba), which led to a lifetime of performing. (MEKS.)

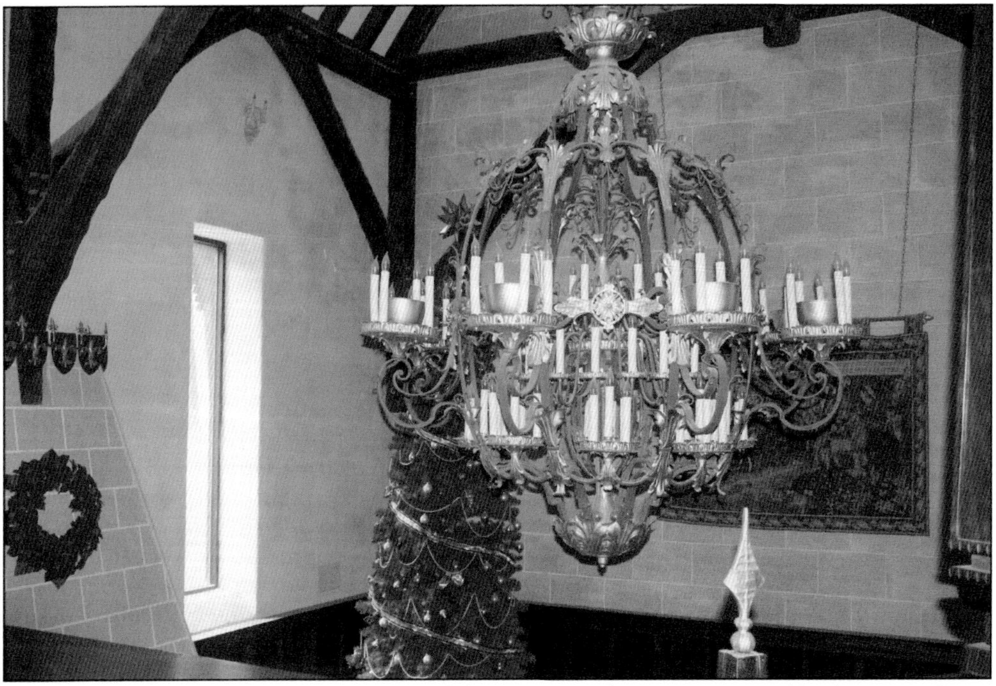

GRAND CHANDELIER. The crown jewel of the Victoria Theater was arguably the magnificent chandelier. Weighing 1,800 pounds and measuring 8 feet wide and 11 feet tall, it had 120 lighted candles and required 5,600 watts to operate. Beautifully restored, it now hangs in the Tudor-style home of Ken and Michelle Boyle. Crystals draped over the chandelier have been removed to better match the style of their home. (KMB.)

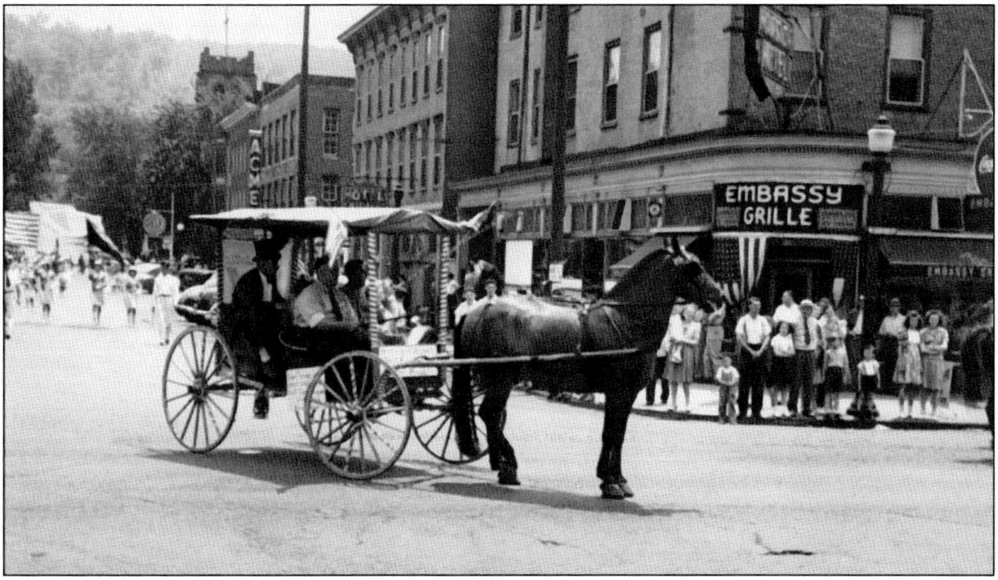

INDEPENDENCE DAY, 1942. Blasts from the whistles of Kaier's Brewery and the Mahanoy City colliery signaled the beginning of the annual July 4th parade in 1942. In the picture, the parade is turning west on Centre Street in front of Gus Simotas's Embassy Grill. At the conclusion of the parade, a flag-raising ceremony was held at the Citizen's Fire Company. Young Hartman Beynon played "Taps," and John Unsinn led the Eagles' Band in the playing of "The Star-Spangled Banner." (JSB.)

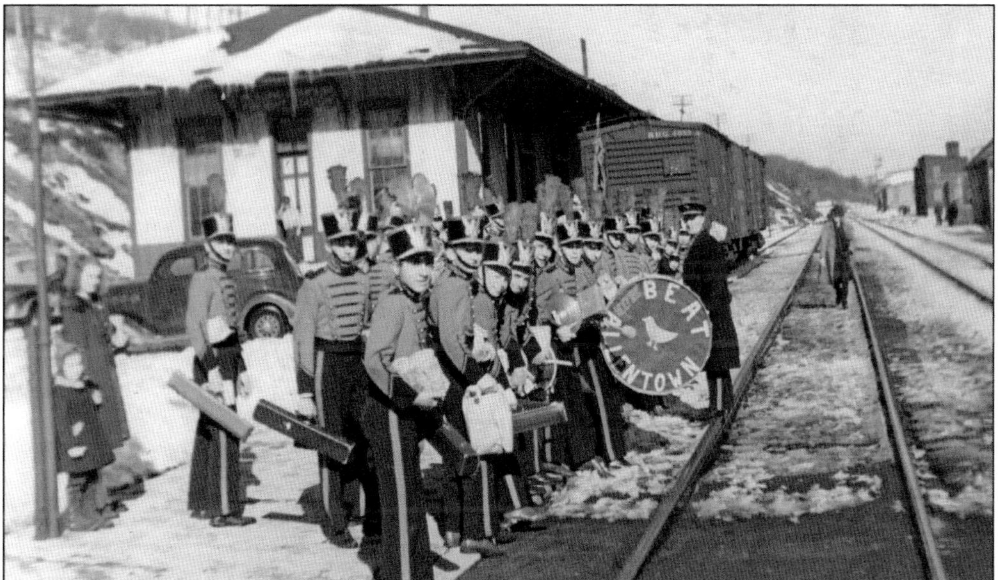

MAHANOY CITY BAND AT TRAIN STATION, 1941. In the winter of 1941, band member and yearbook lensman Joseph Glaudel photographed the band waiting for the train to the Palestra in Philadelphia for the district basketball playoff between Mahanoy City and Allentown. Mahanoy won. Joseph "Swing" Flamini (front, holding lunch) played clarinet in high school and was a member of local bands as an adult. William Becker (facing band members) was band director. (DJG.)

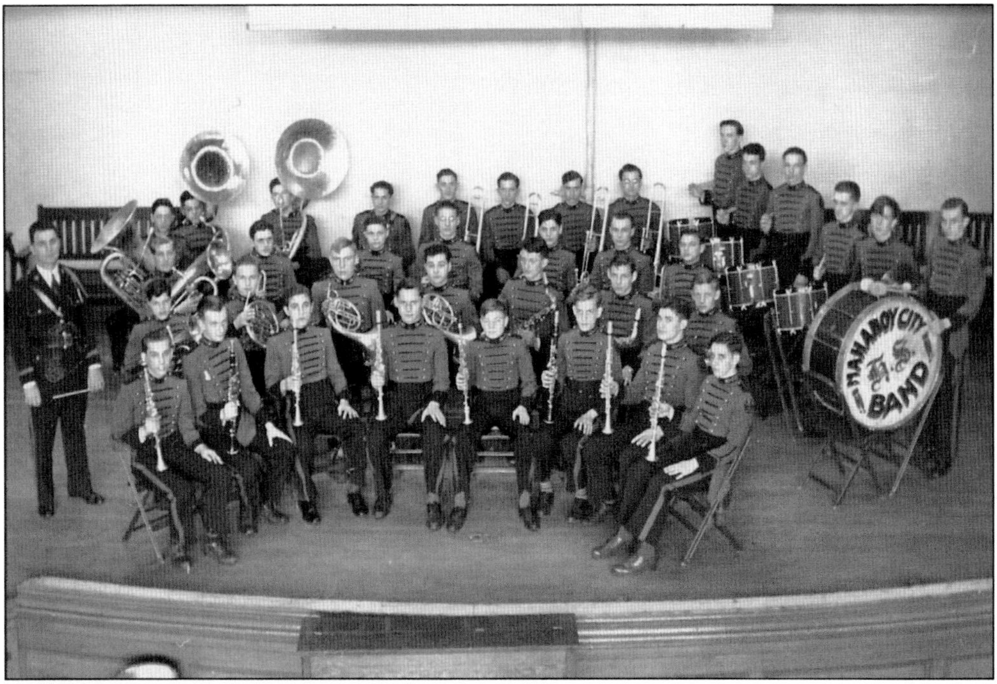

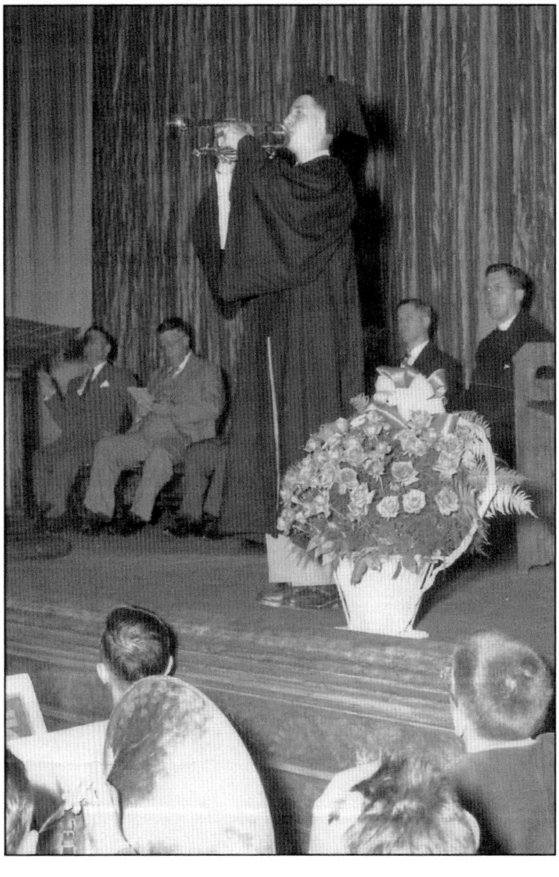

MAHANOY CITY HIGH SCHOOL BAND, 1941. William C. Becker (standing, far left) conducted instrumental music in Mahanoy City schools from 1928 to 1957. Professor Becker, like most in his position, taught all of the instruments. Most children could not afford an instrument and relied on those rented or loaned to them. Often, members played the instrument that was available; sometimes, they played the instrument that they could carry. (DJG.)

BEYNON AT GRADUATION, 1949. On his graduation night in 1949, Hartman Beynon played a cornet solo and was immediately accepted into the 356th Army Band. In 1954, he auditioned and was accepted into "Pershing's Own," the US Army Band, and became a featured soloist. In 1963, Beynon was designated principal bugler of the US Army and, in 1969, was named sergeant major of the US Army Band and enlisted bandleader. (CBS.)

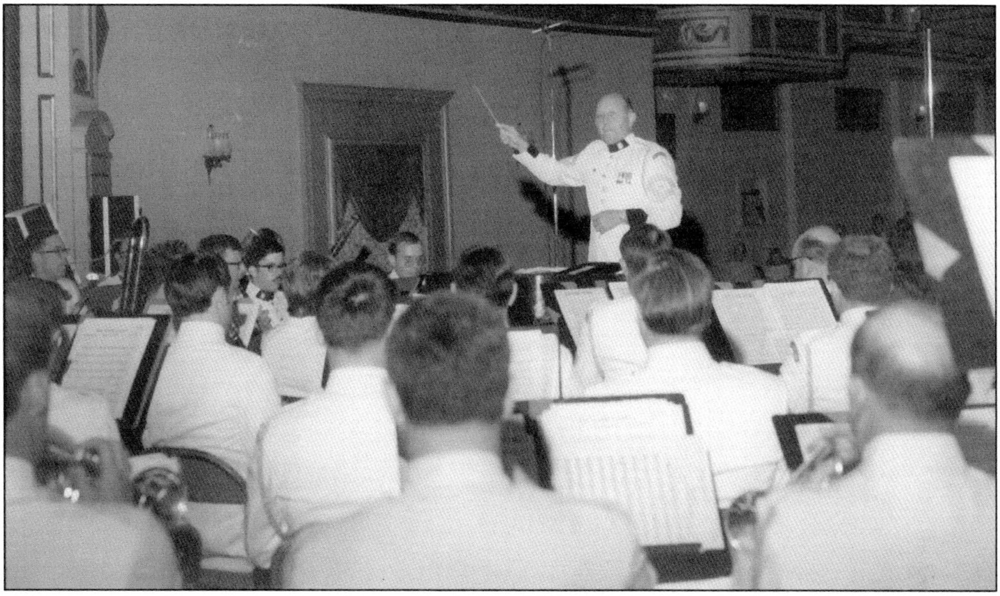

Beynon Conducts, 1976. As a child, Hartman played "Taps" at the graves of those from his hometown who perished in World War II. He also played "Taps" as President Kennedy's body was finally laid to rest in Arlington National Cemetery. Reflecting on his memories, Sergeant Major Beynon recounts his two biggest thrills: conducting his US Army Band on the balcony of the White House and bringing his band to his hometown to perform at the Victoria Theater. (CBS.)

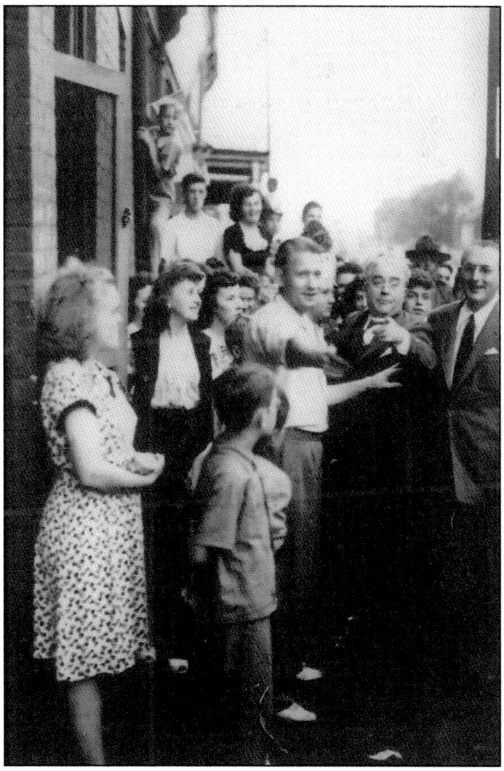

Dorsey in Mahanoy Plane, 1945. A hometown committee invited Tommy Dorsey, seen at the far right, to its Labor Day parade. Hearing about the visit, Lorraine Stanton hiked to "The Foot" from Frackville and witnessed Dorsey borrow a trombone from a Gilberton Band member and delight the crowd by playing "Sentimental Over You" from a nearby porch. Afterwards, Dorsey went for dinner at the home of Francis Brennan, seen to the left of Dorsey, before joining his band at Lakewood Ballroom. (FB.)

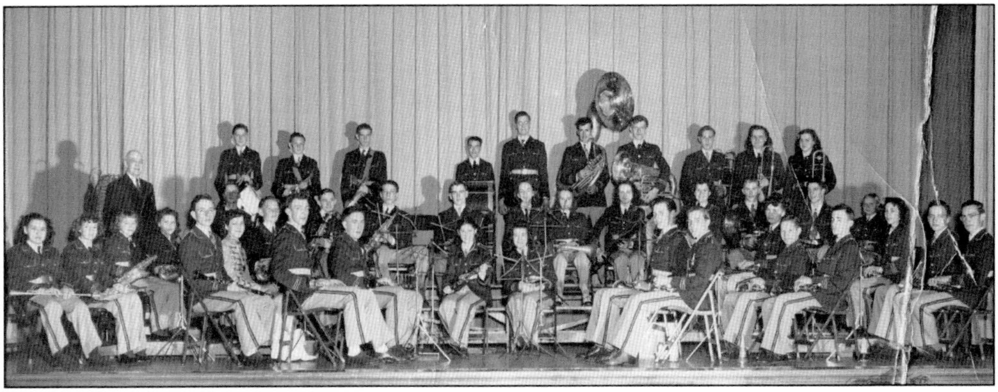

SPRING CONCERT 1948. Prof. Guy Dower, standing at the far left, was band and orchestra director at Mahanoy Township High School from 1926 to 1950. Most members were taught in school by Professor Dower. All of the concerts, outings, parades, and sports appearances were in the hands of the director. Out of uniform is Ann Wahalec Brinsko of Cole's Patch. Ann played with the orchestra but marched with the majorettes to lead the band. (DC.)

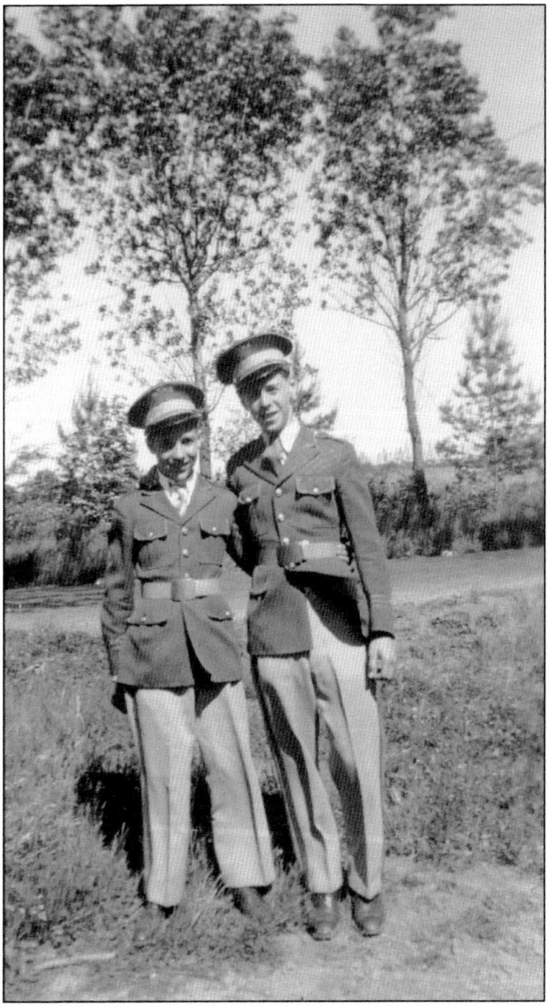

MAHANOY TOWNSHIP HIGH SCHOOL BAND MEMBERS. Pictured here are two freshman members of the 1946 Mahanoy Township High School band. John Kozie (left) of Buck Mountain, took music seriously, earning the lead trumpet chair two years later. John went on to perform with the Pennsylvania State College band. Don Coombe was also a member of the trumpet section. (DC.)

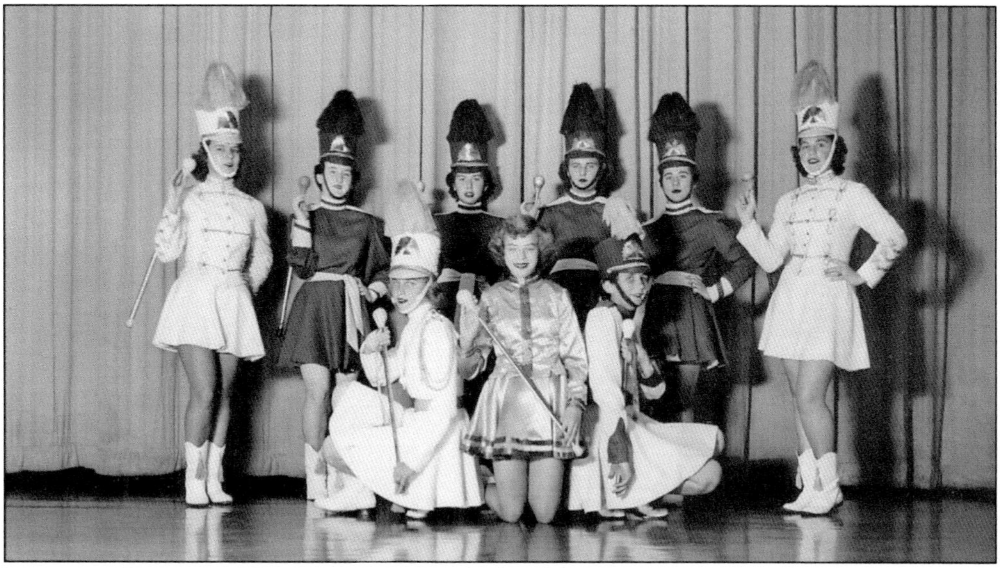

MAHANOY TOWNSHIP MAJORETTES, 1952. The band front was an important part of the marching band and football game performances. 1952 members are, from left to right, (first row) Carol Thompson Wagner, Monica Kardisco, and Marilyn Miller Evans; (second row) Jacqueline Stank, Patsy Kane, Marie Valonis, Cecilia Olinitz, Patsy McNiff, and unidentified. (DA.)

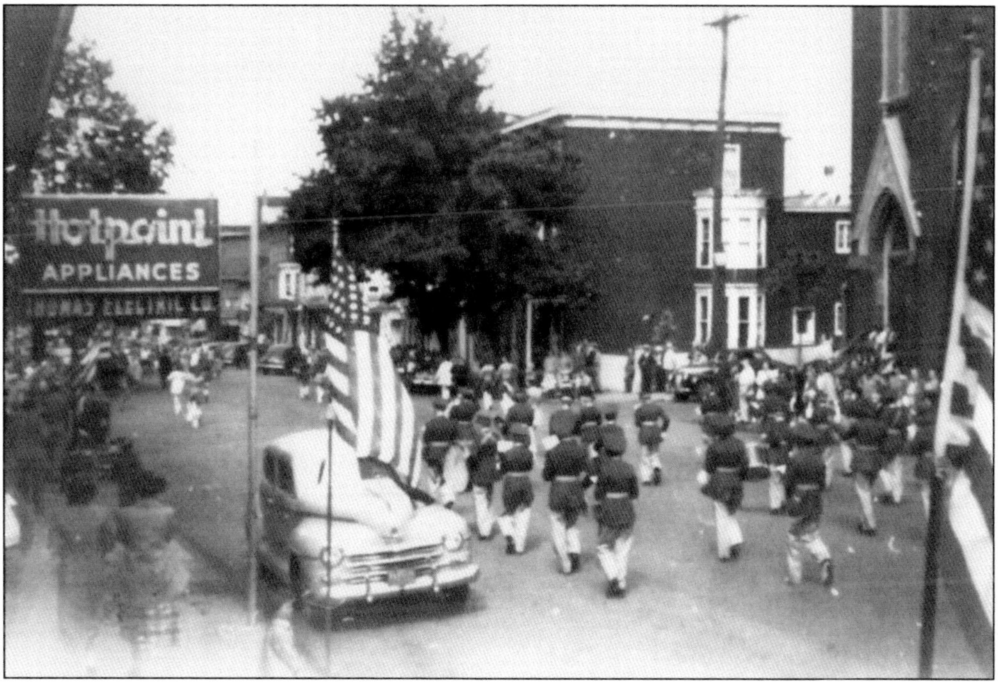

DECORATION DAY 1951. Newspaper accounts indicate Mahanoy City bands played in a Decoration Day parade since 1869. This Memorial Day parade followed the traditional route. From East Centre Street to the west and then back up the mile on Mahanoy Avenue to the east end, the township band marched. This image taken in the 400 block of East Centre Street by Shirley Thomas, age 10, captures the sign for her dad's appliance store as well as the Mahanoy Township High School band. (STR.)

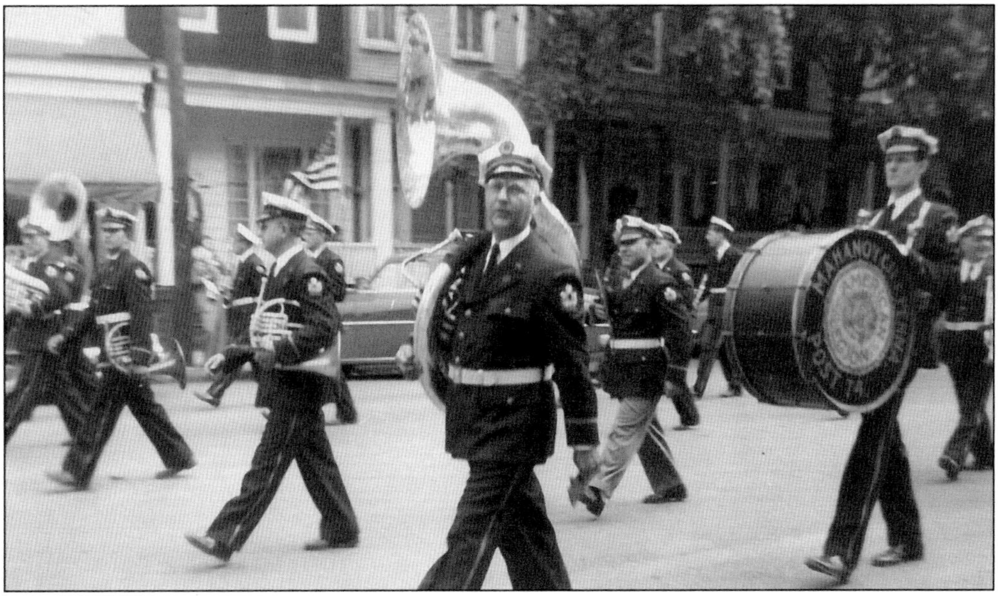

AMERICAN LEGION BAND, MEMORIAL DAY PARADE 1956. Thomas Ward, with his shiny brass tuba, was a member of many local bands, each with a different uniform: Citizens, Germania, Liberty, Eagles, American Legion, Lithuanian, and Italian bands, the Leadercrants, and Professor Dorsey Orchestra. Ward toured with the bands and inspired many of his children and grandchildren to study and enjoy music. (STR.)

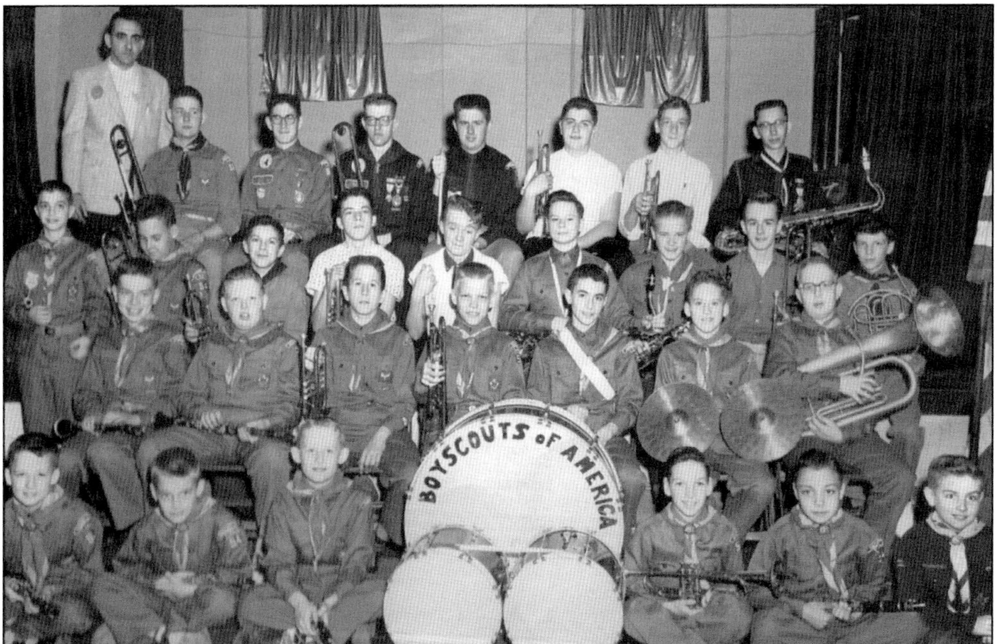

TROOP NO. 54 BAND. From about 1956 through 1959, the Christ Lutheran Church sponsored a band composed of its Troop No. 54 Boy Scouts, with leader Bob Fisher of Mahanoy City. The band met and practiced in the fellowship hall and performed on the church stage. Each member had his own instrument, and most later played in the Mahanoy Area High School band. (JKG.)

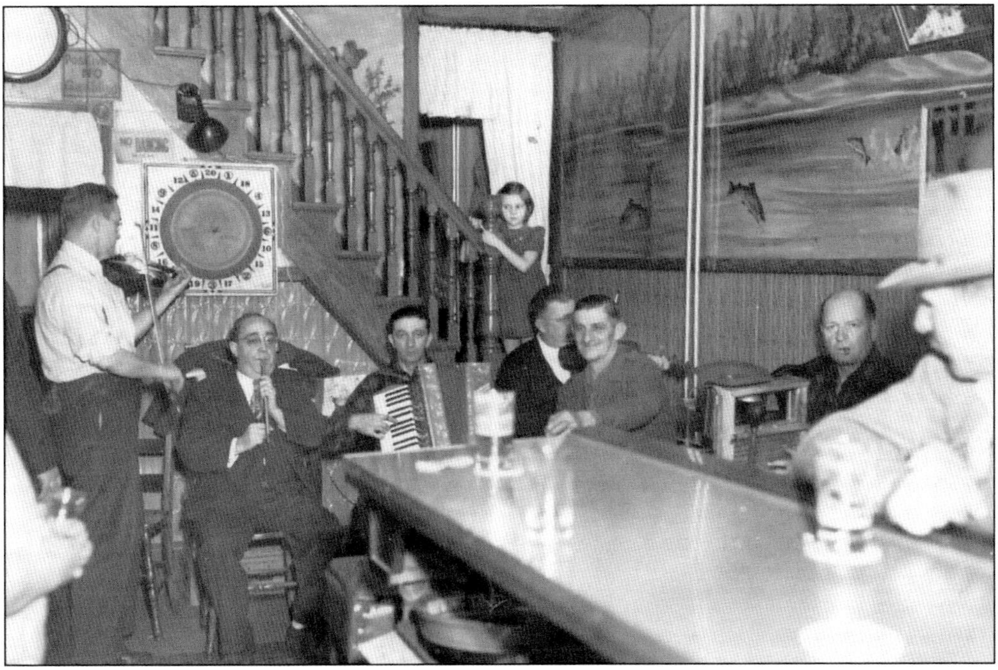

Musicians at Ambrose Café, 1950. Seven-year-old Diane Ambrose, at the banister, recalls that musicians came to her grandfather's bar most Saturdays to play for their own enjoyment. Bob Yienxt, at left, played Diane's grandfather's violin passionately. The musician farthest on the right played a washboard with thimbles on his fingers. As was the custom, men and women in neighborhood bars liked to sing in their own languages. (DA.)

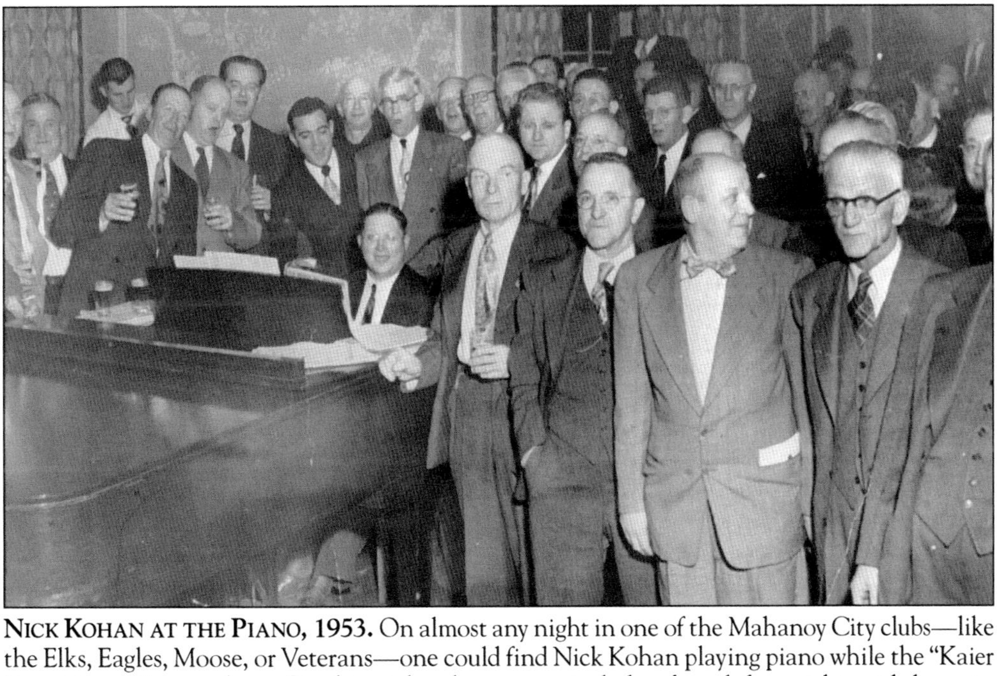

Nick Kohan at the Piano, 1953. On almost any night in one of the Mahanoy City clubs—like the Elks, Eagles, Moose, or Veterans—one could find Nick Kohan playing piano while the "Kaier Beer Quartet" sang along. On this night, the quartet includes, from left to right, with beers in their hands, Leo Doyle, Tom Coombe, Bill Coombe, and Lim Berger. (PC.)

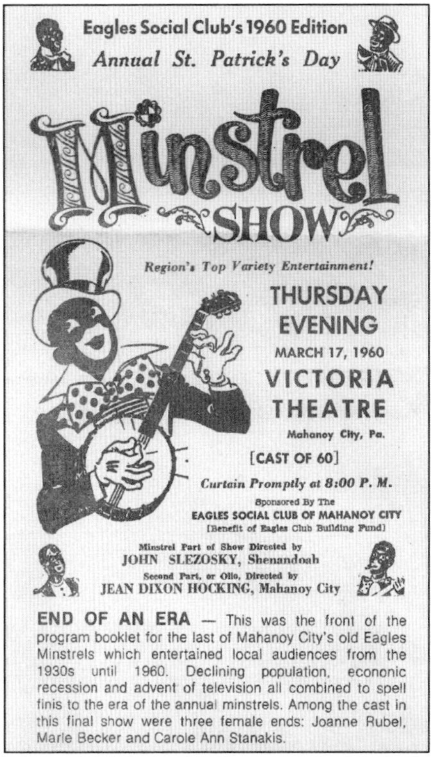

END OF AN ERA — This was the front of the program booklet for the last of Mahanoy City's old Eagles Minstrels which entertained local audiences from the 1930s until 1960. Declining population, econonic recession and advent of television all combined to spell finis to the era of the annual minstrels. Among the cast in this final show were three female ends: Joanne Rubel, Marie Becker and Carole Ann Stanakis.

EAGLES CLUB MINSTREL. The last minstrel show produced by the Eagles Club of Mahanoy City was held at the Victoria Theater in 1960. With a cast of 60, it contained all of the same acts of comedy, music, and dance that the minstrels had included since the 1920s. (MHS.)

BILL MITCHELL WITH THE MAHANOY AREA HIGH SCHOOL MARCHING BAND, 1960. In 1957, Mahanoy City High School hired Bill Mitchell as band director. A trombone student of the famous Professor Dorsey, the service veteran and graduate of Pennsylvania State University was about to revolutionize the performance of high school marching bands. Here, Mitchell, in the first row, far left, marches with his band at the pregame performance at a Philadelphia Eagles football game. (DA.)

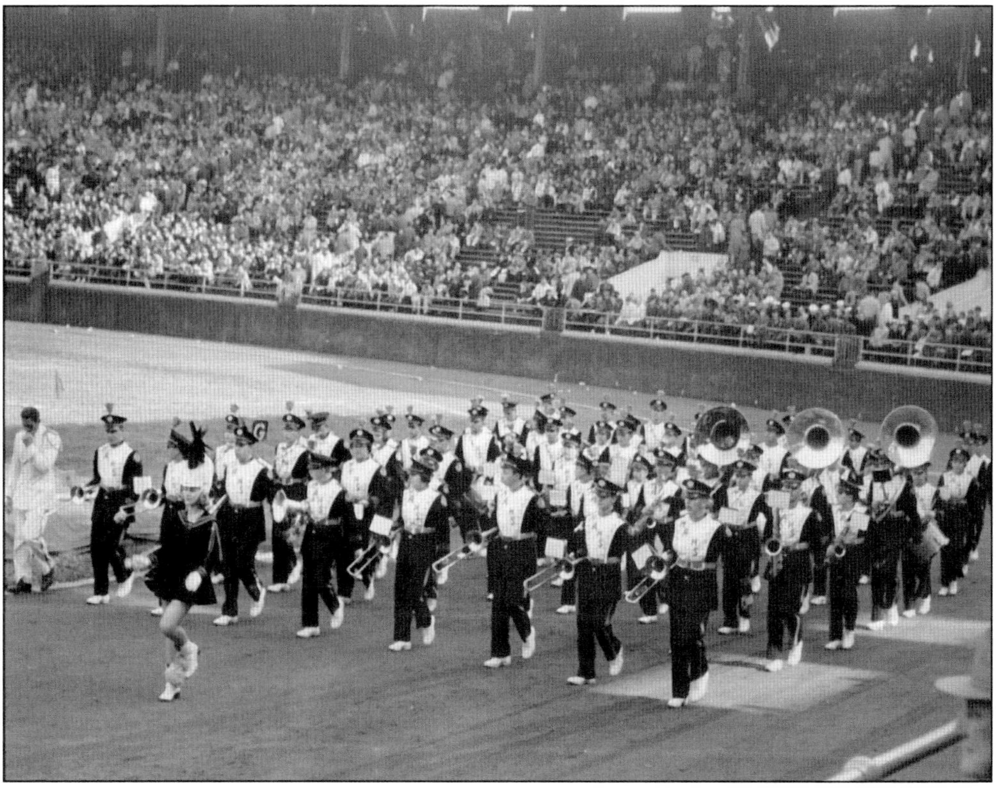

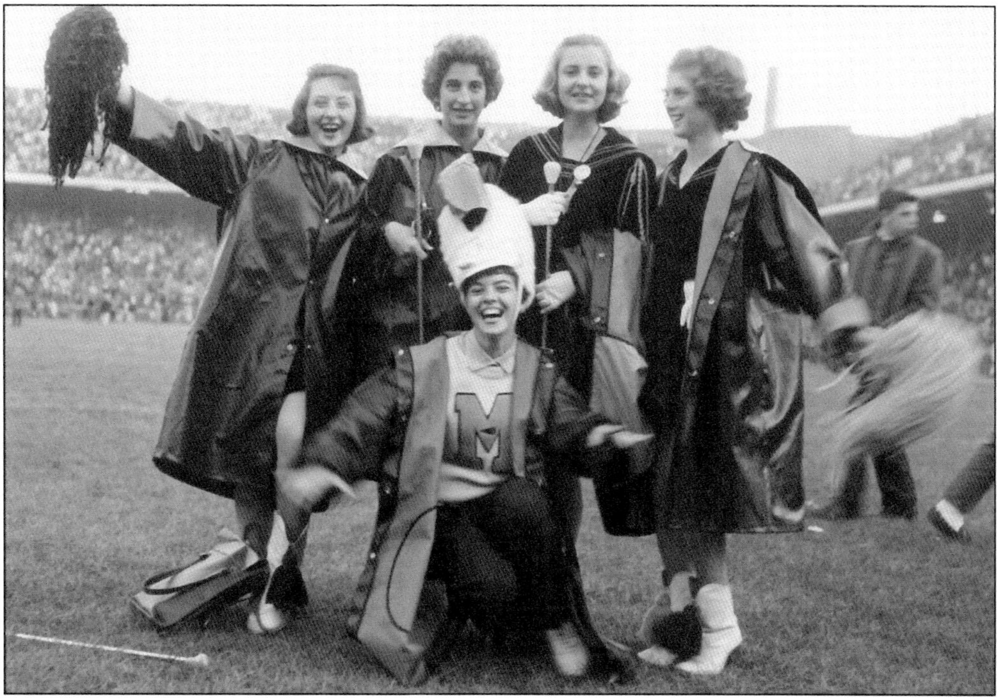

1960 MAHANOY AREA HIGH SCHOOL BAND. From left to right are (standing) majorettes Virgie Decker, Susan Shanfield, captain Diane Ambrose, and Janet Guinan; (kneeling) cheerleader Maria Lawrence. They are celebrating their successful pregame performance at the Eagles vs. Redskins game at Franklin Field in Philadelphia. The 100-member band was invited to perform during the Philadelphia Eagles' National Football League championship season based on its reputation as an outstanding high school band. (DA.)

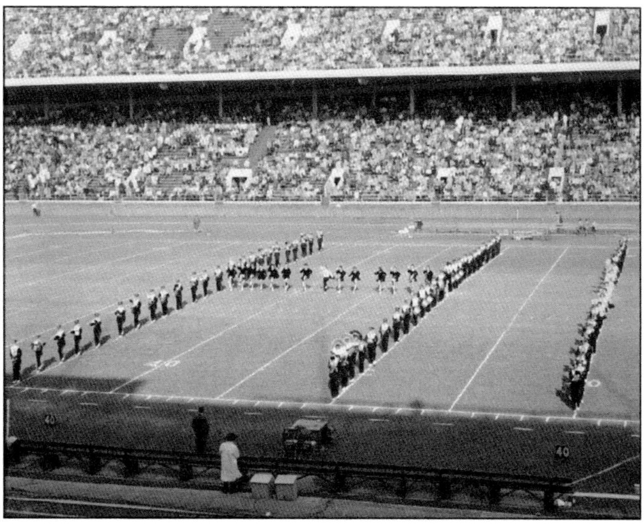

PERFORMANCE FORMATION. The recently formed Mahanoy Area High School Band marches into formations as it plays music in the pregame show at Franklin Field in 1960. Moving into intricate shapes while using dance moves was just an emerging skill in high school bands when Bill Mitchell introduced it not just to the coal regions but also to the national audiences to which his band traveled. (DA.)

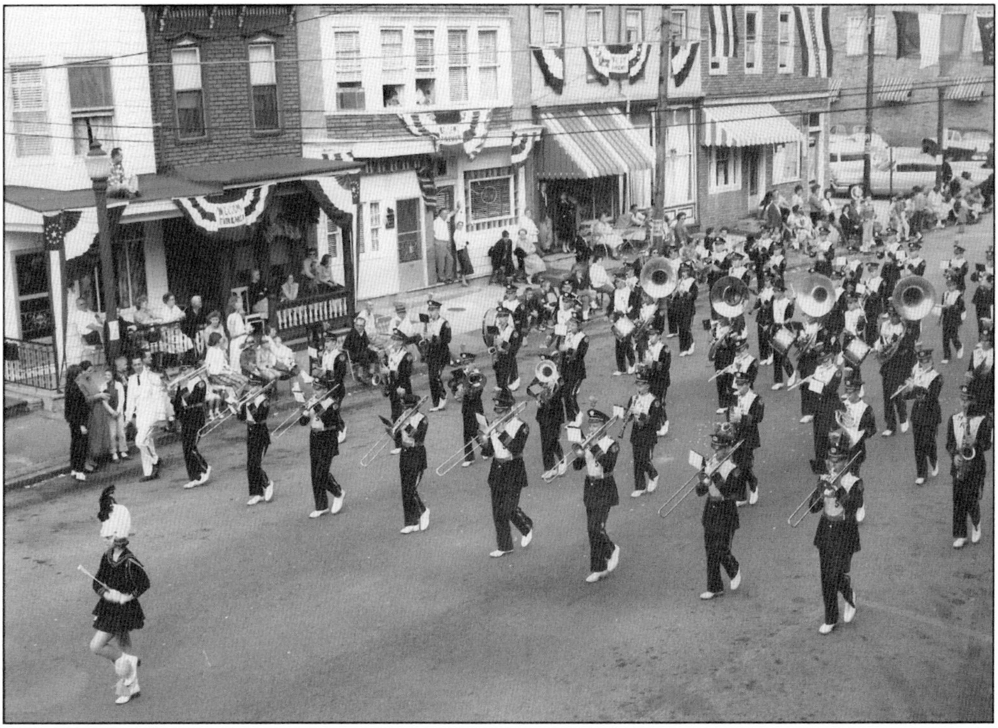

FIREMAN'S PARADE. In 1963, the firemen of Schuylkill County had their convention in Mahanoy City. To celebrate the occasion, the Mahanoy Area High School band marched in a grand parade. Houses were decorated along the two-mile route. Spectators sat on porches and roofs to watch the bands and truck equipment on display. (DA.)

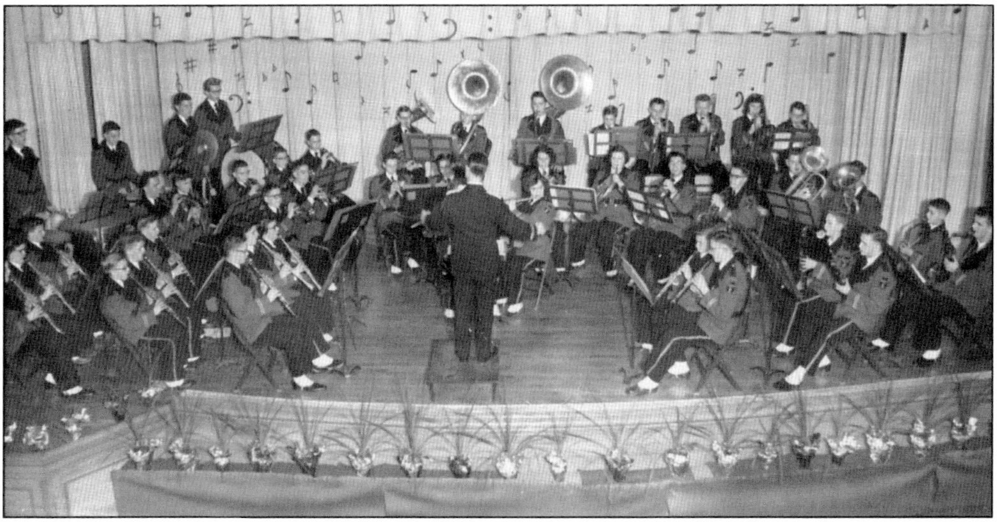

PROFESSOR BECKER, 1952. Onstage at Mahanoy City High School, Becker directs the band at the school's annual concert. Some of those seated in the picture include the following first chairs (best players): Jack Harris (clarinet), Jack Fisher (snare drum), William Richelderfer (trumpet), Bob Yanaitis (oboe), Bob Maurer (saxophone, closest to the audience), Mark Kramer (French horn), Jack O'Connell (tuba, rightmost), Peter Kapo (bass drum), and Eugene Karlick (bassoon). (MHS.)

Three

Take Me Out to the Ball Game

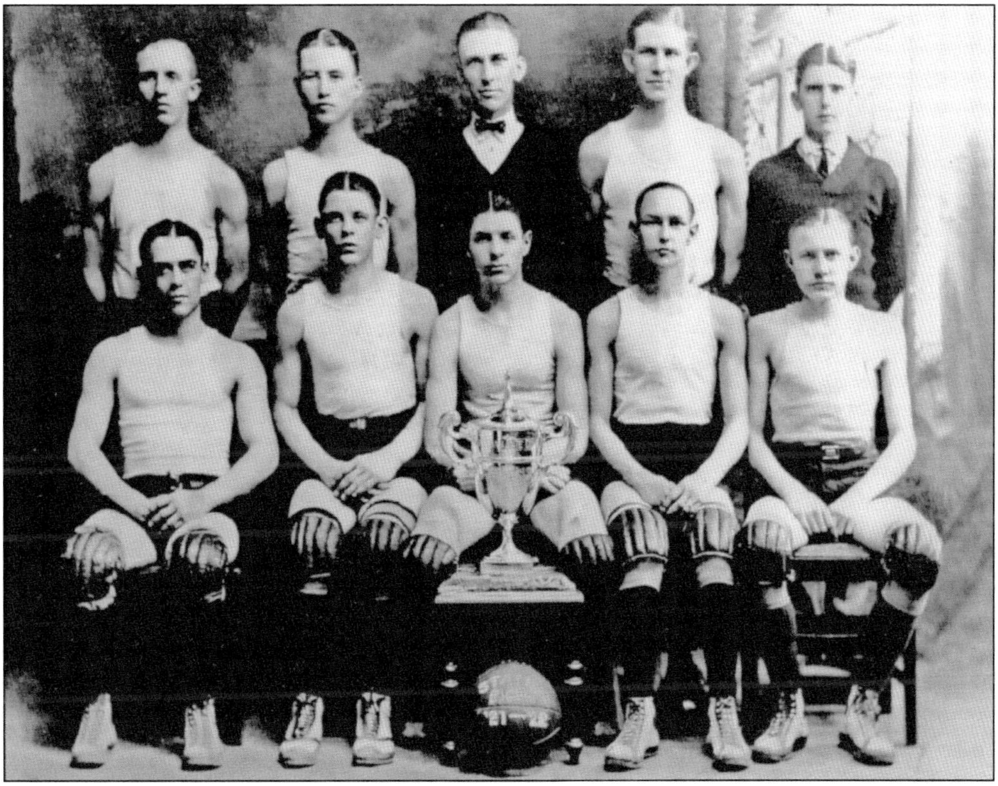

State Champs. Mahanoy City High School's 1921–1922 basketball team completed a 23-3 season with a victory over Harrisburg Tech to win the Pennsylvania Interscholastic Athletic Association (PIAA) state championship. Members of the legendary team that outscored their opponents 1202-564 are, from left to right, (first row) Edward Tolan, Edward August, captain James Leonard, James Deem, and Vladimir Smith; (second row) Peter Kapo, Thomas Courtney, coach John Goepfert, Frank Dawson, and Russell Green. (MHS.)

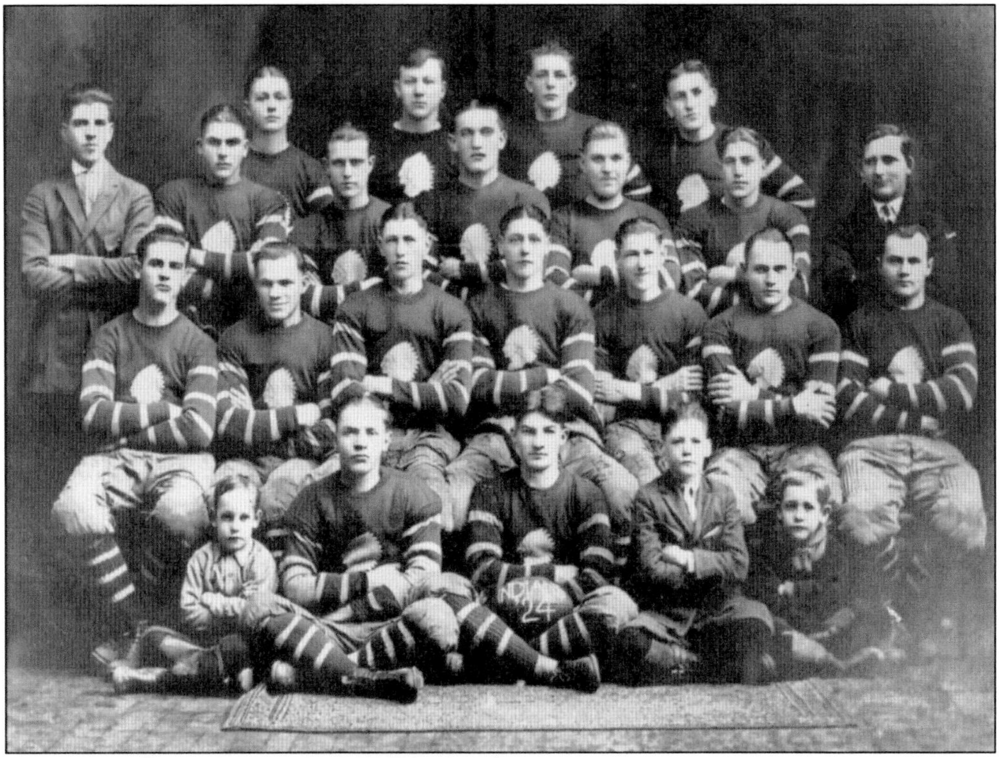

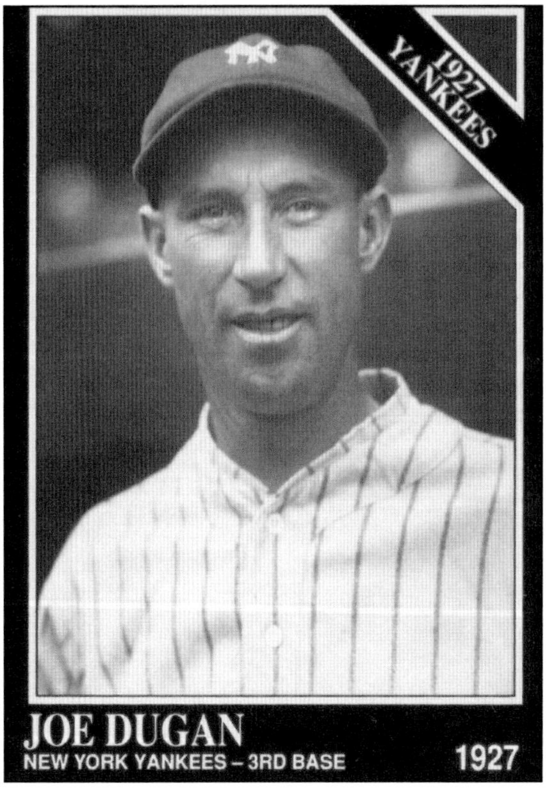

CURLEY INDIANS. The Mahanoy City Indians dominated local football from 1924 to 1927. The town's pride and joy were more commonly known as the Curley Indians because of the team's two star players, quarterback James Curley and his brother John. The team pictured was coached by Frank Sieck. In 1927, under the tutelage of future borough mayor William Sheehan, the Indians won the Coal Region championship. (MHS.)

JOE DUGAN. Mahanoy City's own Joe Dugan played professional baseball from 1917 to 1931. Dugan began his career with the Philadelphia Athletics. In 1923, he helped the New York Yankees win their first world championship. In 1927, Joe played on the Yankee team that some consider the greatest baseball team of all time. He was known as "Jumping Joe" due to his taking unauthorized leaves from the team. (MLH.)

JOE BOLEY. Mahanoy City native Joe Boley played professional baseball from 1927 to 1932 for both the Philadelphia Athletics and Cleveland Indians. Joe was part of the "Million Dollar Infield" that led the Athletics to three pennants and two world championships. In the 1920s, Boley was considered one of the best shortstops in the game. He returned to his hometown following his baseball career and is buried in St. Mary's Slovak Cemetery. (MLH.)

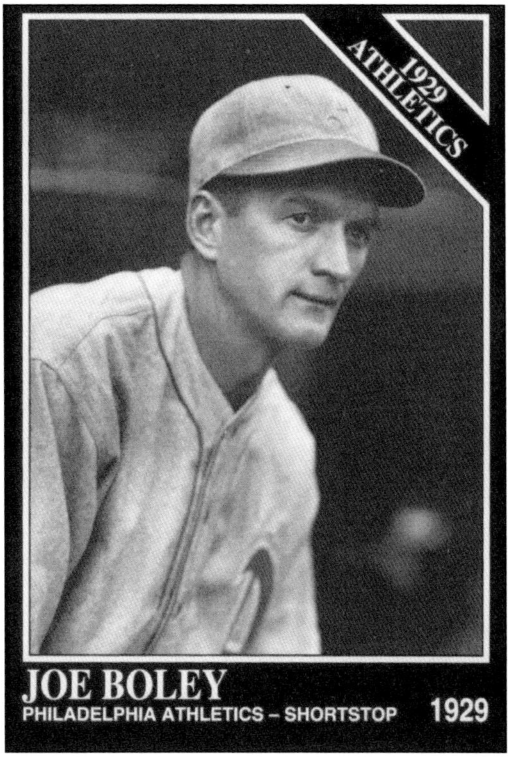

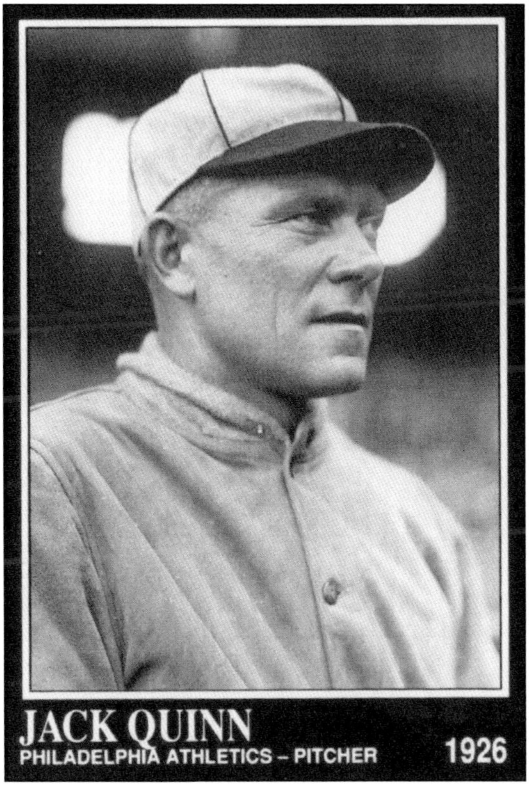

AGELESS WONDER. John Picus Quinn immigrated to America as an infant with his Rusyan parents and was raised in Mahanoy City. In 1909, Quinn began a major-league pitching career that lasted 24 years. The spitball-throwing, ageless wonder won 247 games and played with Joe Boley on the 1929 World Series–winning Philadelphia Athletics. Quinn is still the oldest pitcher (age 46) ever to hit a major-league homer. (PC.)

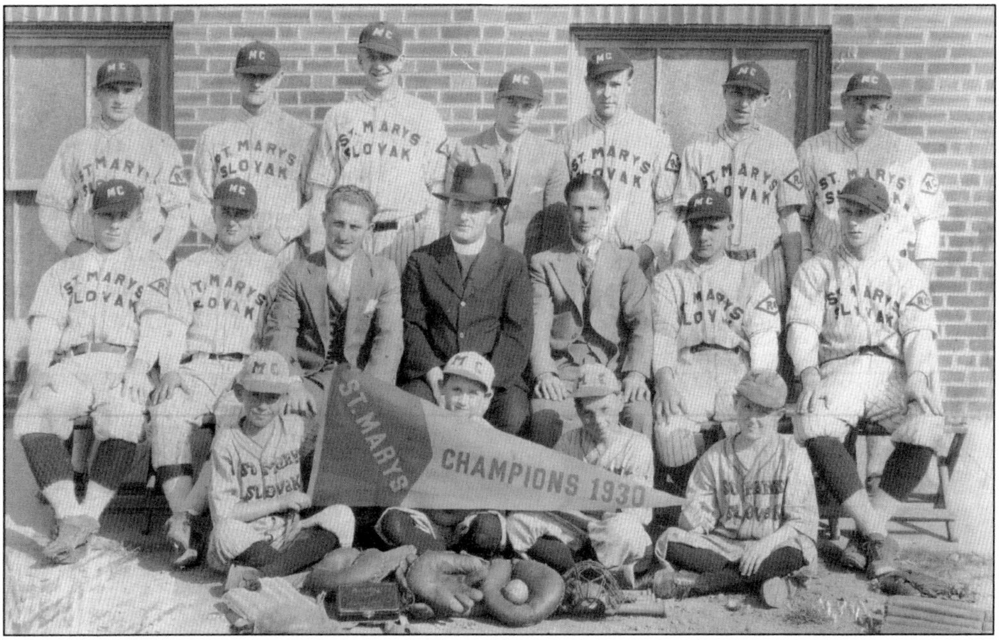

CATHOLIC LEAGUE BASEBALL. The Great Depression was ending its first year in September 1930 when St. Mary's Slovak clinched Mahanoy City's Catholic League championship. Skippered by Fr. Stephen Valesek, St. Mary's finished the season 16-2 and went on to the win the Inter-league championship by defeating the Welsh Congregational team in a five game series. (MHS.)

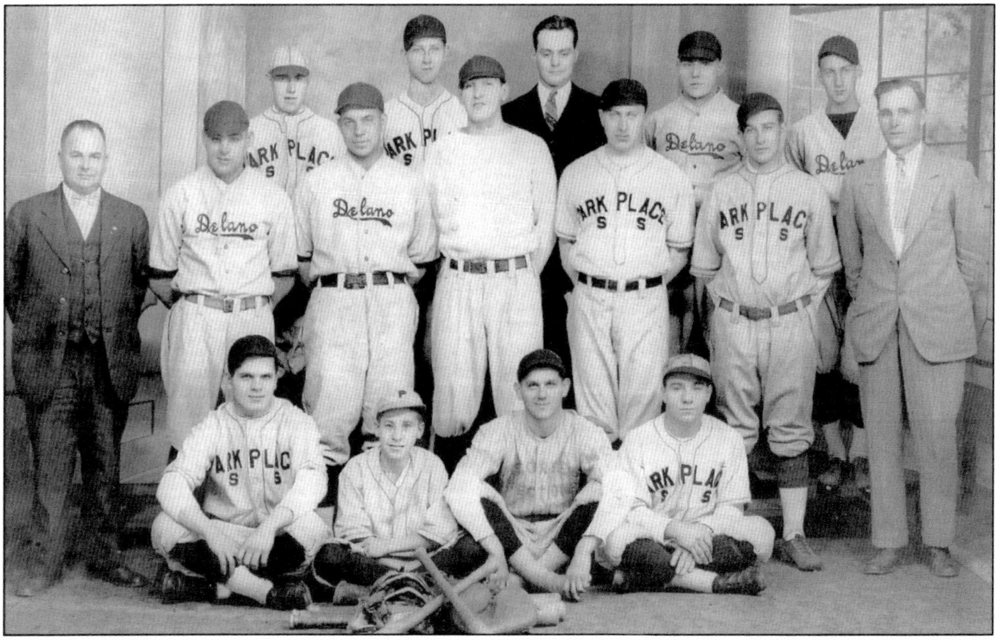

SUNDAY SCHOOL LEAGUE. This team from Park Place dominated the Sunday School League in the late 1920s. Pictured are, from left to right, (first row) Harry Gaval, batboy Charles Humes, Walter Gaval, and Clarence Osenbach; (second row) assistant manager Ellsworth Wolfe, Andy Steiner, Bock Perry, Laverne Sticher, Al Faust, Frank Olin, and manager Bill Powell; (third row) Milt Kline, Ed Burgess, Ralph Applegate, Rube Steiner, and Clarence Houser. (MHS.)

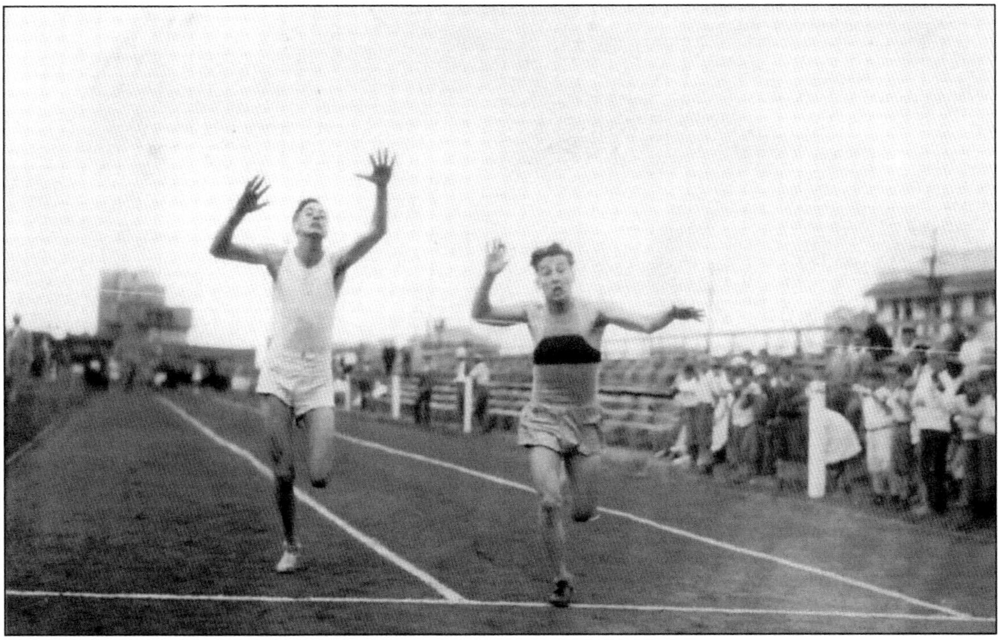

JOHN ZEMELAVAGE. Mahanoy City High School's John Zemelavage won a heat of the 75-yard dash in 8.2 seconds at the National Junior Olympic All-Around Competition in Atlantic City on July 11, 1928. Zemelavage placed second to Californian John Falcon in the five-event competition. In 1930, Zemelavage, the national chin-up record holder, set Mahanoy City High School records in the 100- and 220-yard dashes. (MCPL.)

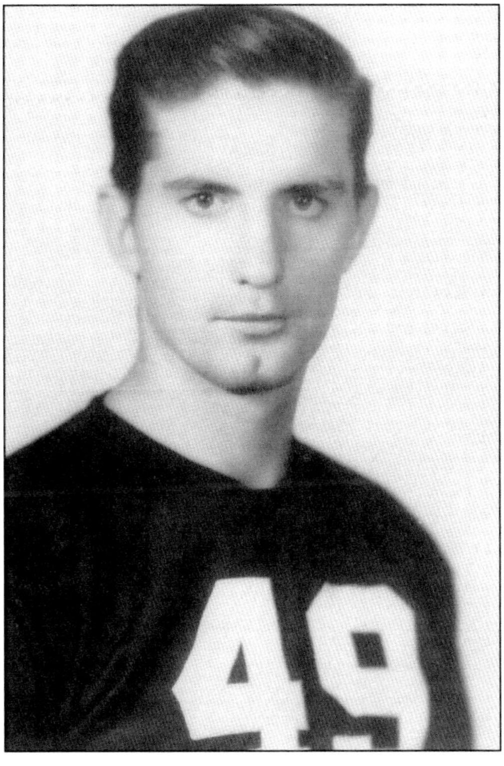

JOSEPH W. SETCAVAGE. Led by quarterback Joe Setcavage, the 1936 "Praying Miners" of Mahanoy City High School won all but one game. The team captain and quarterback shared the field with his brother George and cousins Stanley and Frank Setcavage. After graduating from Duquesne, Joe played professional football and later became a successful high school football, basketball, and track coach. He was inducted into the Pennsylvania Hall of Fame in 1984. (JS.)

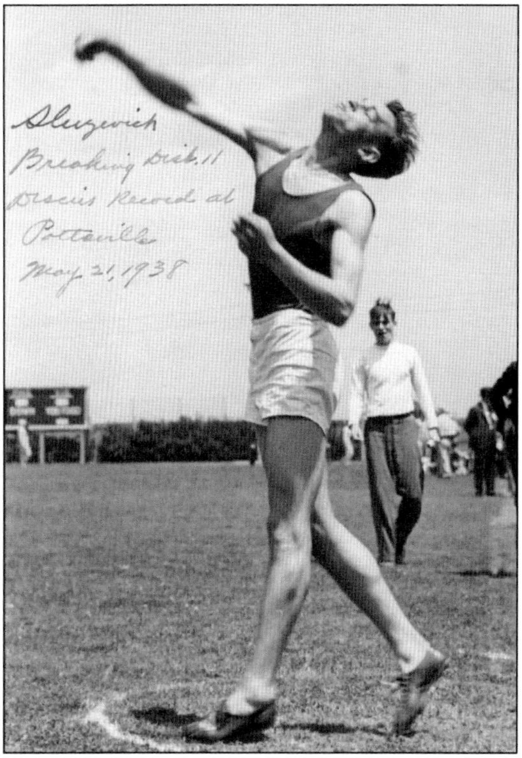

JOHN SLUZEVICH. "John, in my estimation, is one of the greatest athletes to attend Mahanoy High." Those words of legendary coach John Goepfert summarize the high school athletic career of three-sport letter-winner John Sluzevich. Sluzevich's shot put toss of 48 feet 6 3/4 inches still stands as a Mahanoy City record 75 years later. The picture shows John winning the 1938 District XI discus throw. First Lieutenant Sluzevich was killed in action in Holland on October 9, 1944. (MCPL.)

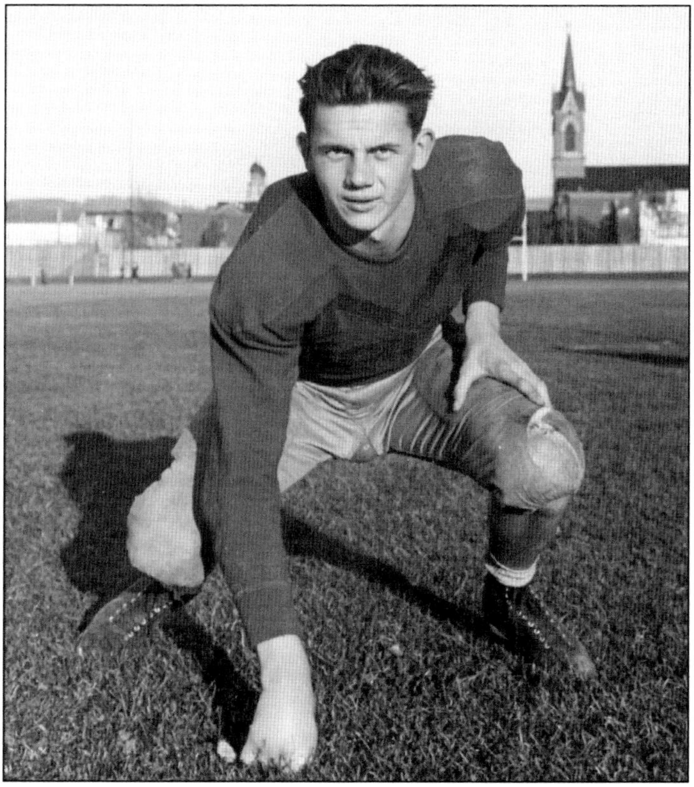

BILL KUBILIS. Mahanoy City High School's Bill Kubilis scored the first touchdown in the first Dream Game played on December 2, 1938. Kubilis scored when he pounced on the South's bad snap from center in the end zone. The North All-Stars defeated the South All-Stars 13-7 on an ice-covered field at Pottsville High School Stadium. (MHS.)

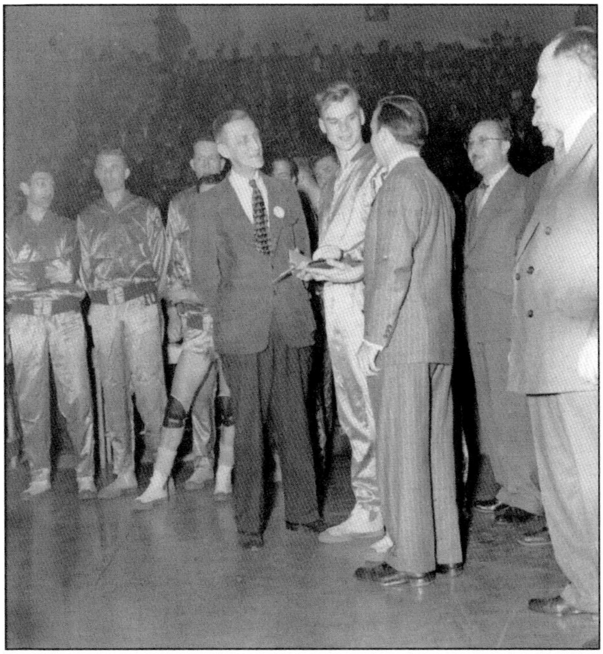

GOEPFERT AND SENESKY. Two Mahanoy City basketball legends were present at the Philadelphia Arena on March 27, 1947, on the occasion of the Philadelphia Warriors' George Senesky Night. Coach John Goepfert, who, in 34 years as coach at Mahanoy City High School, amassed a total of 834 wins, a state championship, a district title, and 17 league titles, congratulates his star pupil George Senesky. (DJG.)

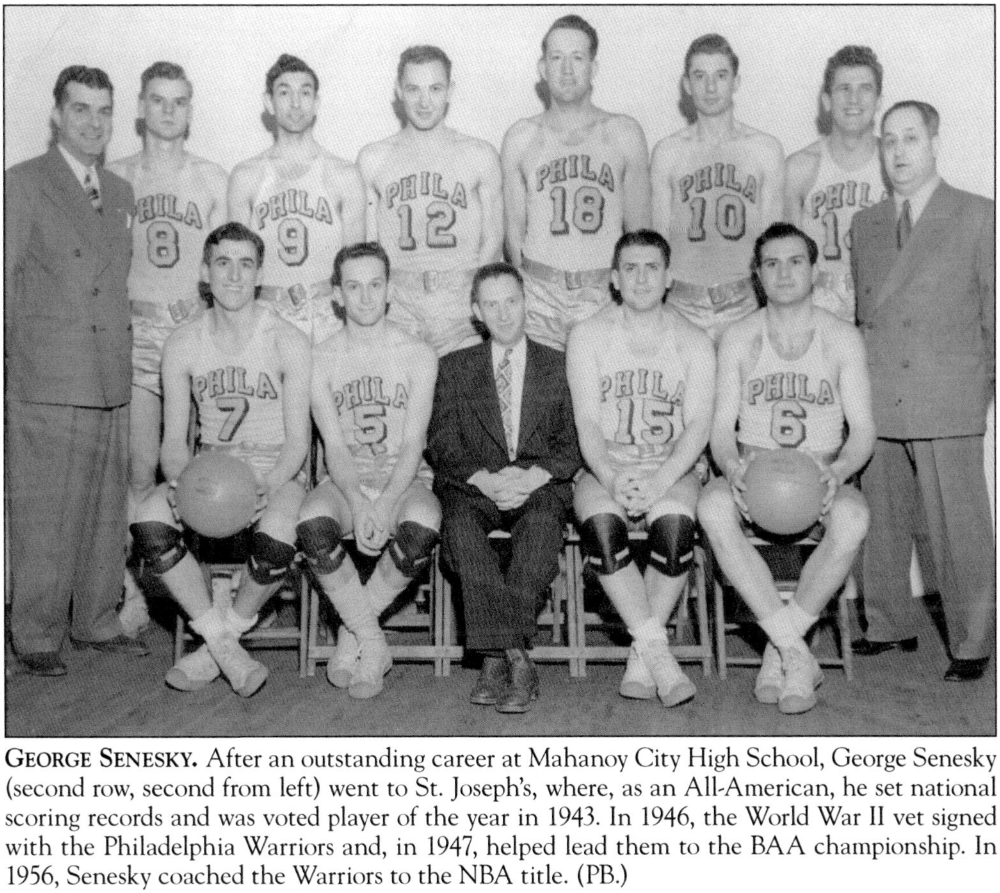

GEORGE SENESKY. After an outstanding career at Mahanoy City High School, George Senesky (second row, second from left) went to St. Joseph's, where, as an All-American, he set national scoring records and was voted player of the year in 1943. In 1946, the World War II vet signed with the Philadelphia Warriors and, in 1947, helped lead them to the BAA championship. In 1956, Senesky coached the Warriors to the NBA title. (PB.)

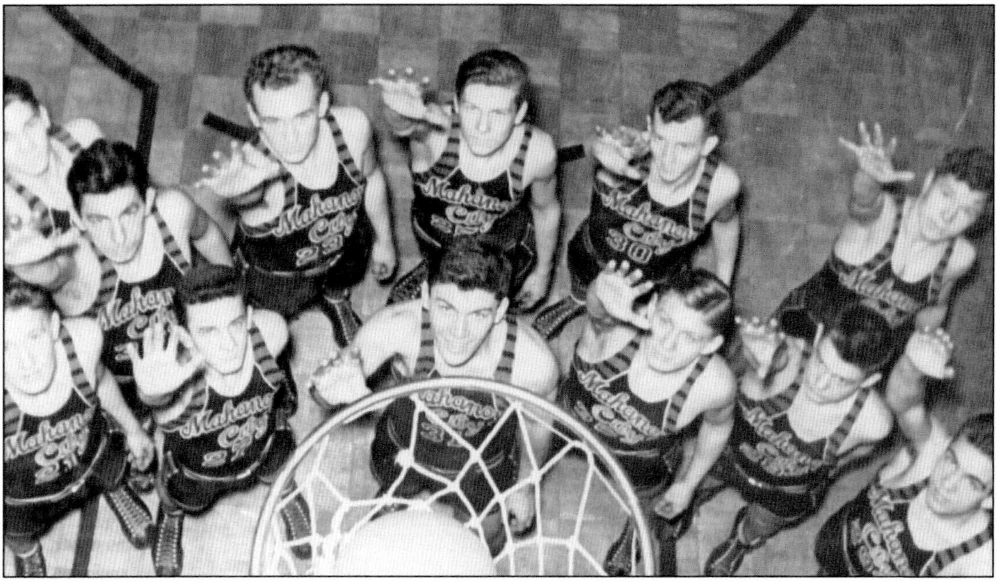

DISTRICT BASKETBALL CHAMPIONS. Coach John Goepfert's Mahanoy City High School Maroons finished the 1940–1941 season 18-1 to win their third consecutive Black Diamond League title and defeated Allentown High at the Palestra in Philadelphia to win District XI laurels. Pictured, from left to right, are (first row) John Fletcher, Steve Wasilini, John Goepfert Jr., Leonard Sebalowski, Francis Richards, and Michael Jacubac; (second row) Michael Baranusky, Martin Hanrahan, Albert Glaudel, Francis Dziadosz, Paul Rajkowski, and Francis Malinowski. (MERP.)

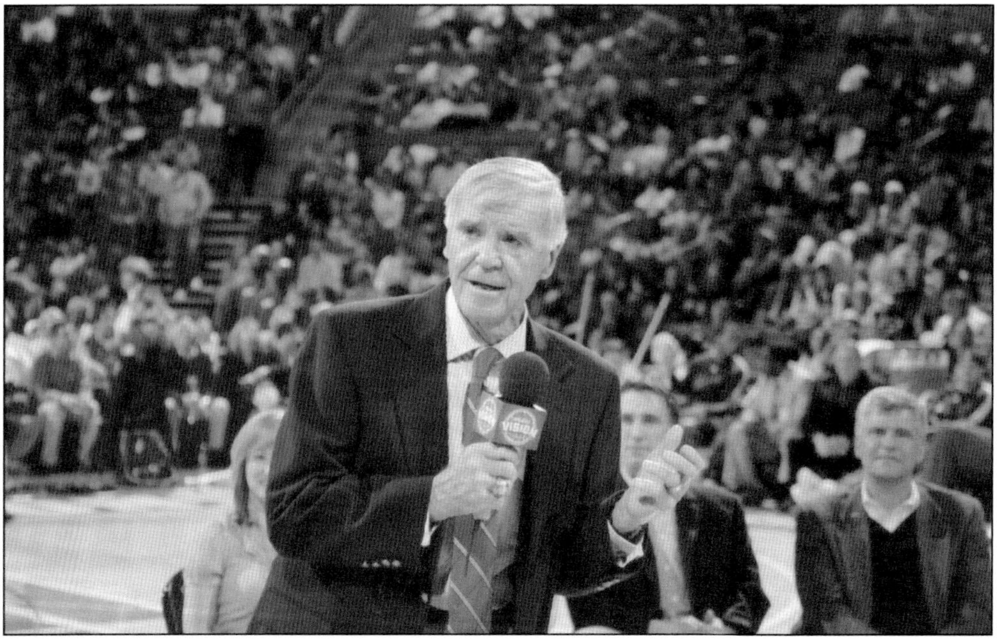

JACK MCCLOSKEY. A 1942 Mahanoy Township graduate, Jack McCloskey became a force in the National Basketball Association following his college graduation and a stint in the Navy during World War II. Known as "Trader Jack," he made numerous trades during his tenure with the Detroit Pistons. Eventually, those trades paid off as the Pistons under his leadership won the National Basketball Association championship in both 1989 and 1990. (JMcC.)

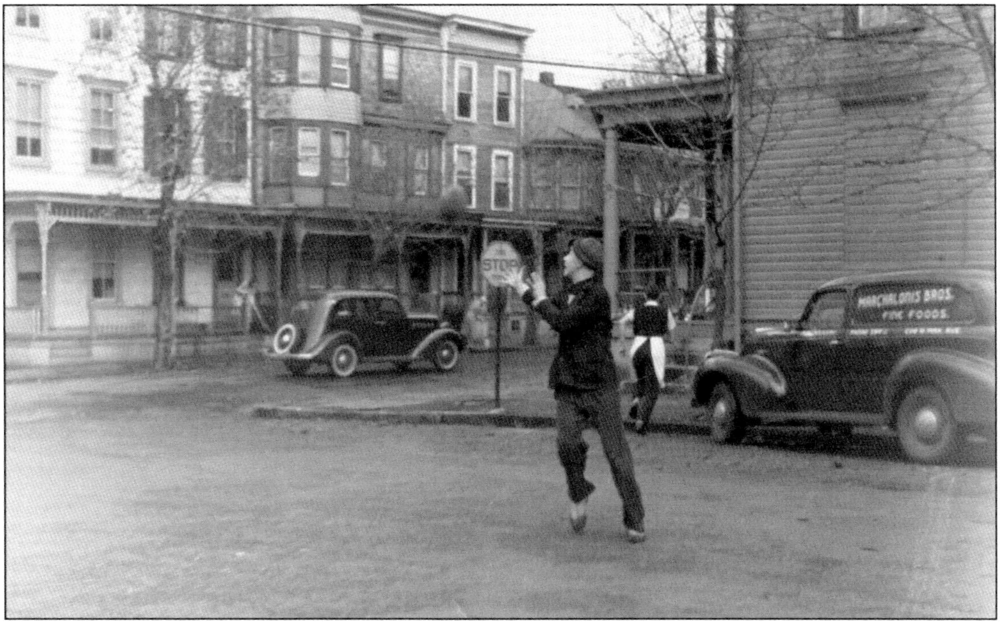

STREET FOOTBALL. A familiar sight in the 1940s on any street in Mahanoy City or the surrounding patches was a group of kids playing. In the days before electronic media, most leisure hours were spent outdoors. This scene was shot at the corner of Catawissa Street and Mahanoy Avenue, near the Marchalonis grocery store in the early 1940s. (DJG.)

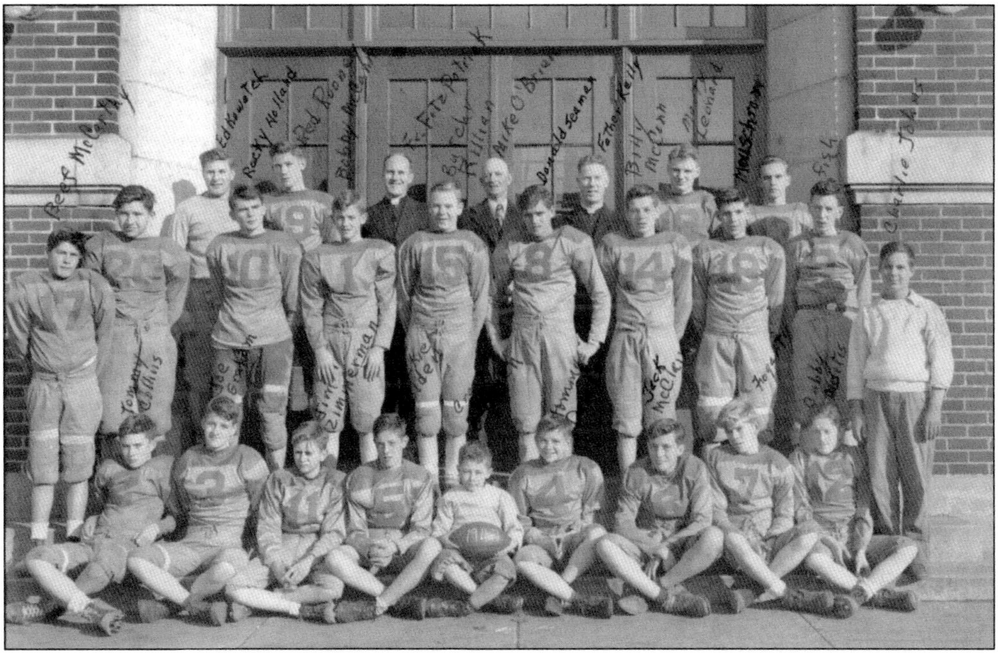

ST. CANICUS FOOTBALL. In the fall of 1947, St. Canicus Parish had a school with 303 students in the first through tenth grades and a football team that played home games in the East End Park and practiced on the dirt playground across Catawissa Street from the school. In the first game of the season, coach Mike O'Brien's Irish defeated St. Francis of Orwigsburg 12-6 on two touchdowns scored by quarterback Charlie Johns. (MHS.)

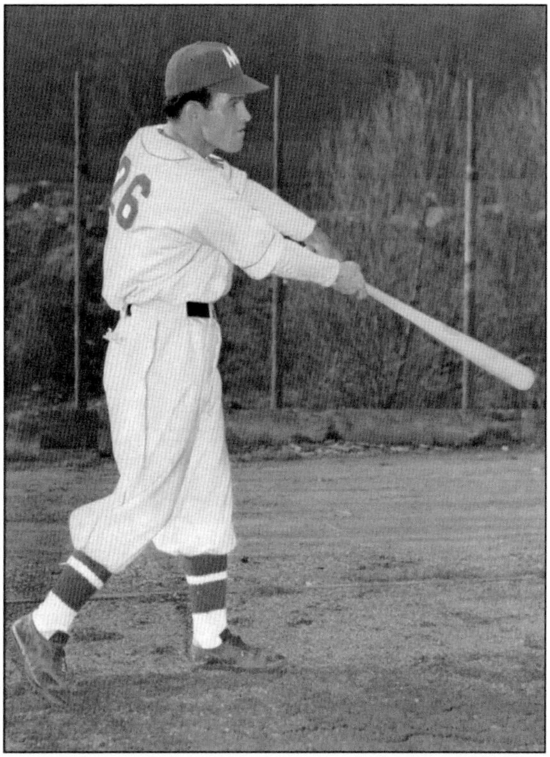

BREWERS BASEBALL. Professional baseball came to Schuylkill County for the first time when Mahanoy City joined the North Atlantic League. The Brewers played a 126-game schedule against teams from Pennsylvania, New York, and New Jersey. One of the stars of the Brewers was Mahanoy City's own Tom Murphy, a hard-hitting third baseman who later became the borough's police chief. (AM.)

ACADEMY FOOTBALL. In 1952, Immaculate Heart High School in Fountain Springs became the site of a football program that had originated in Mahanoy City. After St. Canicus eliminated its freshman and sophomore classes, coach Mike O'Brien and many of his players formed a new program at the academy. Pictured are, from left to right, (first row) Albert Palonis, Charles Rice, and John Miller; (second row) Thomas Whalen. (TWH.)

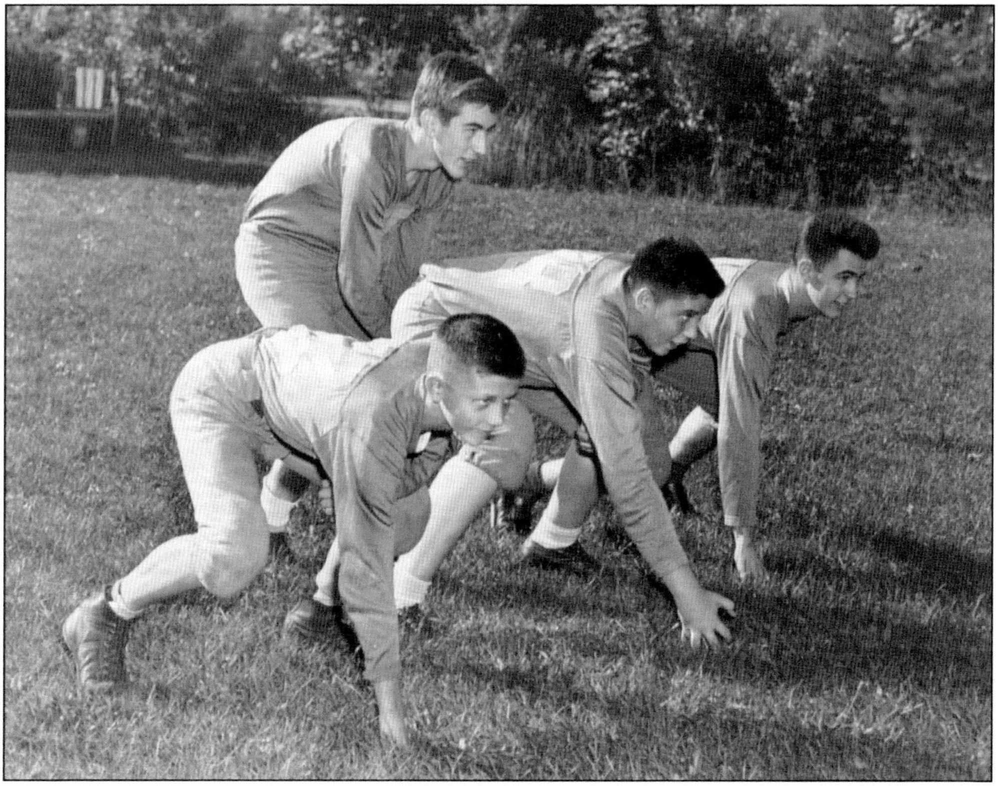

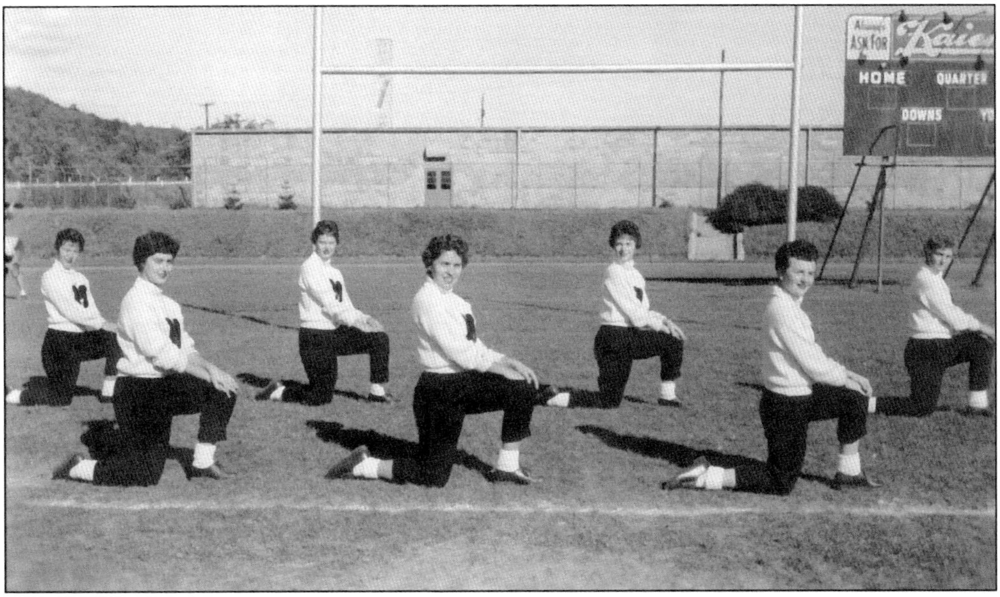

CHEERLEADERS. Cheerleaders have always been a large part of any sporting event. Shown here are the Mahanoy City High School cheerleaders of 1956–1957. They are, from left to right, Gail Richards, Marilyn Early, Patricia Conrad, Dorothy Wirtz, Doris Llewellyn, Mary Edith Holland, and Sandra Lezousky. (MHS.)

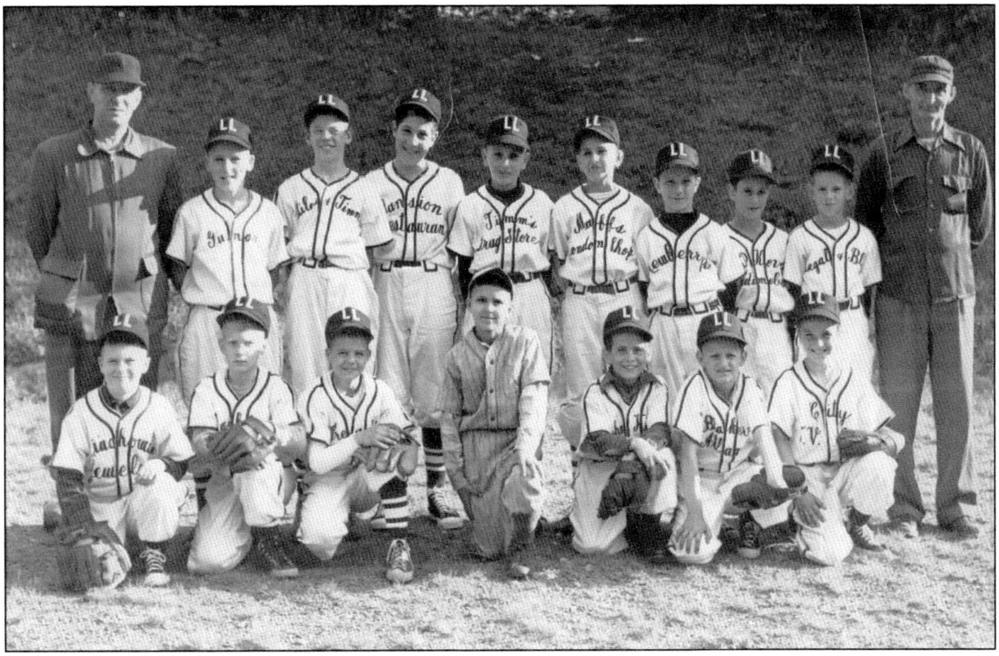

LITTLE LEAGUE. Little League baseball came to Mahanoy City in 1955. Directed by Dr. Mark Holland, the league was made up of four teams. Pictured are the Merchants, from left to right, (first row) Howell Davis, Joseph Nolter, Kenneth Hall, batboy Robert Wargo, Ernest DiLabio, Thomas Puidokas, and Edward Sabol; (second row) manager William Leskie, Robert Kurzinsky, John Murtin, Robert Guzinsky, Edward Fernandez, Michael Wargo, Joseph Anceravige, William Tarn, Joseph Alansky, and coach Andrew Wargo. (JM.)

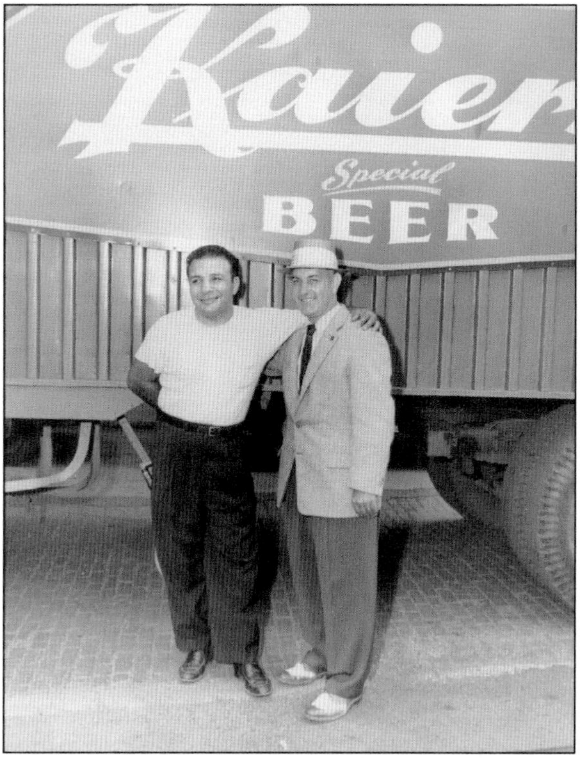

JAKE LAMOTTA. In 1957, former World Middleweight Boxing champion Jake LaMotta (left) visits Kaier Brewery along with Ed Romance, a WPPA radio sportscaster. LaMotta was the subject of the 1980 film *Raging Bull*, in which his portrayal by Robert De Niro earned De Niro the Academy Award. Romance, a legend in local sports circles, was the host of the long-running *Kaier's Sportsbook*, which aired on WPPA, Schuylkill County's first radio station. (MHS.)

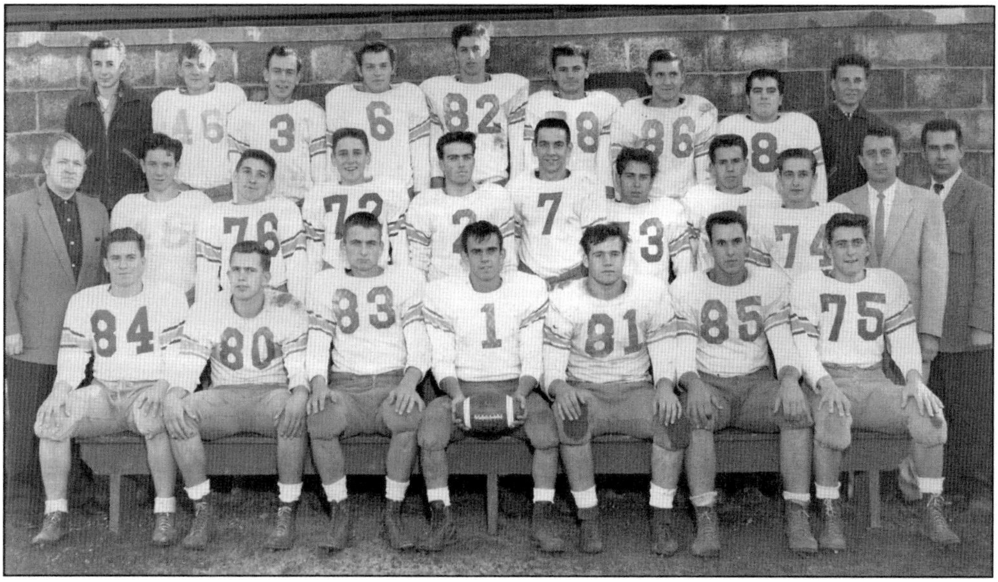

1958 PURPLE LARKS. Pictured, from left to right, are (first row) William Zellner, John Goshiney, Randolph Kurzinsky, Lee Houser, Bernard Boyle, Thomas Hayes, and Douglas Fristick; (second row) coach William Jones, James Shea, Edward Gnall, Robert Kurzinsky, William Brennan, John Museosky, Glenn Fegley, Ronald Bowman, John Thornton, assistant coach David Linkchorst, and assistant coach Elbur Techentin; (third row) Francis Whalen, John Gmitter, Arthur Frey, Larry Fenkner, Frank Mroczka, John Pascavage, James Mitchell, Robert Mongrain, and Andrew Stofanick. (MHS.)

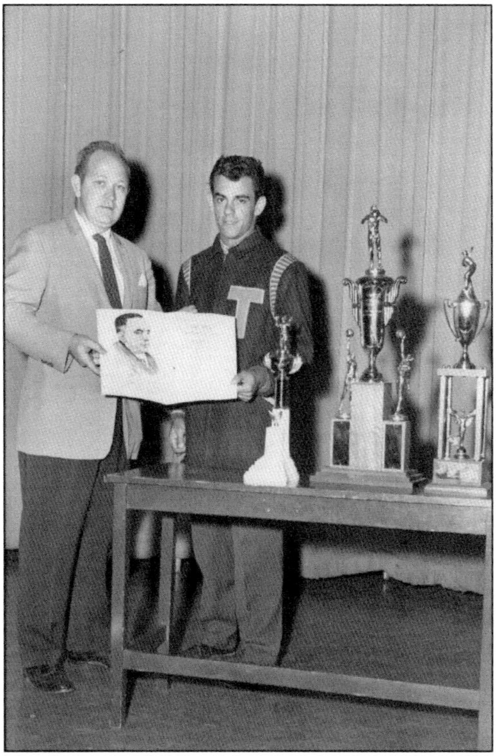

Lee Houser. Mahanoy Township High School football coach William "Buck" Jones and star quarterback Lee Houser display the January 27, 1959, edition of the *Sporting News*, in which Houser is listed as an honorable mention All-American along with Mahanoy City High School's quarterback Ed Dougherty. Dougherty's Maroons defeated Houser's Larks 20-13 in the last football game ever for both teams before the establishment of the combined Mahanoy Area High School. (AWH.)

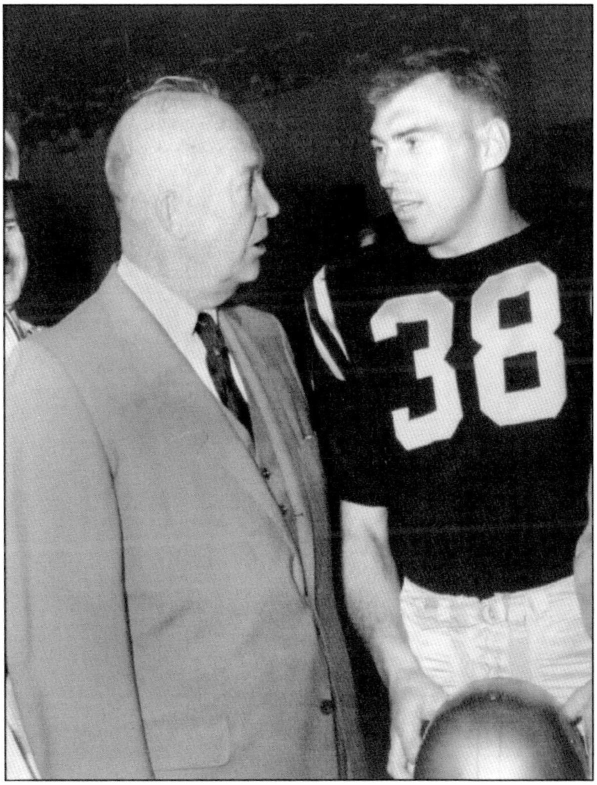

Joe Matalavage. Navy football captain and 1956 Mahanoy City High School graduate Joe Matalavage greets Pres. Dwight Eisenhower at the 1960 Army-Navy game in Philadelphia. Navy beat Army and finished the season with a 9-1 record, earning the right to appear in the 1961 Orange Bowl, where the Midshipmen lost to Missouri in a game attended by the newly elected president, John F. Kennedy. (JMA.)

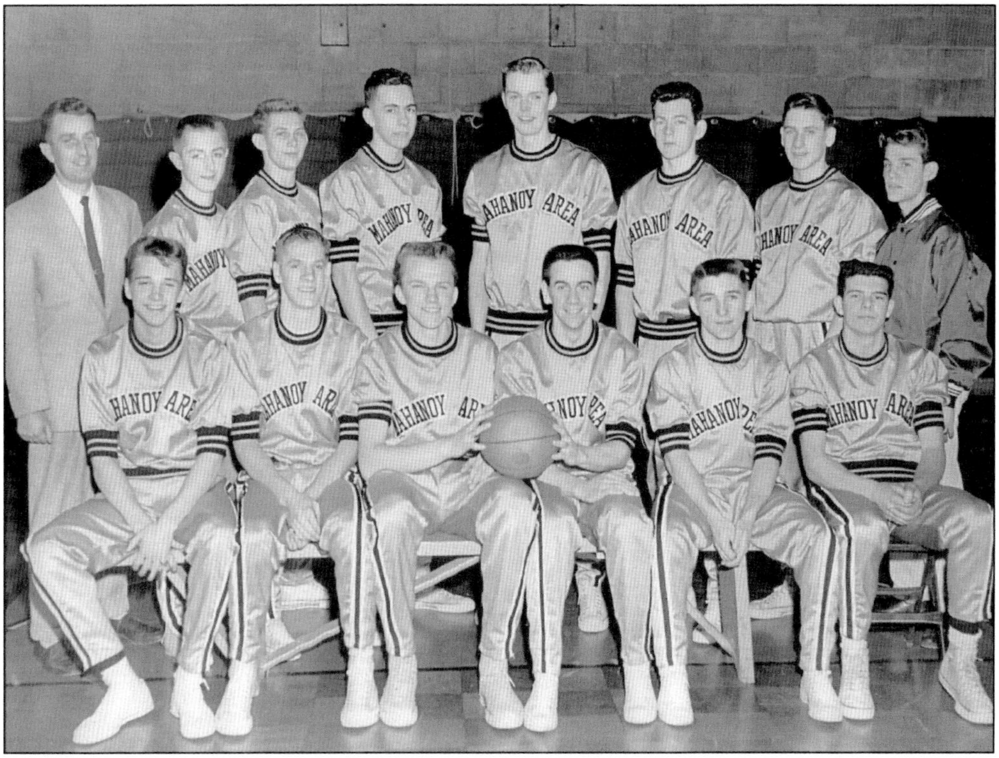

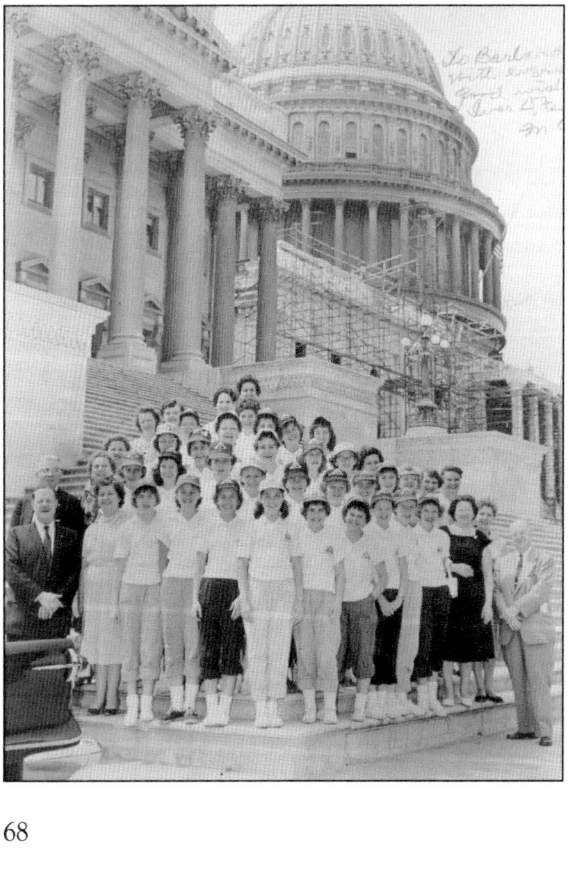

GOLDEN BEARS. The first Mahanoy Area Golden Bear basketball team won the North Schuylkill championship and went 23-0 before falling to Hazleton in the district semifinals 62-60 in overtime. Pictured, from left to right, are (first row) Leonard Yedsena, Eugene Miller, Gerald Stefanic, John Museosky, Edward Gnall, and George Cunningham; (second row) coach Dave Linkchorst, Francis Meade, Paul Petrucka, Robert Blue, Edward Kubert, Joseph Galvin, Robert Kurzinsky, and Gerald McCabe. (MHS.)

LASSIE LEAGUE. In 1958, Elsie Tolan and others began to organize Lassie League softball for girls in Mahanoy City and surrounding communities. Pictured is a group of players who traveled to Washington, DC, to meet with Congressman Ivor Fenton and Sen. Hugh Scott. Also pictured are Elsie Tolan and one of the league's founders, Peter Mahalage. (BND.)

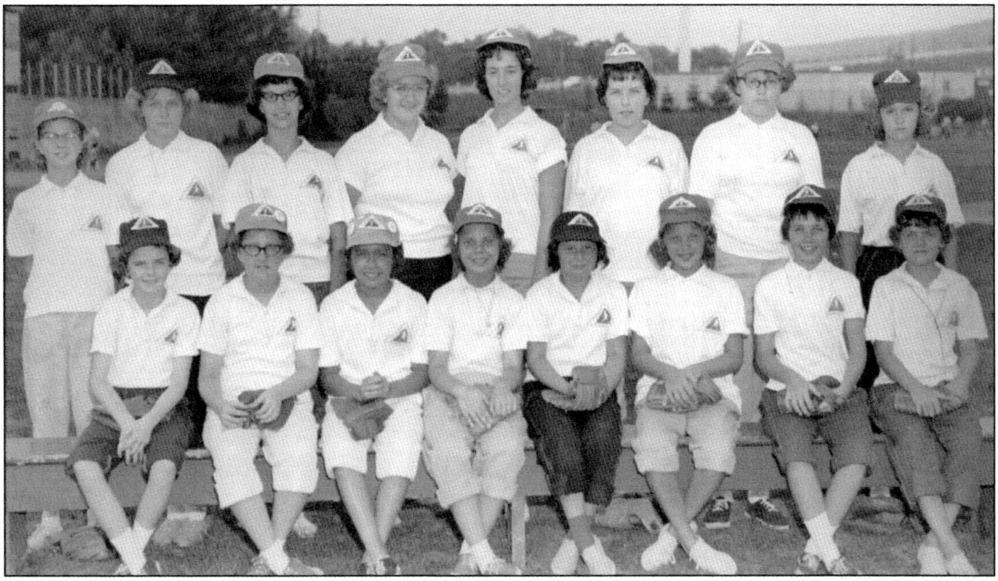

JUNIOR ALL-STAR LASSIE LEAGUE. Mahanoy City's All-Star teams competed in communities including Forestville, New York; Collegeville, Pennsylvania; and Bordentown, New Jersey. Pictured are members of 1962 team. They are, from left to right, (first row) Anne Holland, Kathy Karetsky, Marylou Wellington, Elaine Mack, Jane Waseline, AnnaLee Wagner, Michelle Wargo, and Kay Wagner; (second row) Carol Dainauski, Ruth Roman, Kathy Malasavage, Louise Teter, Stephanie Perry, Sharon Keilman, Louise Krause, and Patricia Harviletz. (ET.)

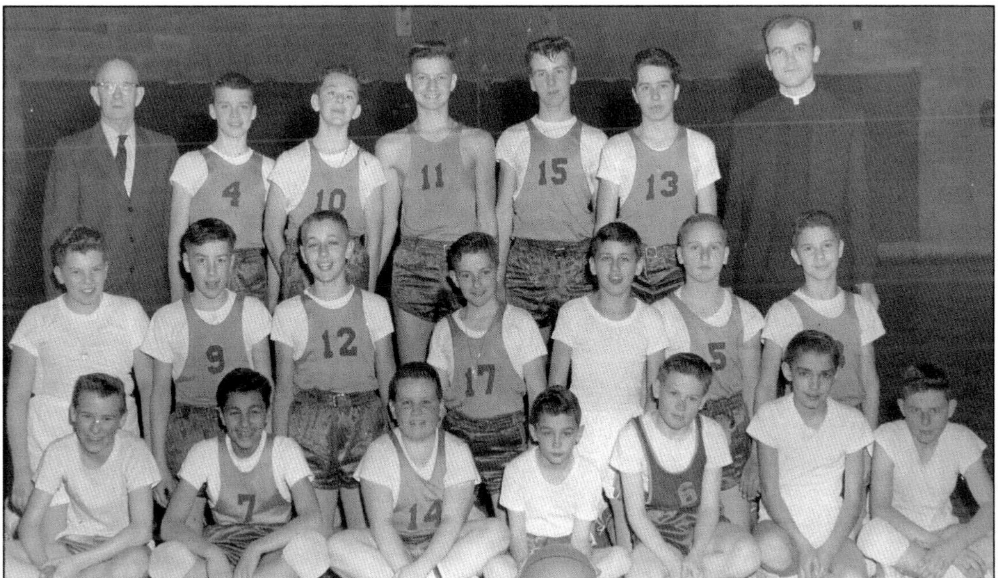

CYO BASKETBALL. In 1962–1963, St. Canicus boys won the District Catholic Youth Organization (CYO) championship. Pictured, from left to right, are (first row) Nestor Gnall, James DeAngelo, Joseph McCall, Francis Kane, John Bayliff, Michael Jacubac, and Andrew Yankus; (second row) James Lucas, John Mellon, Lawrence Souchak, Gerald Lotwick, Andrew Wargo, George Karetsky, and Ronald Bulcavage; (third row) coach Michael O'Brien, Mark Holland, Martin Galvin, John Chilinskas, John Cavanaugh, Paul Coombe, and Rev. Steven Halabura. (PC.)

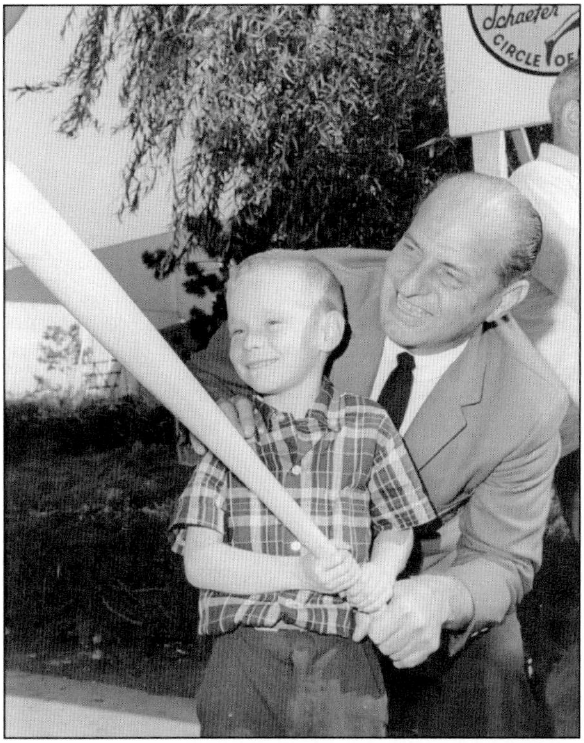

YANKEE GREAT. The world's fair in Flushing, New York, was the place to be in 1964. A group of parishioners from Assumption BVM Church in Mahanoy City traveled to the fair that September. Here, second-grade student Ricky Wellington is given some batting pointers from Tommy Henrich of the New York Yankees. Nicknamed "Old Reliable," Henrich played 11 seasons for the Yankees and was an All-Star five times and a member of five World Series winners. (MLH.)

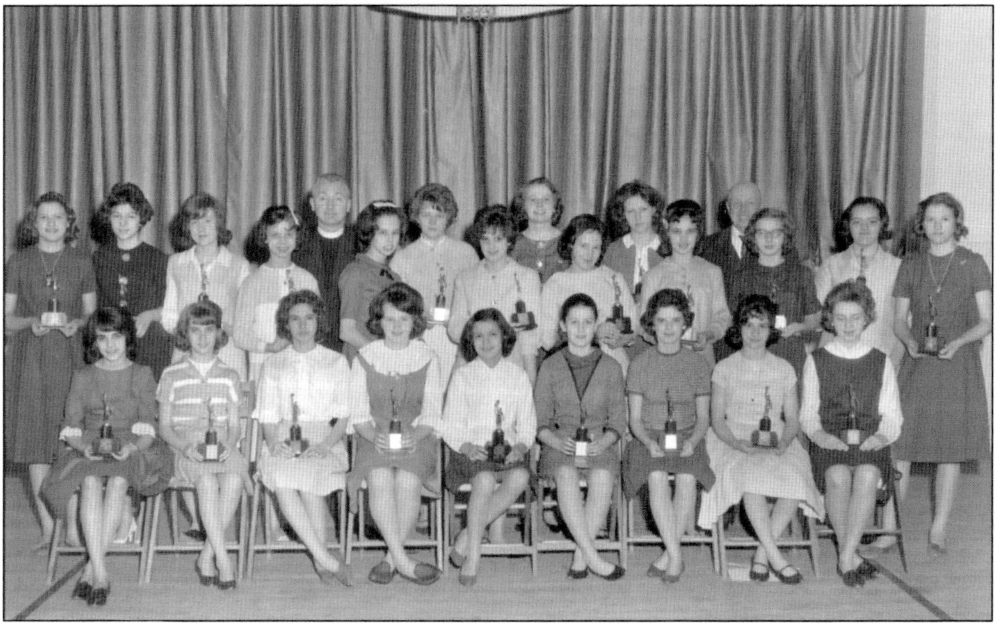

CYO GIRLS' BASKETBALL. Pictured are the 1964 graduates of CYO girls' basketball. They are, from left to right, (first row) Rosemary Sebastian, Joanna Chesko, Helene Forgotch, Karen Cavanaugh, Sharlaine O'Brien, Agnes Whitaker, Anne Holland, Anne Webb, and Cathy Setcavage; (second row) Karen Engle, Connie Bulcavage, Diane Yuditsky, Elaine Mack, Father McPeak, Gena Neddo, Ruth Roman, unidentified, Beverly Yutko, unidentified, unidentified, Edwina Holloway, unidentified, Carol Dainauski, unidentified, and Kathy Engle. (EML.)

Four

OVER THERE

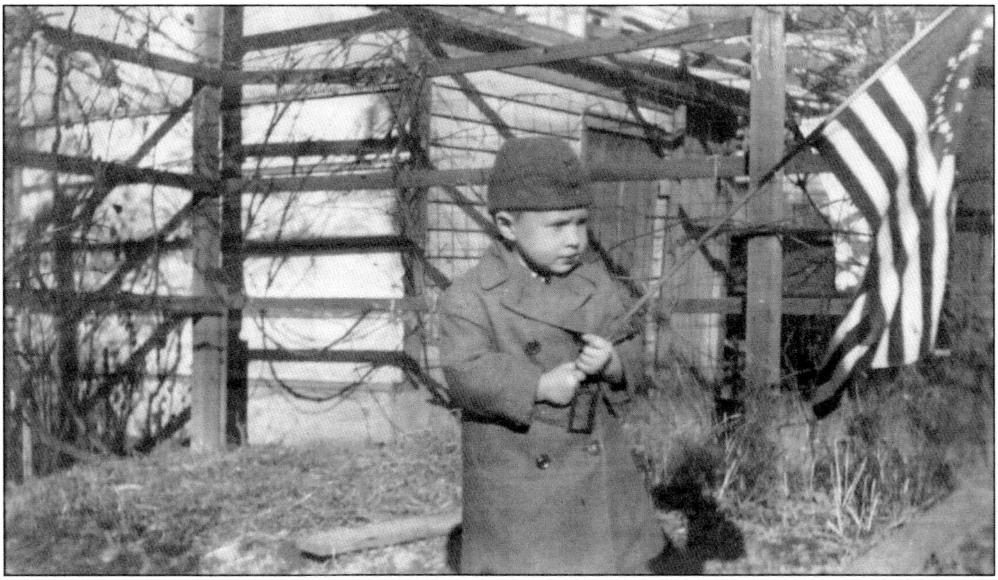

NOVEMBER 11, 1918. In 1917, the Pennsylvania Guard (former Silliman Guard) was called up to serve as Company E in the US Army during World War I. When their service was over, this young Klitsch boy welcomed them on Armistice Day, November 11, 1918, with a peace flag. Designed by W. Whipple to celebrate the end of the war, it contained 48 stars with the original 13 states placed in a central position. (PGG.)

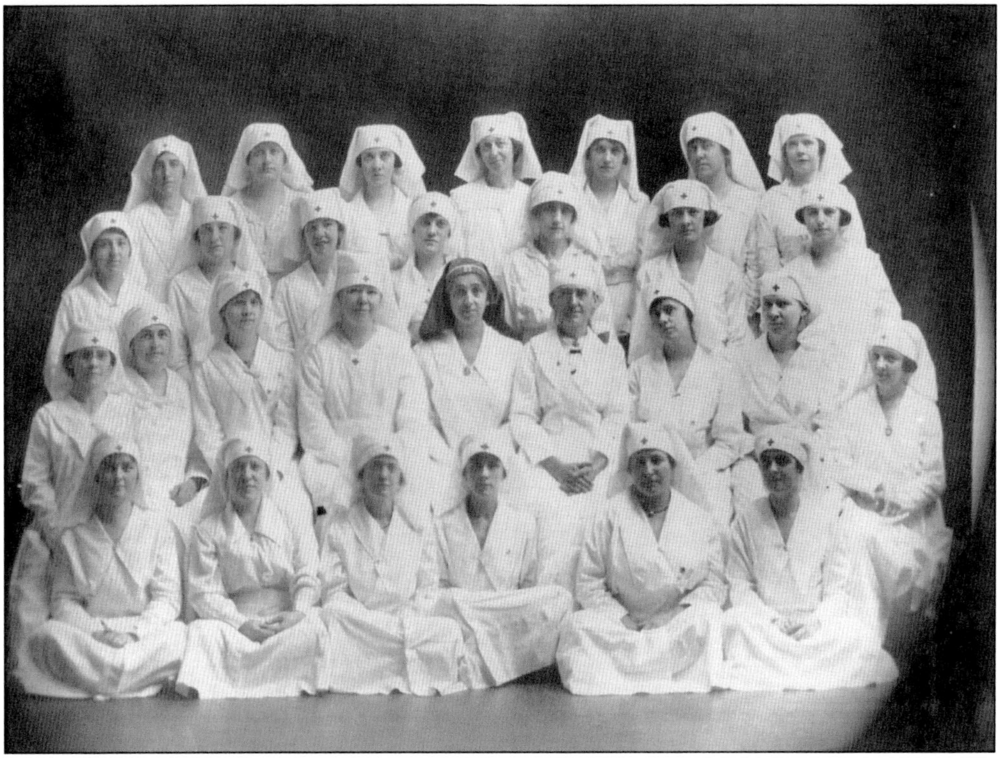

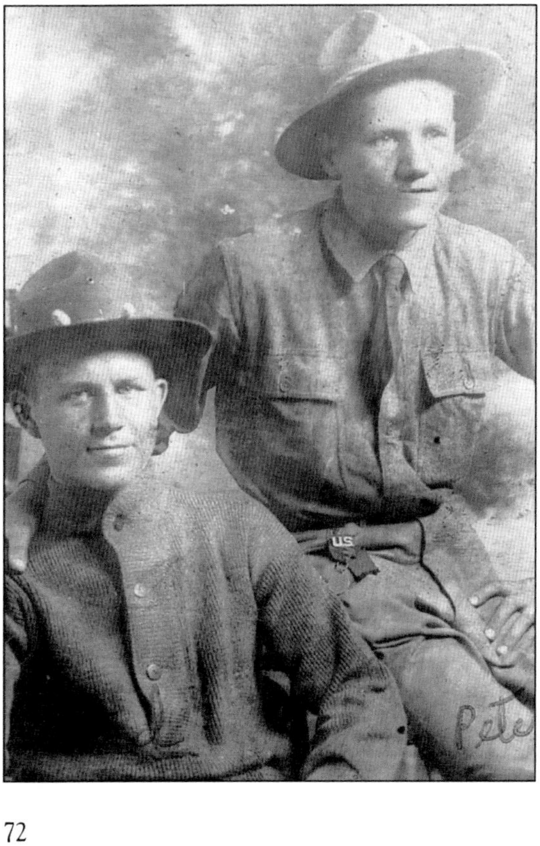

MAHANOY CITY CHAPTER OF THE AMERICAN RED CROSS. Within two months of war being declared, Augusta Thomas, author of the history of Mahanoy City, and her team of Rev. George Smith, Daniel F. Guinan, and Catherine Horan had recruited and organized the Mahanoy City Chapter of the Red Cross. They raised $40,000 and organized volunteers into a cohesive group of mostly women and students who completely outfitted 584 recruits by making them sweaters, mittens, socks, wristlets, helmets, and afghans. (MCPL.)

ROMANOFSKY BROTHERS. Brothers Edward (left) and Peter Romanofsky served in the US Army during World War I. Edward was killed while trying to retrieve equipment between the trenches in Fismes, France. Peter was severely wounded and blinded by poison gas. He is buried at St. Joseph's Cemetery. (DJK.)

LEO J. KISSINGER. Pvt. Leo J. Kissinger joined the US Army Air Service on December 15, 1917. He served with the 258th Aero Service Squadron until his discharge in 1919. After the war, he served his community as commander of American Legion Post No. 74 and chairman of the American Red Cross blood drive committee. (PGG.)

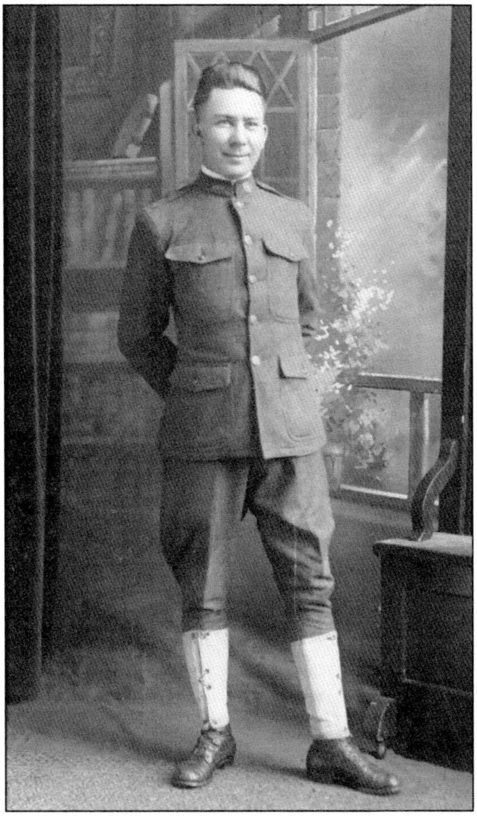

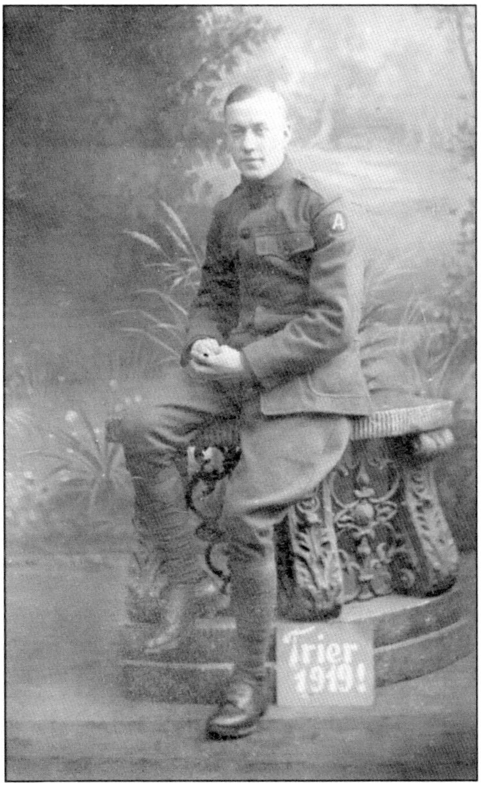

JOHN H. EVANS. Jack Evans was the son of Evan and Ann Lewis Evans. He loved music and was the piano player for the town's silent movies. He was an Army veteran of World War I, having served in France and Germany (1918–1919). In 1932, he became transportation manager at Maple Hill Colliery for the Philadelphia & Reading Coal and Iron Company. He was seriously injured in a colliery accident on February 22, 1944. (AKE.)

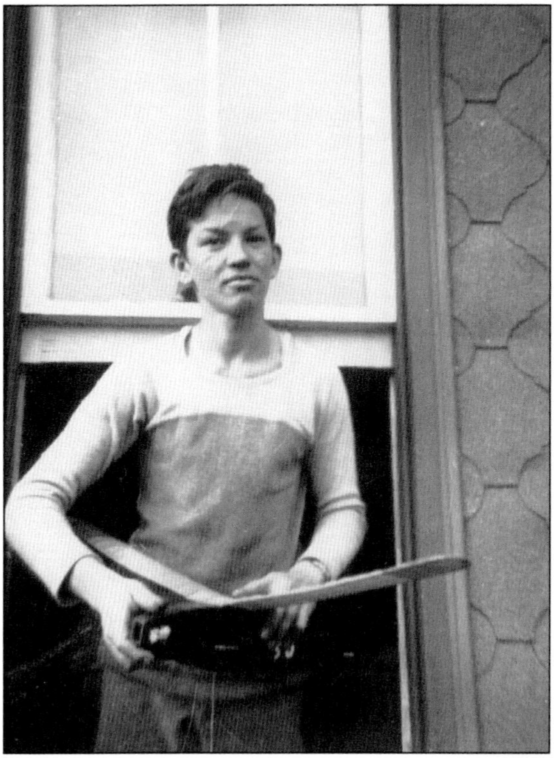

First Casualty of World War II. Jerome Szematowicz (Mahanoy City High School class of 1938) joined the Army Air Corps before the war. He was killed at Hickam Field during the Japanese surprise attack on Pearl Harbor on December 7, 1941. He was Mahanoy City's first casualty of World War II. His brother S.Sgt. Stanley J. Szematowicz was killed in action in Italy on September 14, 1944. (DJG.)

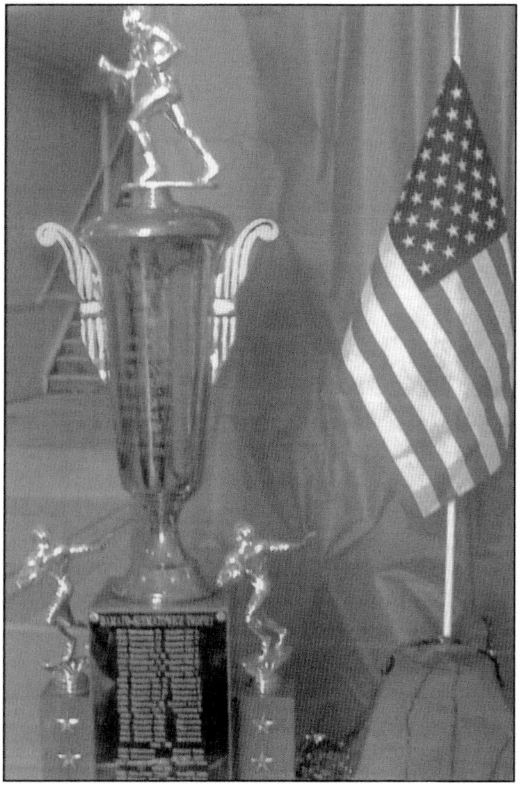

Damato-Szematowicz Trophy. After the war, the American Legion posts of Mahanoy City and Shenandoah created the Damato-Szematowicz Trophy honoring the first men from each community killed in action in World War II. The "black-and-blue" trophy is awarded annually to the winner of the Mahanoy Area/Shenandoah High School football game. Beginning in 1899, this game is one of the nation's oldest rivalries. The 2012 game was the 104th contest between both teams. (MHS.)

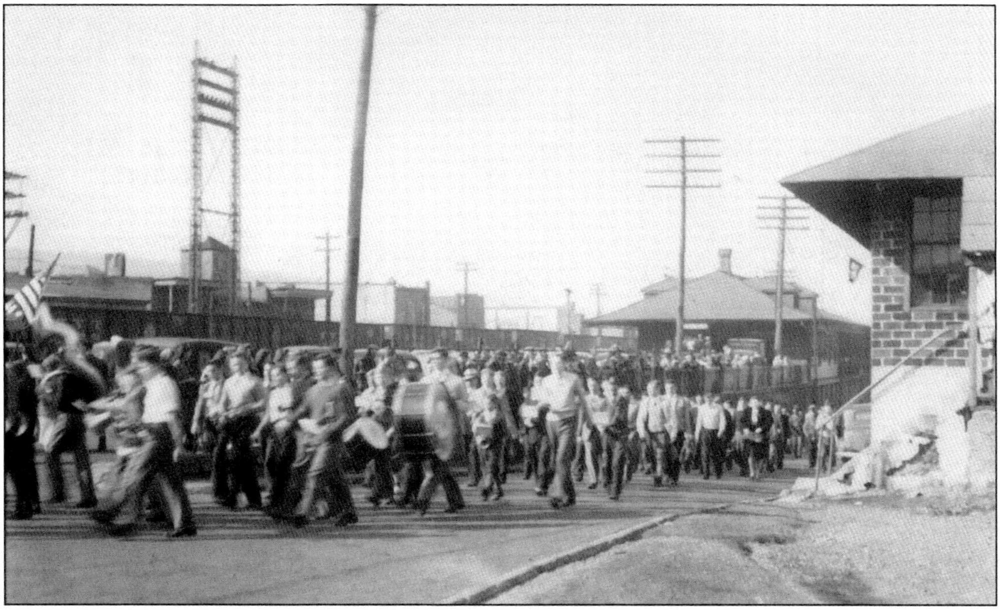

Patriotic Send Off. Hundreds of Mahanoy area residents and the Mahanoy City High School band turned out at the North Main Street Reading Railroad Terminal on October 9, 1942, to send off 41 local recruits to the US Army induction center at New Cumberland. The train left to the cheers of onlookers after a patriotic band concert. (MHS.)

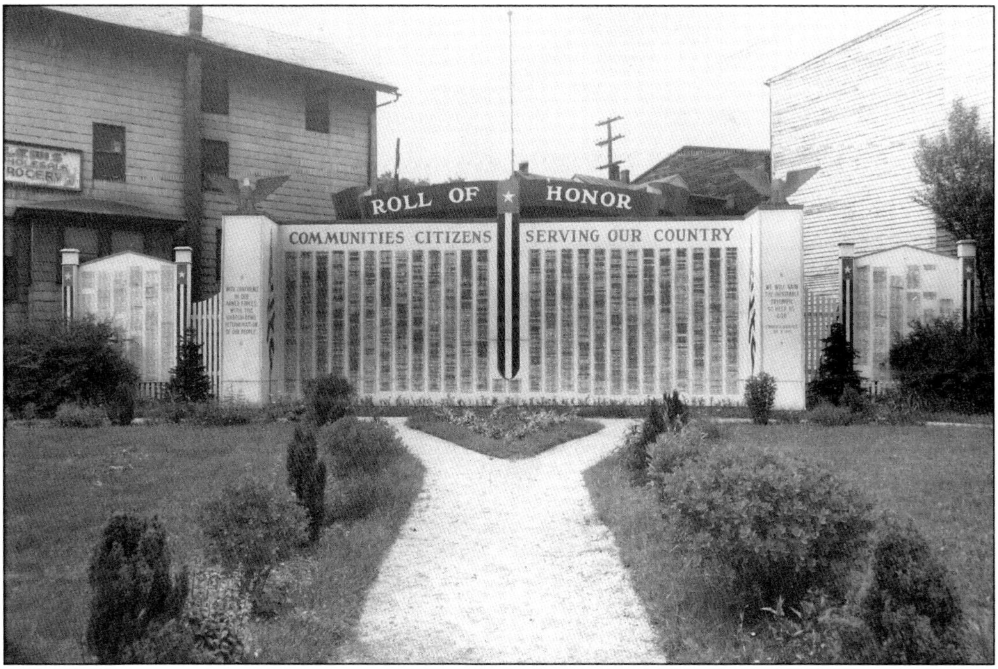

Community Honor Roll. James G. Miles was the chairman of the committee responsible for erecting the community's honor roll. Dedicated on June 1, 1943, the honor roll contained the names of community members serving in all areas of the armed forces. It stood proudly on the corner of Second and Centre Streets. A large crowd gathered for the dedication, and the town's dignitaries spoke reverently of the sacrifices of the town's heroes. (JKG.)

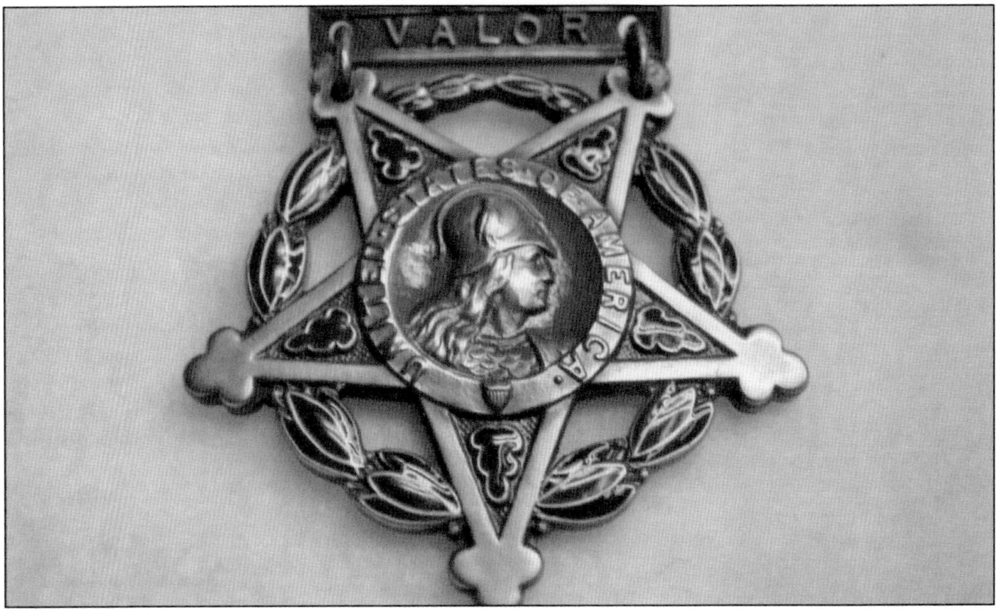

MESSERSCHMIDT. Sgt. Harold Messerschmidt of Grier City was killed in action in France on September 17, 1944. He served in North Africa, Italy, and France with the US Army 3rd Division. Sergeant Messerschmidt was awarded the Congressional Medal of Honor (above) for his bravery. "His sustained heroism in hand-to-hand combat with superior enemy forces was in keeping with the highest traditions of military service," said Pres. Harry Truman. His body was returned to the United States in 1948, and he was reburied with full military honors at the Christ Evangelical (White Church) Cemetery in Barnesville (below). The American Legion in Quakake, Rush Township, bears his name, and a street in Grier City Barnesville is named after him. (Both, JSH.)

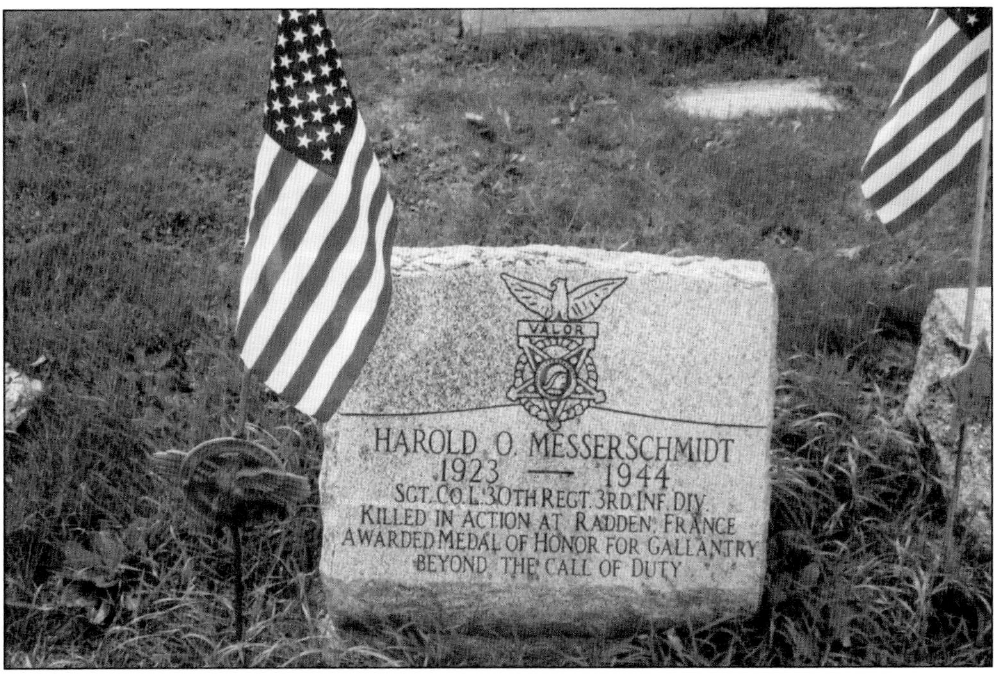

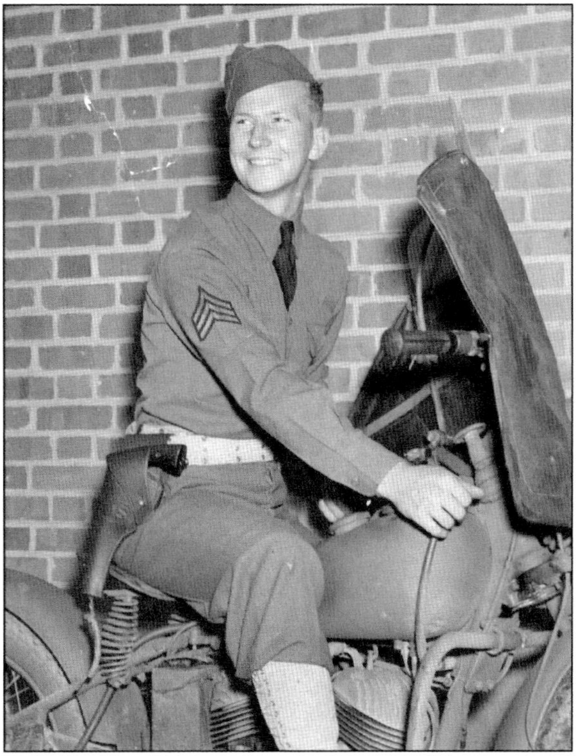

SGT. FRANCIS TRUSKOWSKI. Francis graduated from Mahanoy City High School in 1940 and was a B-29 radar operator with the 421st Bombardment Squadron. On April 24, 1945, while attacking targets near Tokyo, his bomber suffered a direct hit by an antiaircraft shell, severing the tail section from the aircraft. Sergeant Truskowski and the entire crew died in the crash. (DK.)

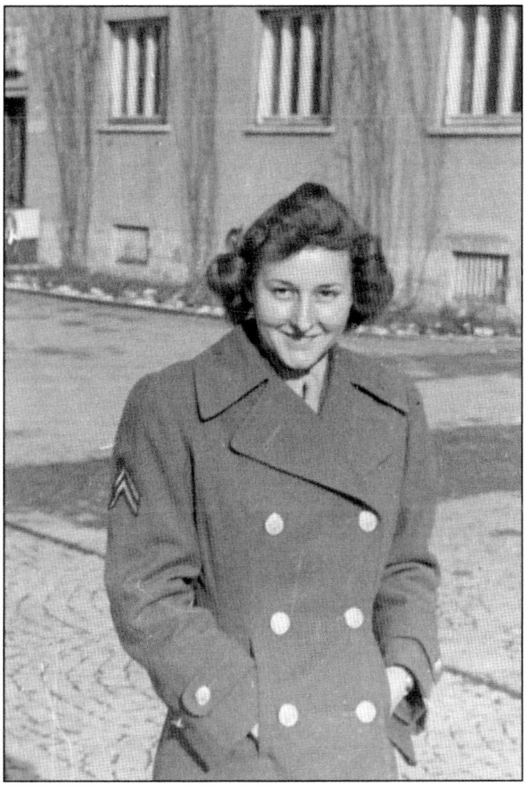

DOROTHY CROGLE BROWN. Glendon resident Dorothy Crogle graduated from Mahanoy Township High School in 1938. In September 1943, she volunteered for the Women's Army Corps (WAC) and after some time at Fort Oglethorpe, Georgia, was assigned to a military post office in devastated postwar Munich. While in Munich, Dorothy visited the recently liberated Dachau concentration camp and viewed the infamous ovens long before much of the world knew of the Holocaust. (BG.)

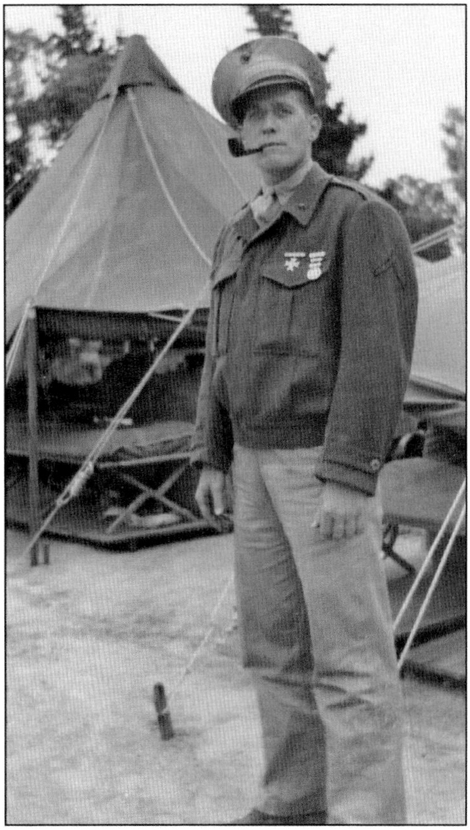

Robert Fletcher. Robert Fletcher enlisted as a US Marine shortly after the attack on Pearl Harbor. Robert served with the heroic 1st Marine Division. While outnumbered and lacking food, supplies, and ammunition, they captured and held a strategic airstrip, Henderson Field, at the South Pacific Battle of Guadalcanal during September and October 1942. Here, Robert and his fellow Marines endured an intense bombardment by several Japanese battleships and heavy cruisers that is said to be the worst bombardment endured by any Marine unit during World War II. (MF.)

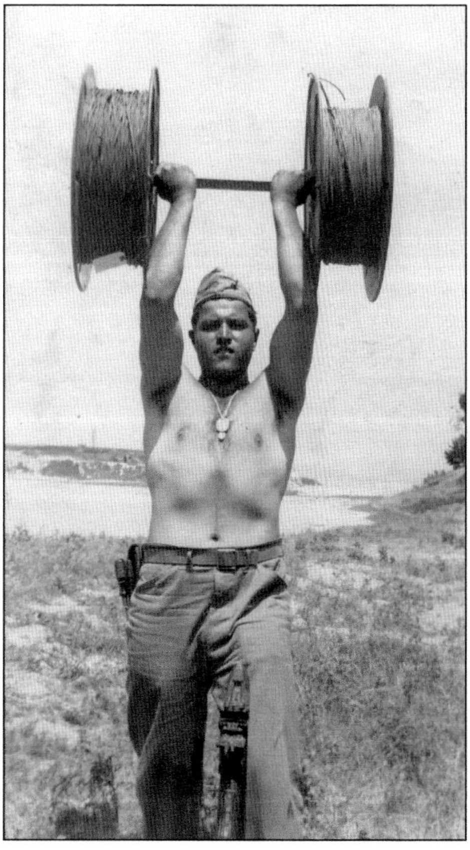

Gino Capone. Gino Capone volunteered to join the Marine Corps on May 10, 1943. He saw action at Quagelline, Saipan, Guam, and Okinawa. After the war, he worked for PPL and volunteered to serve his community in Scouting, Little League baseball, and sports training and as an ambulance trainer, American Red Cross first aid and sports medicine technician, and member of the Good American Hose Company No. 3. In 2006, he received the President's Award for community service. (MMC.)

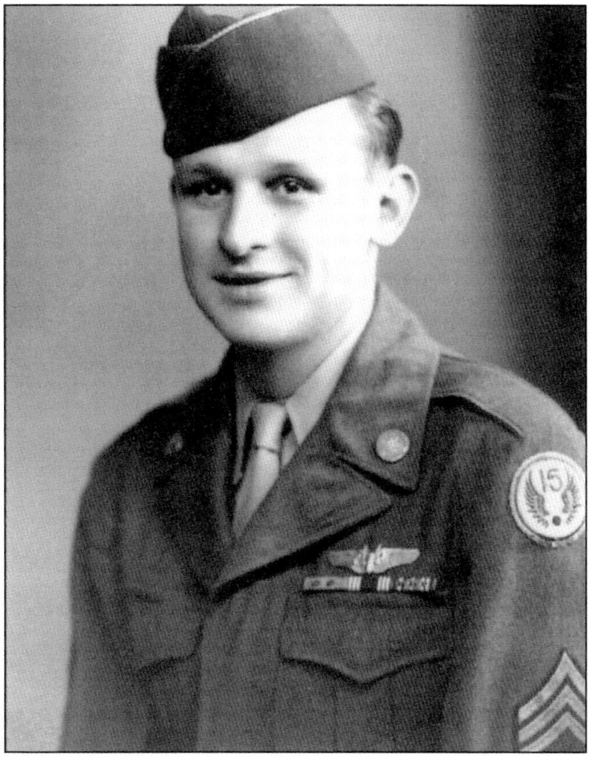

FRANK LASHINSKY. Frank Lashinsky graduated from Mahanoy City High School in 1942; he was a B-24 tail gunner attacking Nazi oil facilities in Yugoslavia. After he bailed out of his crippled bomber, local partisans helped him evade capture, and he eventually returned to his unit to rejoin the fight. On his 25th mission, he bailed out again and was captured by the Germans and made a prisoner of war (POW). Gen. George Patton's 14th Armored Division liberated his prison camp in April 1945. (FL.)

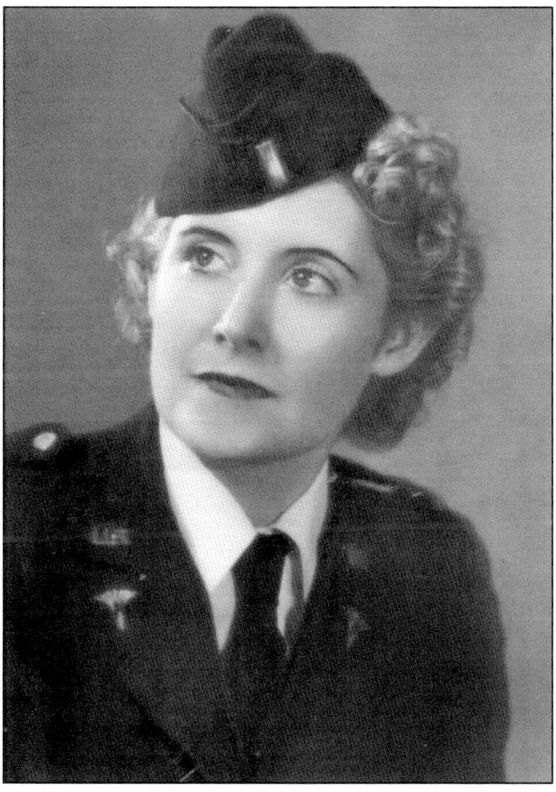

JULIA MCGROARTY. After graduating from Mahanoy Township High School, Morea native Julia McGroarty received her bachelor of nursing degree and enlisted in the US Army. During World War II, Lieutenant McGroarty cared for battle-fatigued soldiers in England and later cared for German prisoners of war on Staten Island, New York. After the war, Julia received a master's degree from Columbia University and continued her career working for the Veterans Administration. (KME.)

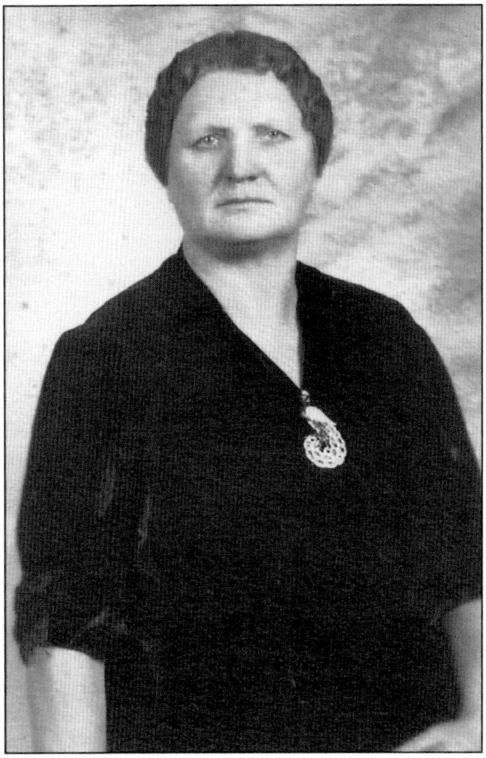

JOSEPHINE MILUNAS DERISCAVAGE. When her seventh son enlisted in the armed forces, Josephine was a proud mother indeed. Her husband died young from meningitis, and she raised her eight sons and three daughters by herself. From eldest to youngest, her sons were Julius, 34, a seaman second class; Joseph, 31, infantry; George, 29, a Merchant Marine; William, 27, Army Air Forces; Peter, 25, a Merchant Marine and later a lieutenant in the Navy; Algird, 20, infantry; and Daniel, 19, armed services. All of Josephine's sons survived the war. (PGG.)

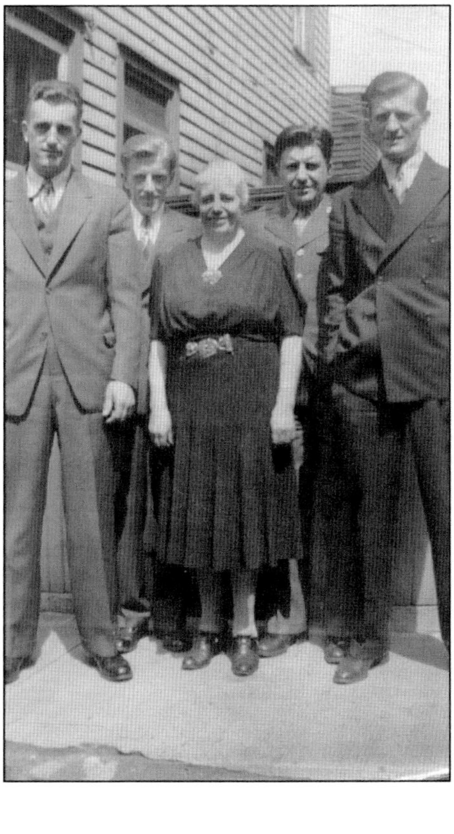

THE CAPITANIO BROTHERS. All four sons of Norina and Dominick Capitanio served in World War II. Pictured with their mother, Norina, they are, from left to right, Louis, Arnold, James, and Thomas. James served with the Army Judge Advocate Corps. Louis spent most of his days with the Navy in Bermuda. Thomas was an Army engineer serving in the European theater, and the youngest son, Arnold, enlisted in the Navy and served in the Pacific theater. (MC.)

FRANCIS CHESKO. Francis Chesko served as a combat engineer with the 148th Engineer Battalion. After D-day, he served in France, Holland, Germany, Belgium, and Luxembourg and fought in the Battle of the Bulge. Of the 700 men serving in his battalion in France, 49 were from Mahanoy City and surrounding patches and four from his Mahanoy Township High School class of 1942. (FC.)

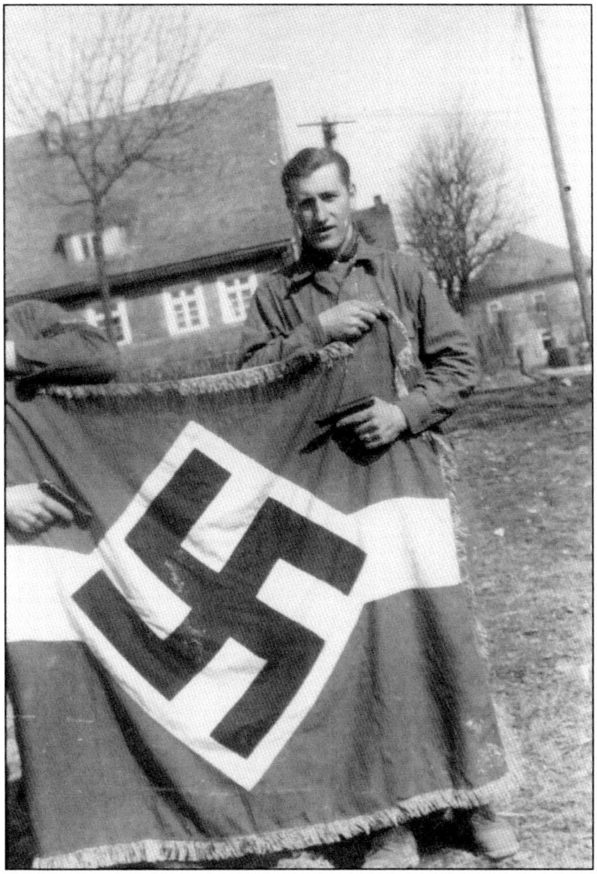

NEW HEBRIDES. A 3rd class petty officer, Joseph Katchmaric relaxes from his duties on the island of New Hebrides during World War II. The Americans arrived there in 1942 before the Japanese invaded and created a safe haven for the natives. The islands were only bombed once by the Japanese after the Americans set up camp. That Japanese plane was shot down, and there was only one casualty, Bessie the cow. (FW.)

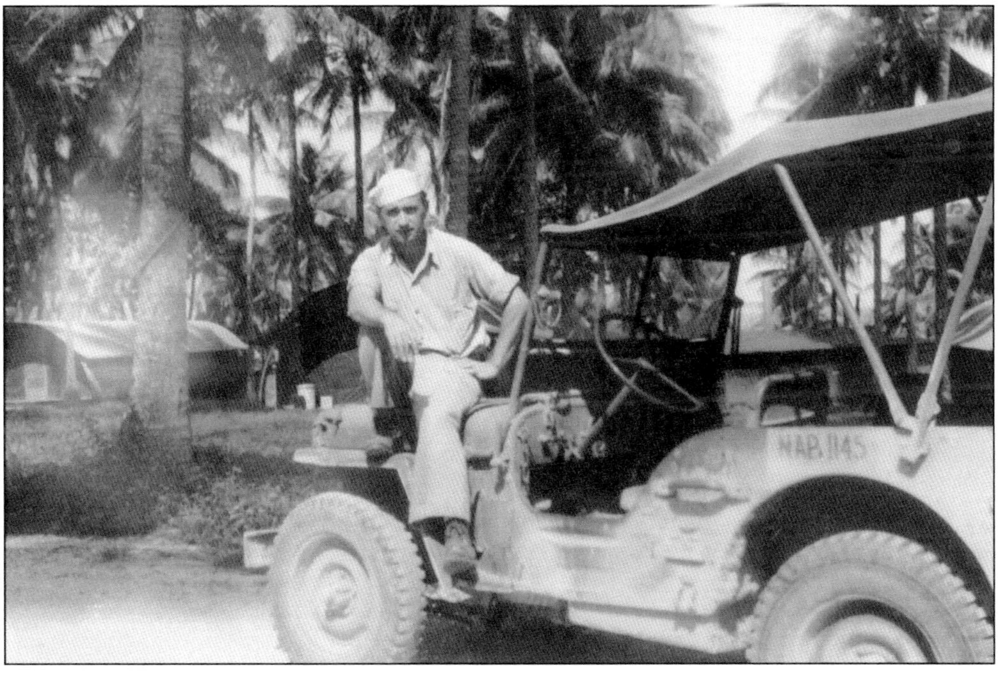

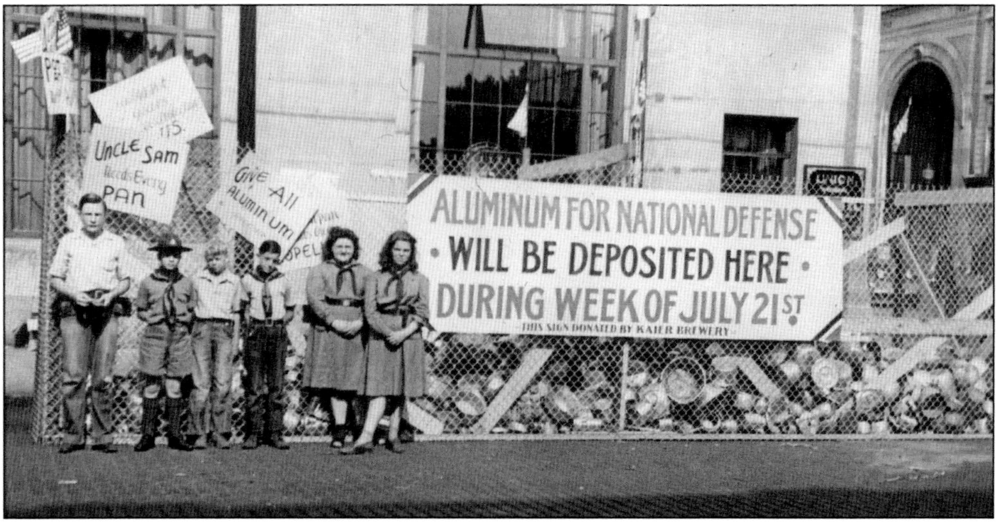

CONSERVATION FOR WAR. Scrap metal drives, similar to the one led by the Boy Scouts and Girl Scouts from the Mahanoy area, helped build war morale at home and helped to illustrate and encourage conservation of scarce resources that were necessary for the war effort. Saving aluminum cans meant more aluminum for the soldiers. Other recycling drives included rubber, paper, and waste oil. (JSK.)

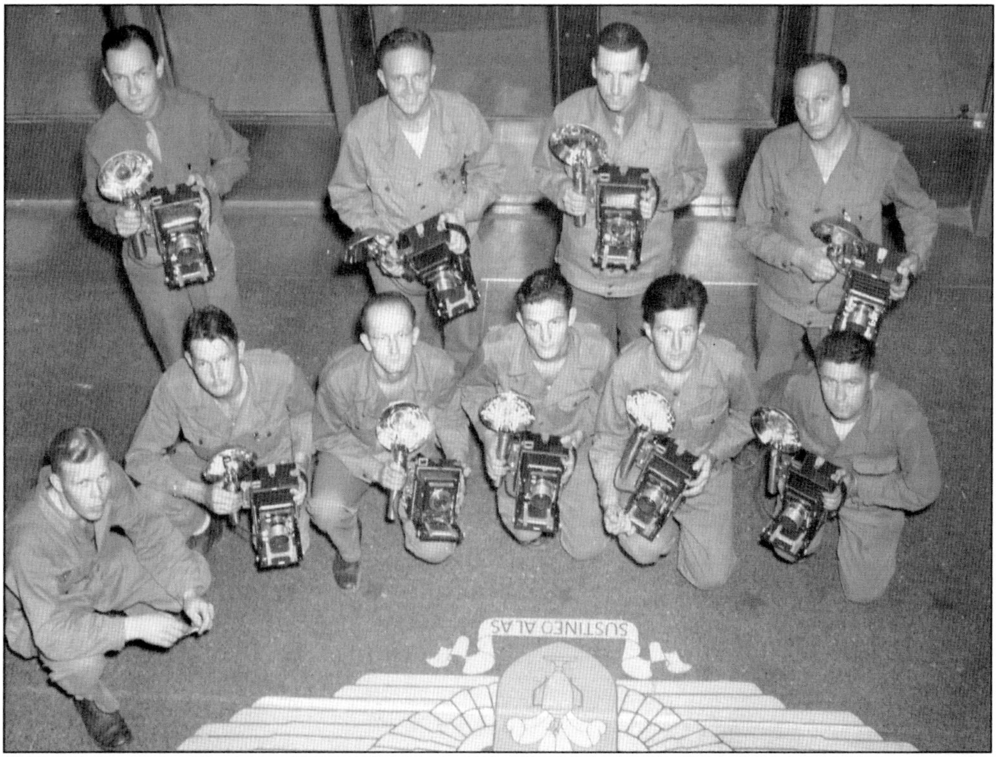

RECONNAISSANCE PHOTOGRAPHER. Maurice Pedriani (first row, fifth from left) served in Europe as an Army Air Corps reconnaissance photographer. After the war, Maurice ran a popular barbershop on East Centre Street. Maurice was also an accomplished photographer who snapped many of the photographs in this volume. (JKG.)

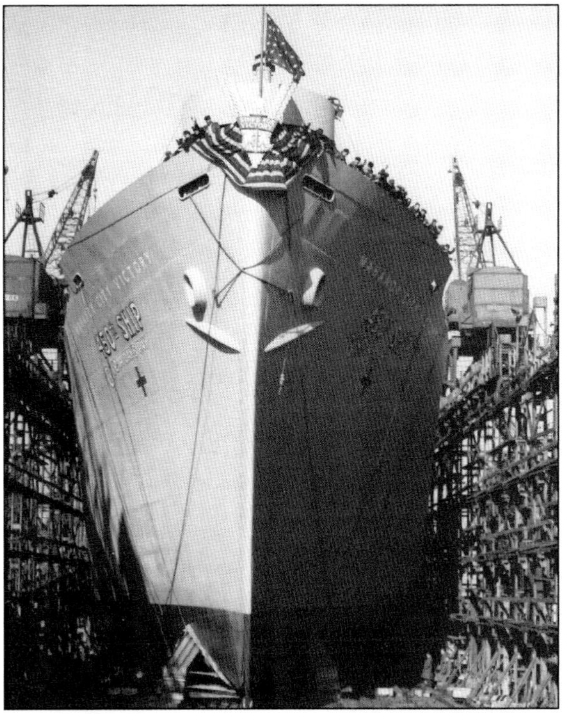

A Victory Ship for Mahanoy City. The SS *Mahanoy City Victory* was a World War II cargo ship designed and produced to replace shipping losses caused by German submarines. The SS *Mahanoy City Victory* was faster and larger than the older Liberty Ship design. It displaced 15,200 tons and was 455 feet long. (MHS.)

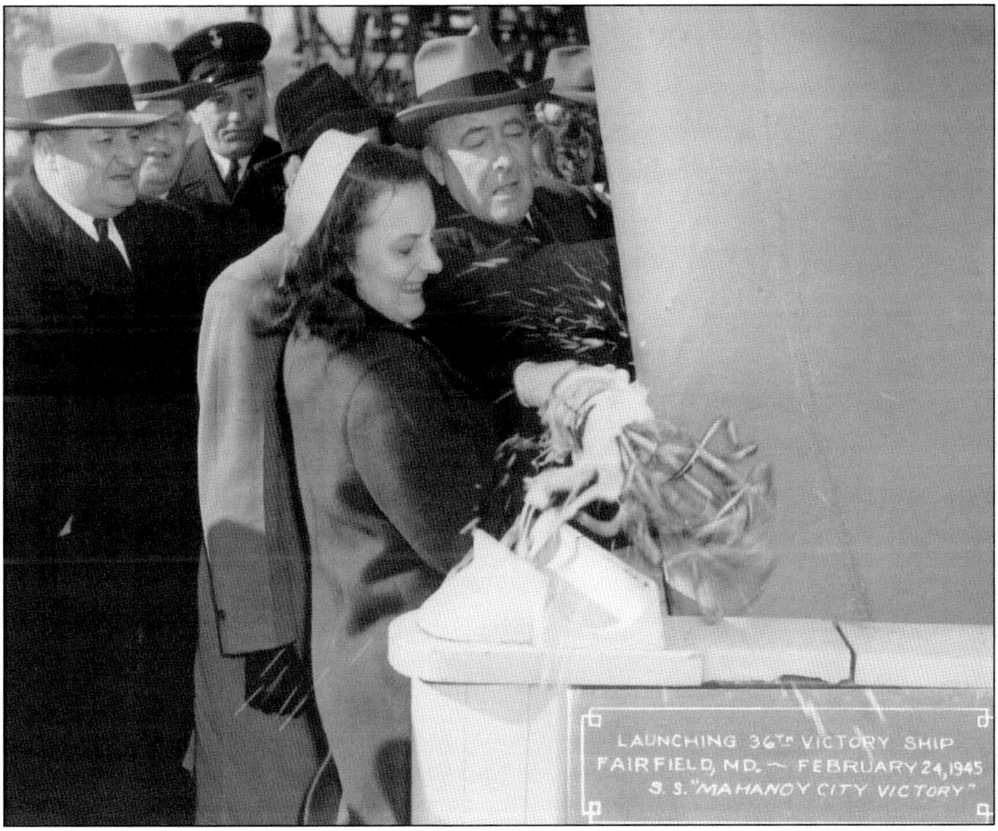

Launching 36th Victory Ship. The SS *Mahanoy City Victory* was launched at the Bethlehem Fairfield shipyard on February 24, 1945. This 15,200-ton Victory Ship was christened and named by sophomore Rosanne Konsavage (Mahanoy City High School class of 1948) as a prize for winning an essay contest sponsored by the United Mine Workers Union. This vessel was one of only three warships named after Pennsylvania coal region communities. (MHS.)

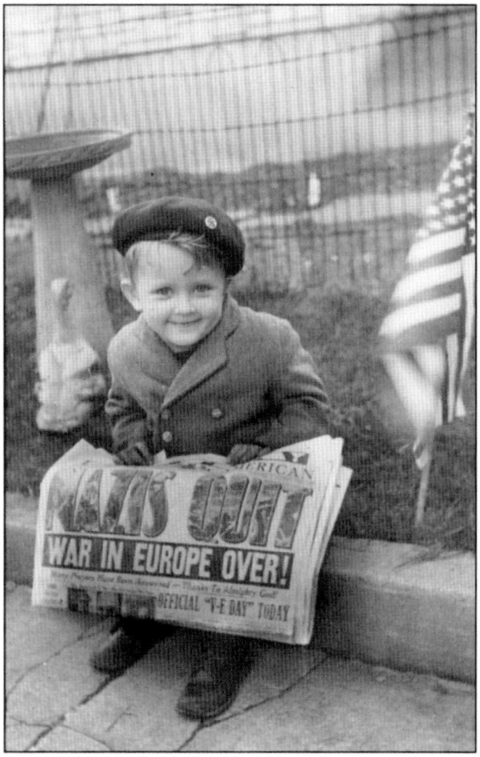

V-E Day. The *Record American* provided the community detailed and timely reports on the progress of the war, as well as the status of local servicemen. Here, an unidentified child holds a special edition published just after V-E Day in May 1945. (JSK.)

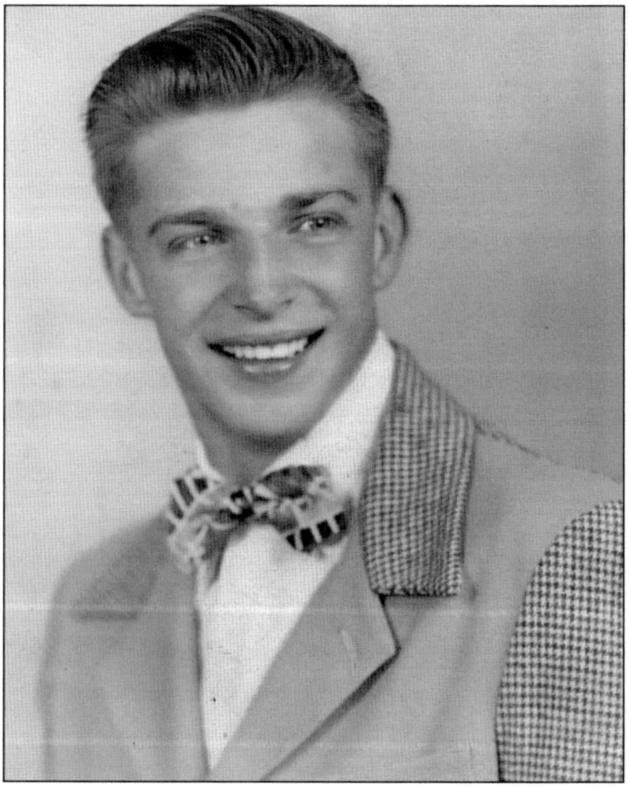

Stephen Gavula. The September 22, 1953, *Mahanoy City Record American* reports the following: "There seldom ever was a celebration in Mahanoy City to equal the public ovation tendered Cpl. Stephen Gavula, repatriated Korean POW." US Army corporal Stephen Gavula, a 1949 Mahanoy City High School graduate, was welcomed by a throng of over 10,000 Mahanoy area residents, family, and friends after spending 33 months in captivity. (AGM.)

Five

SENTIMENTAL JOURNEY

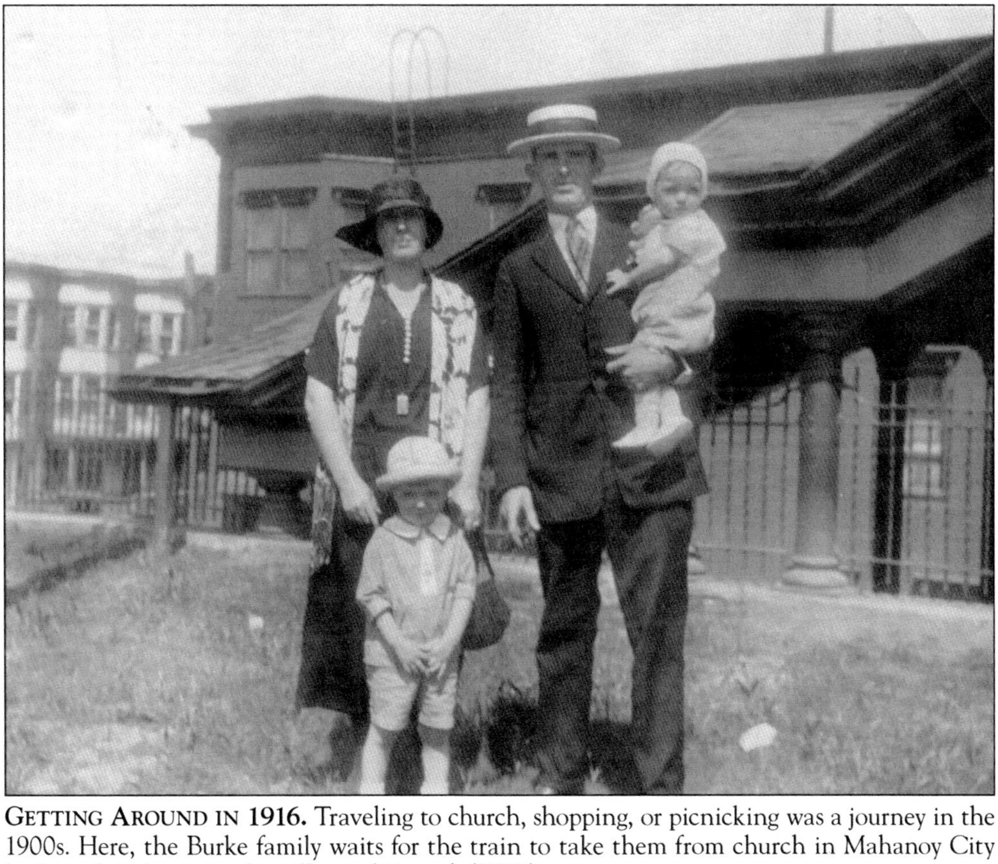

GETTING AROUND IN 1916. Traveling to church, shopping, or picnicking was a journey in the 1900s. Here, the Burke family waits for the train to take them from church in Mahanoy City back to their home in the village of Tunnel. (JBW.)

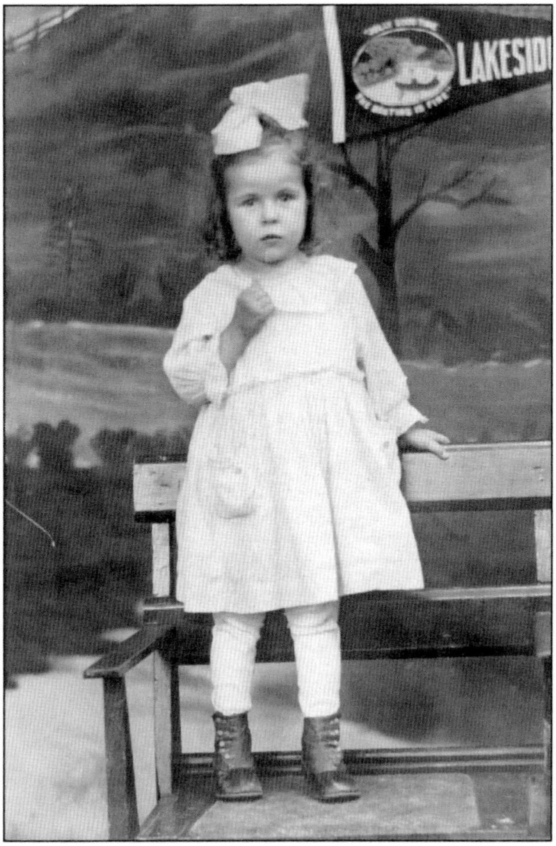

CHILDHOOD MEMORY AT LAKESIDE. Mahanoy City had two nearby bathing and picnic areas, both at East Mahanoy Railroad Junction. The first, Lakeside Park, was begun in the 1880s. Here, Janet Kline's mother, Rita Post, born in 1916, is photographed with a painted background identifying the location of the day of fun. (JSK.)

BOATING AT LAKESIDE. By train or even by foot, young men made their way to Lakeside on a Sunday to picnic with their church group or civic organization. Usually dressed in shirt and tie, a fellow would take his gal for a ride past the bathhouse. (JBW.)

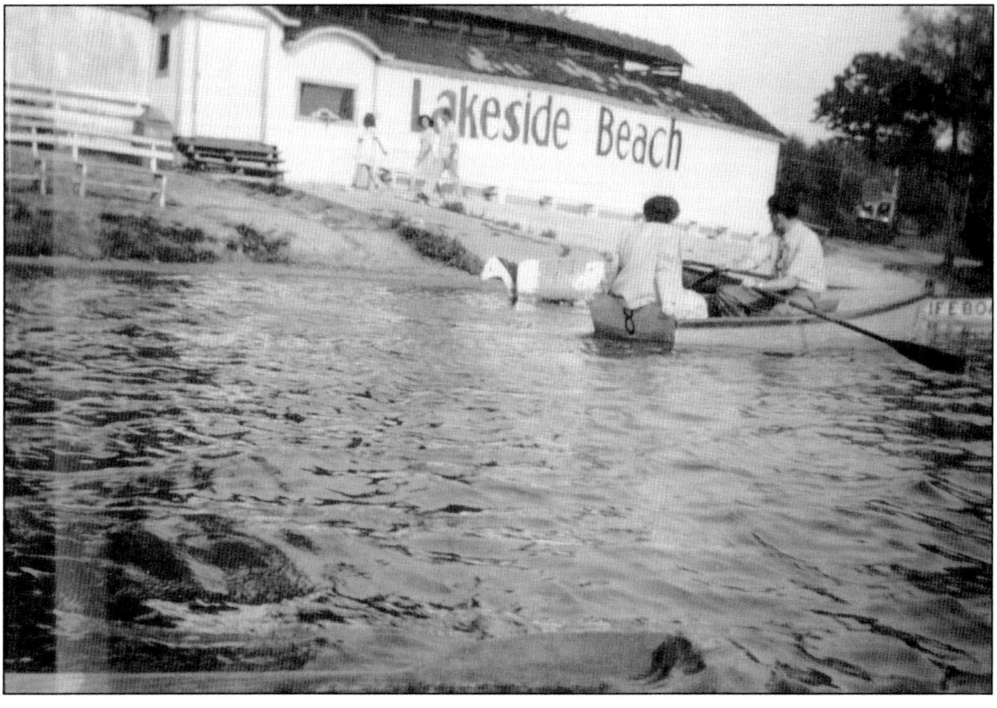

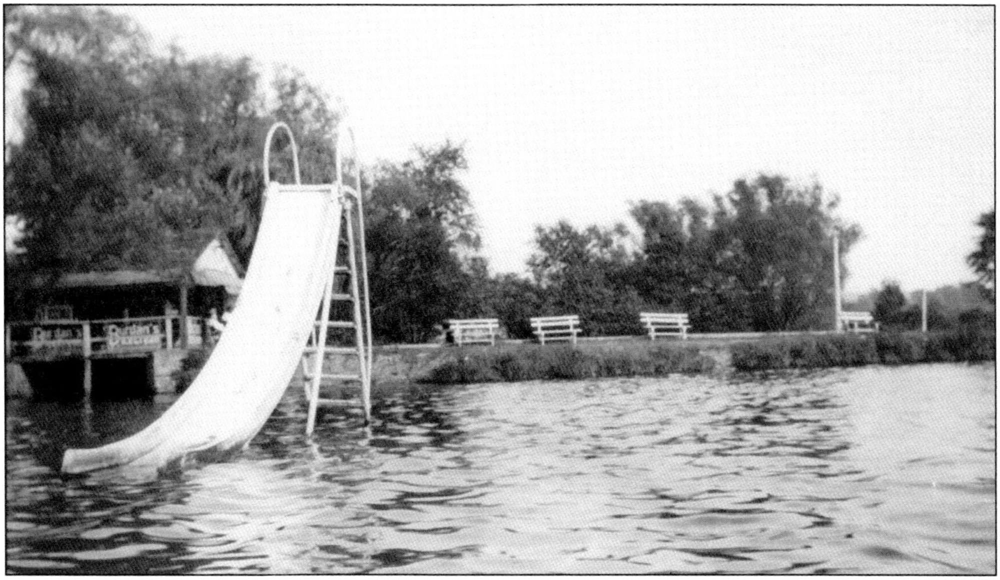

SWIMMING AT LAKESIDE. Part of the fun of swimming at Lakeside was sliding into the water on this metal slide. How hot it must have been on an August day! (JBW.)

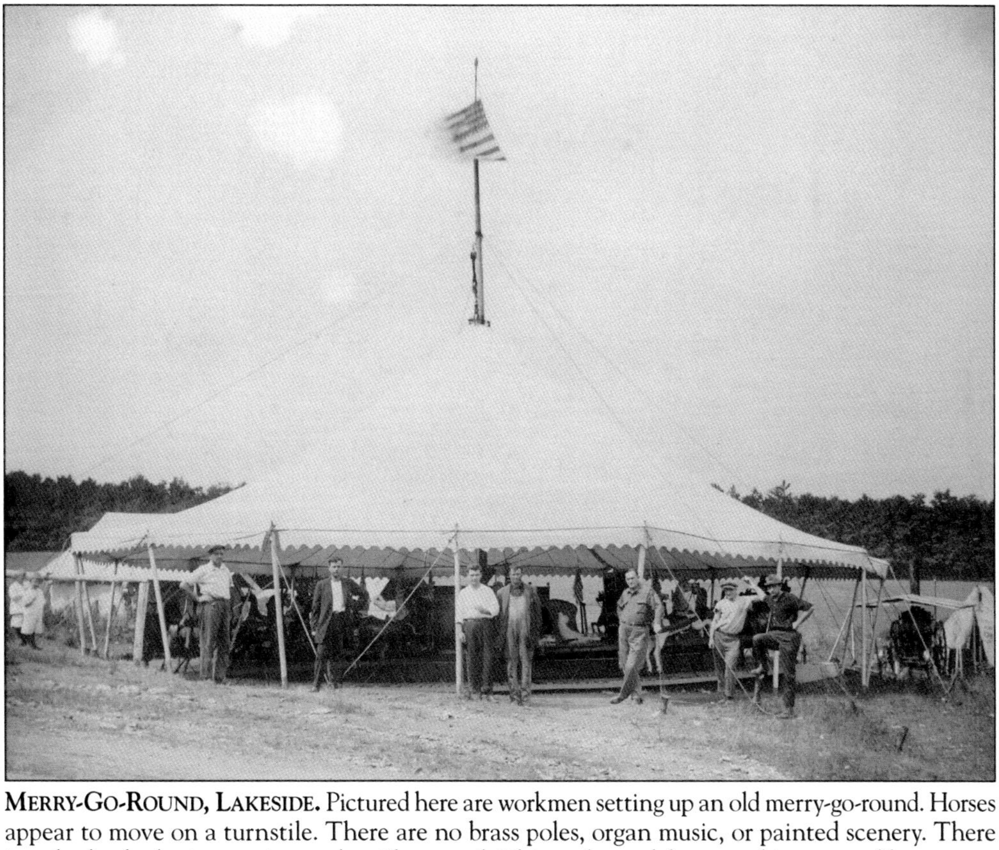

MERRY-GO-ROUND, LAKESIDE. Pictured here are workmen setting up an old merry-go-round. Horses appear to move on a turnstile. There are no brass poles, organ music, or painted scenery. There is only the fresh air to enjoy as the ride moved. This early-model carousel is powered by a steam engine, seen on the right, along with its equipment in the tent posted "KEEP OUT." (SF.)

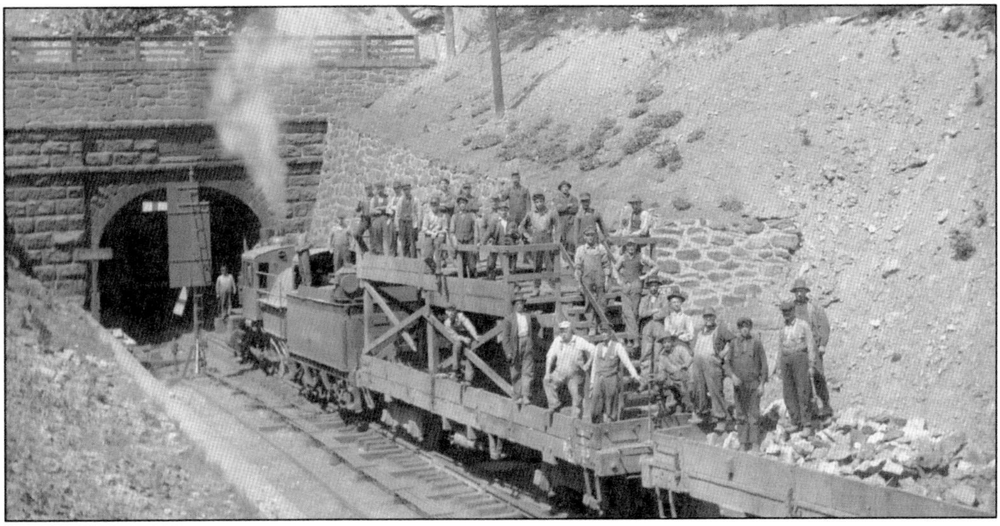

MAHANOY TUNNEL CREW. Before 1917, travelers who did not walk from Shenandoah and Mahanoy City to the lakes came by the frequent and sometimes specially run trains. Steam from train engines had impeded visibility and accumulated on the wall of the tunnel. In approximately 1916, a project to ventilate the tunnel was underway. Pictured above is the crew who installed huge exhaust fans in the tunnel. (JBW.)

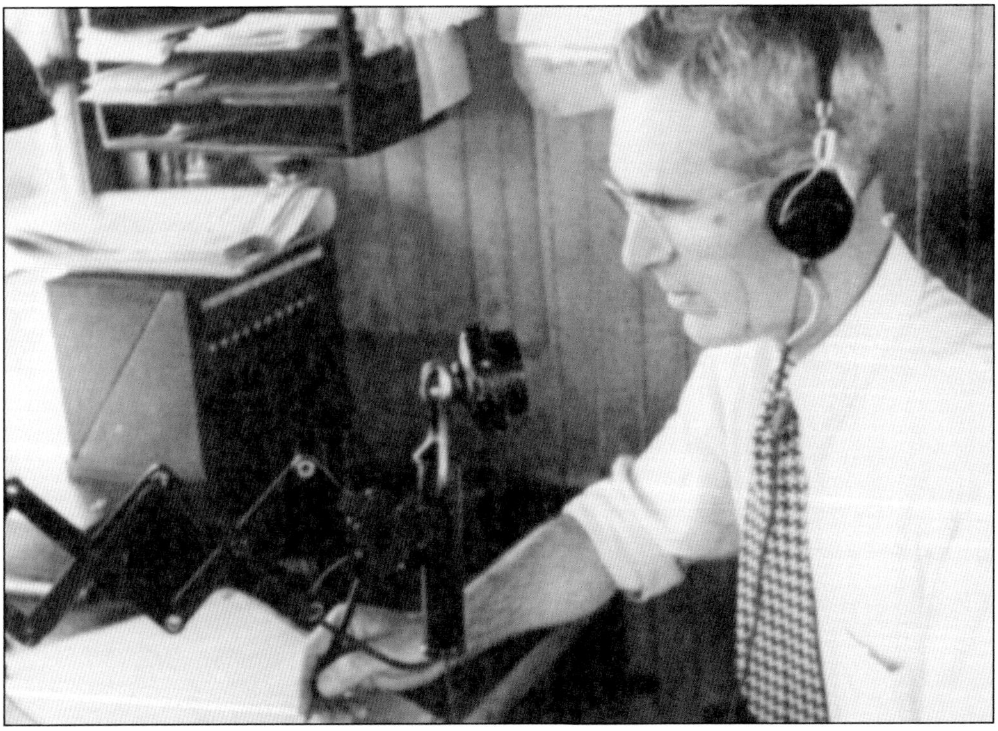

TUNNEL TRAIN STATION. Pictured is Stephen Burke, a telegraph-communication official at the Tunnel Train Station. The Burke family lived in the village of Tunnel located next to this site. Telegraphers transmitted information mainly via Morse code and were responsible for the general safety of train traffic, including routing and track switching. Elizabeth Burke's brother Daniel McCarthy photographed the construction of the tunnel and of Route 45. (JBW.)

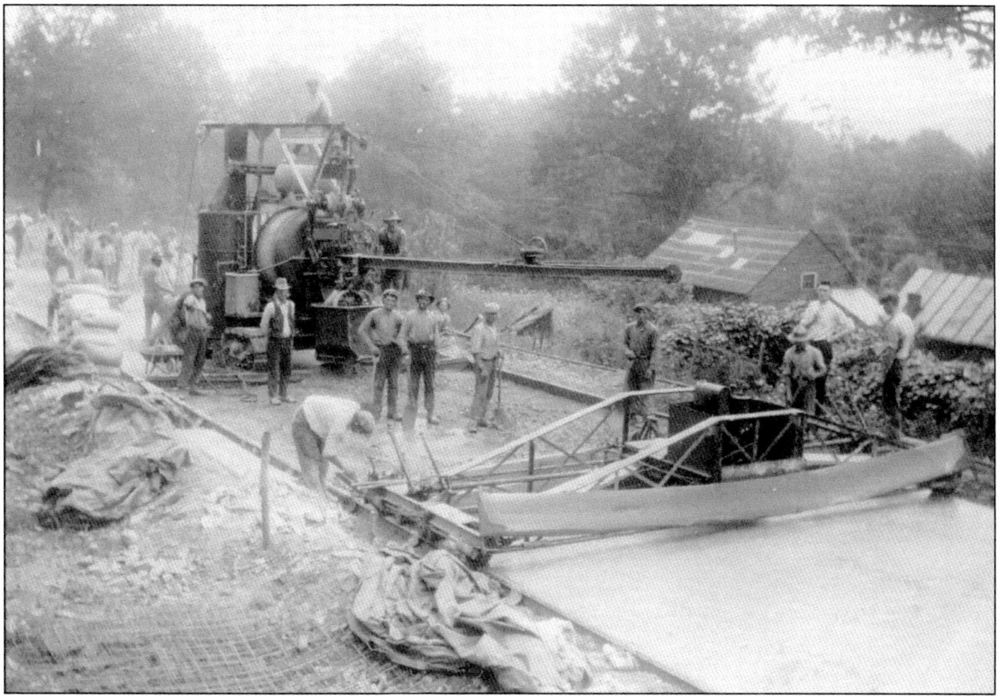

PAVING OF ROUTE 45 (54). In 1917, the Pennsylvania State Highway paving project reached the Mahanoy City area. Its impact on the local geography is best described in Joseph H. Zerby's *History 1934*: "Park Crest owes its origin to the building of state highway No. 45 and Lakewood Park (and Lakeside)." The picture looking east shows the Tunnel homes on the right, the cement mixer at rear, and the cement leveler near. (JBW.)

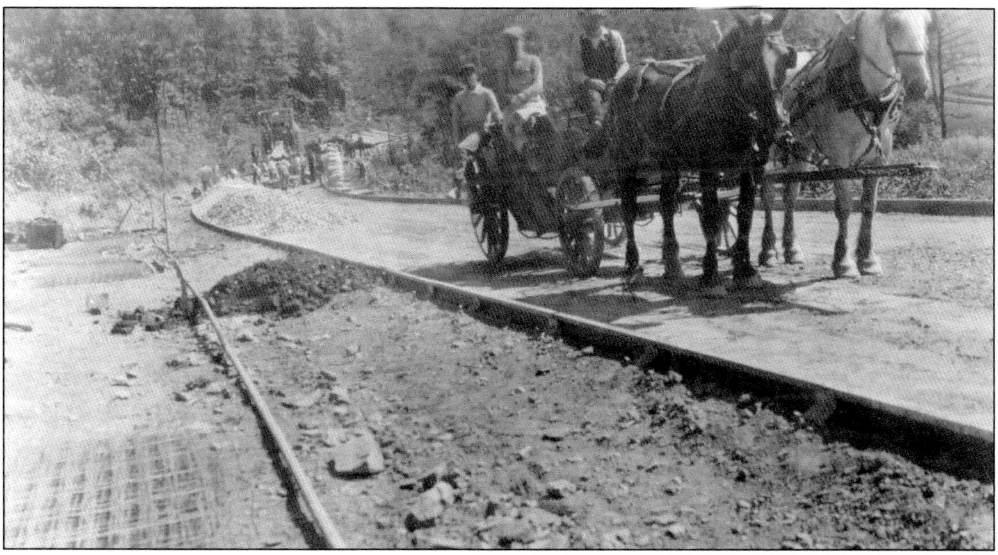

HORSE AND WAGON ASSIST. Paving a short stretch of road was a long process. Men drove a wagon over a stone roadbed carrying supplies to the cement mixer. The Burke family, who lived in the village of Tunnel located adjacent to Route 45 where this work was done, took this photograph and the one above. (JBW.)

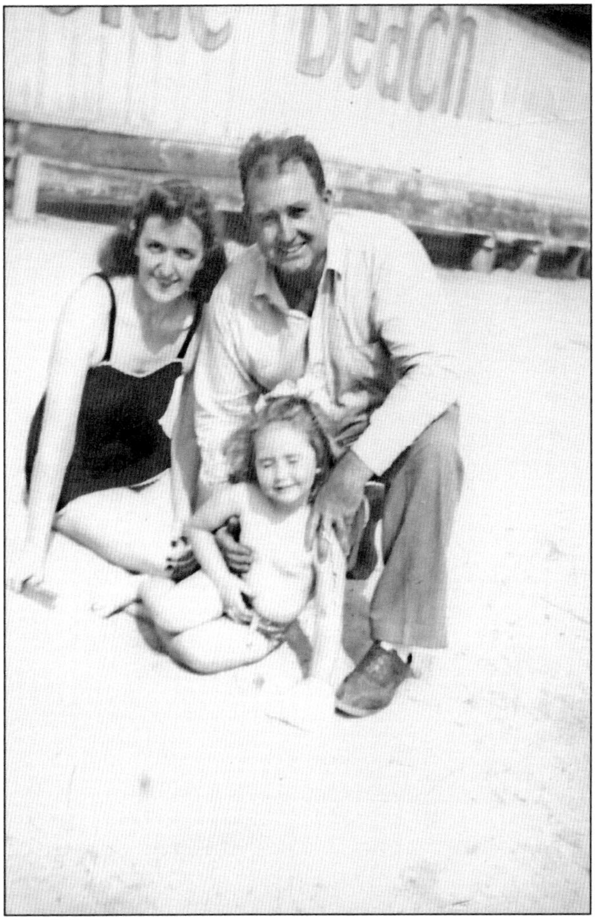

HART PHOTOGRAPH. In 1901, Harry Hart Sr. and William Lewis purchased Lakeside's 188 acres from Robert Roth. In 1912, Hart bought out Lewis, and on the death of Hart in 1928, the park passed to his five children. Active in the operation of Lakeside during the 1930s and 1940s was Harry's son William, seen here on the Lakeside beach with his wife, Ruth, and their daughter Ruth Hart (Wildoner). (RHW.)

RUTH FLETCHER HART. Ruth Hart and an unidentified companion enjoy swimming in the lake. They are using an inner tube, commonly used as a flotation device. (RHW.)

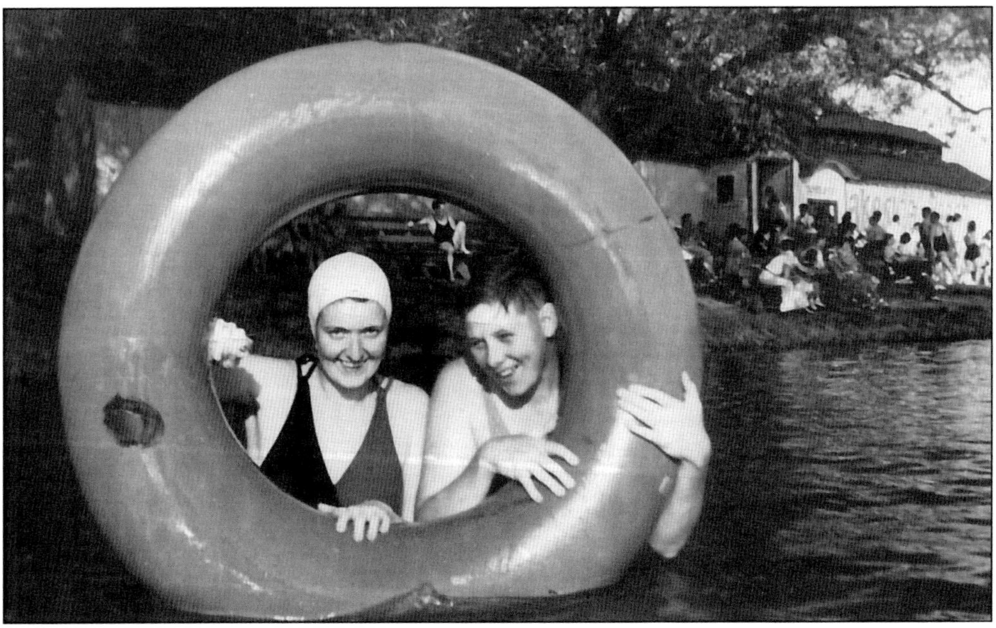

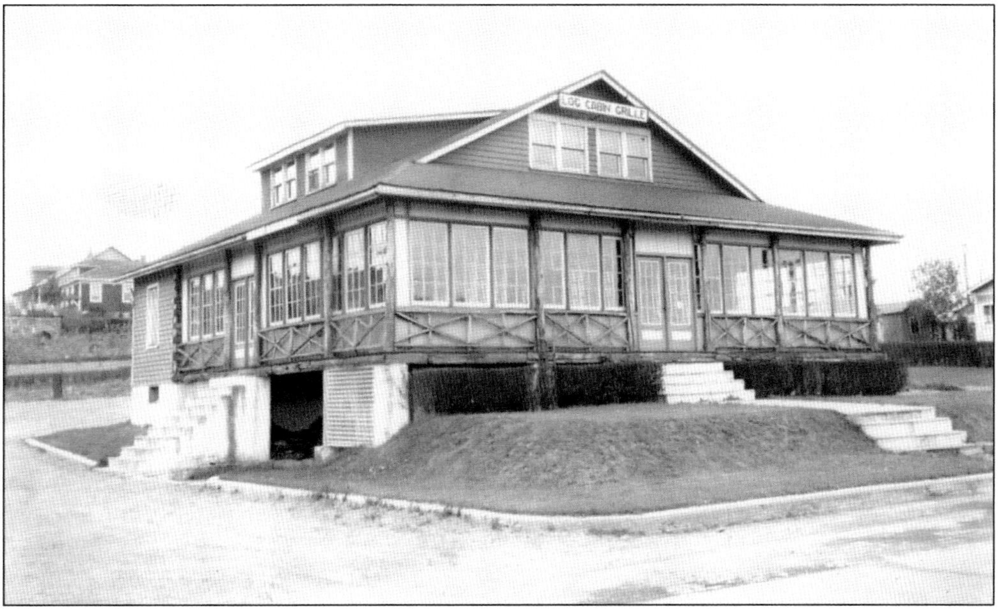

Log Cabin Inn Park Crest. The Surfield family operated the Log Cabin Inn from the 1920s until 1959. The establishment had a staff of cooks, waitresses, bartenders, and housekeepers. Open for late lunch and dinner, the Surfields maintained a fine restaurant where their son and daughter earned enough money to pay for college. Across the highway from the Log Cabin was the entrance to Lakewood Park. (ES.)

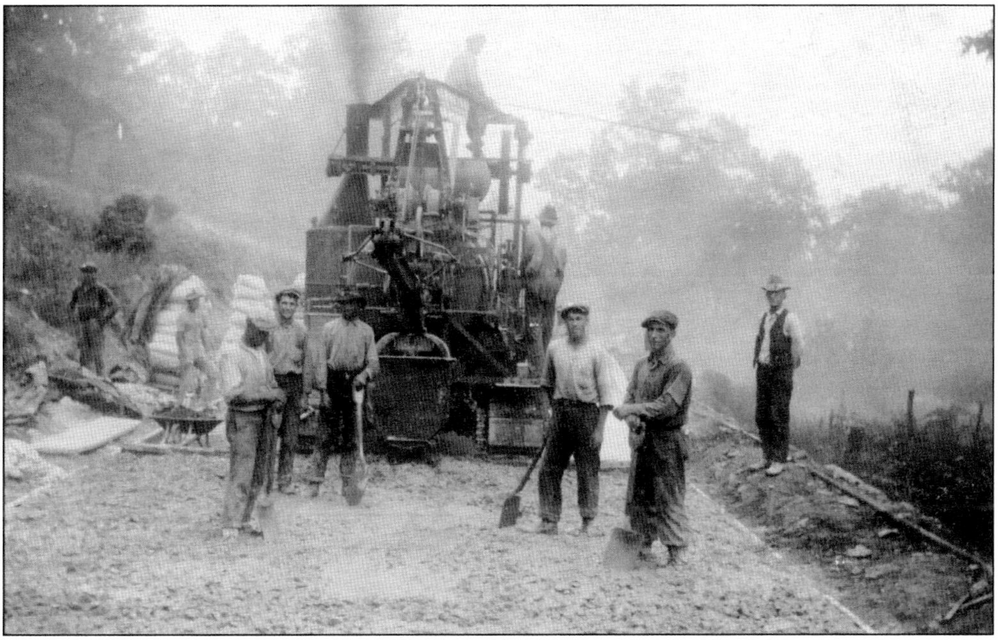

Continuing the Modern Highway. In 1920, infant Frank Selgrath and his family moved to Barnesville, six miles east of Mahanoy City. Route 45 was finished up to that point, and his family could travel all the way to town on a paved road. In this picture, the cement mixer that is run on steam dwarfs the workmen in front of it. Although assisted by a mixer, shoveling and leveling were both done by hand. (JBW.)

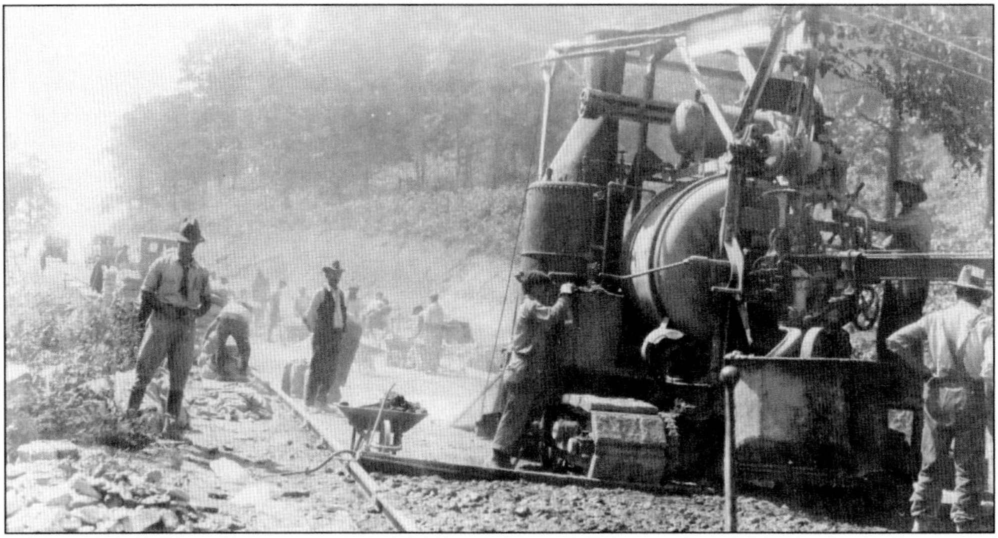

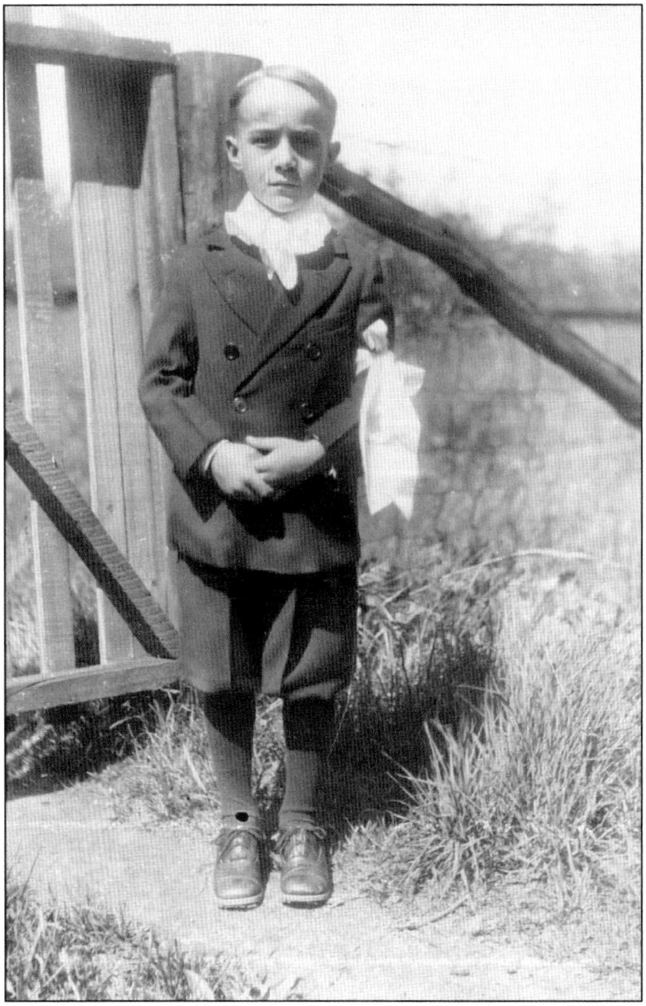

The Vulcan Mountain. One of the most difficult sections of roadway construction was the Vulcan Hill. Here, the cement mixer and workmen are in the foreground while very early model trucks can be seen traveling up the hill to get more supplies. (JBW.)

Frank Selgrath. The Selgrath family belonged to St. Canicus Catholic Church when they moved to the village of Barnesville. With no Catholic church nearby, the family continued to worship in Mahanoy City seven miles away. Here is seven-year-old Frank in 1927 on his way to his First Holy Communion. (FAS.)

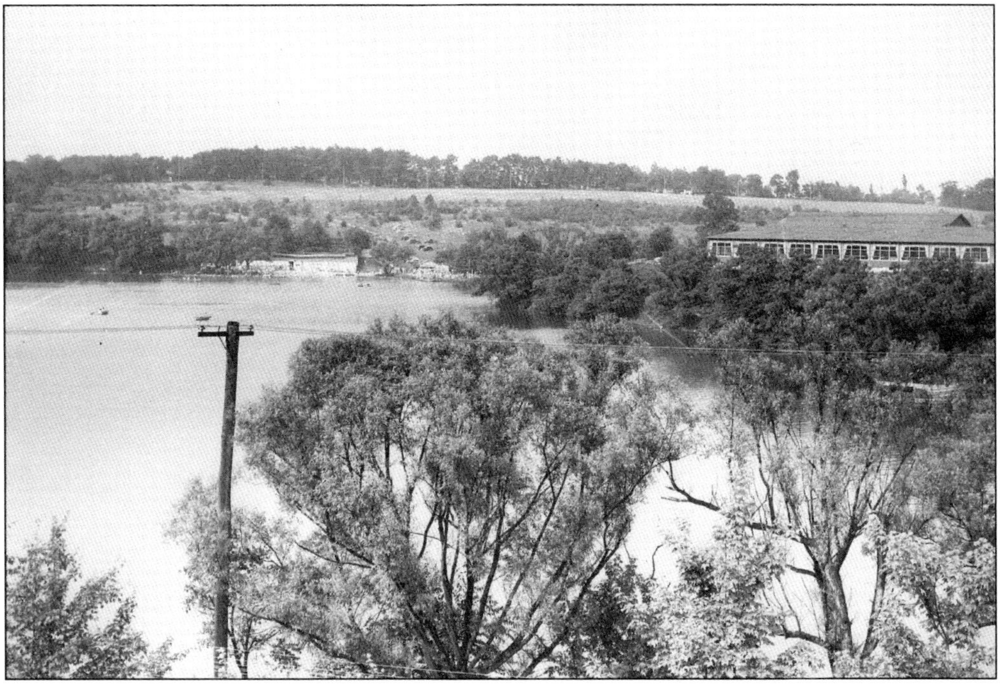

VIEW OF LAKESIDE. From 1924 to the 1970s, this view of Lakeside remained unchanged. Bathers and boaters used the large lake, with its sandy beach and bathhouse in the distance. On the right is the large ballroom, which exists today. In 1924, Harry Hart made $20,000 worth of improvements to his pavilion and created a ballroom with an arched ceiling covered in silk, a crystal ball, and a large wooden floor. (JKG.)

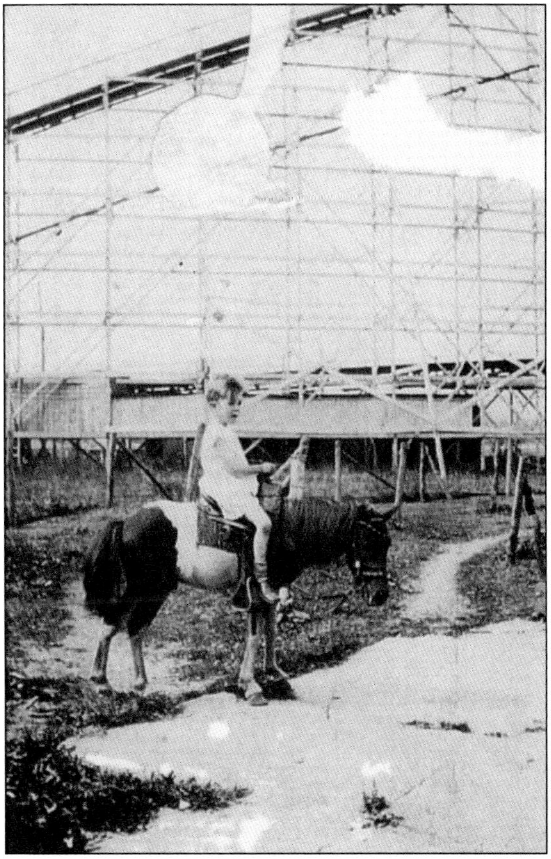

THE COASTER, 1929. Arthur Brill, age six, pauses on his ride to watch the new coaster (built in 1925). He saw men and women dressed in their best clothes on two-person seats. Each car of six seats was pulled up the first hill by chain and motor. Momentum carried the loaded car down the next three hills. As the coaster neared the end, a brakeman pulled on the gears to stop the moving car. (BF.)

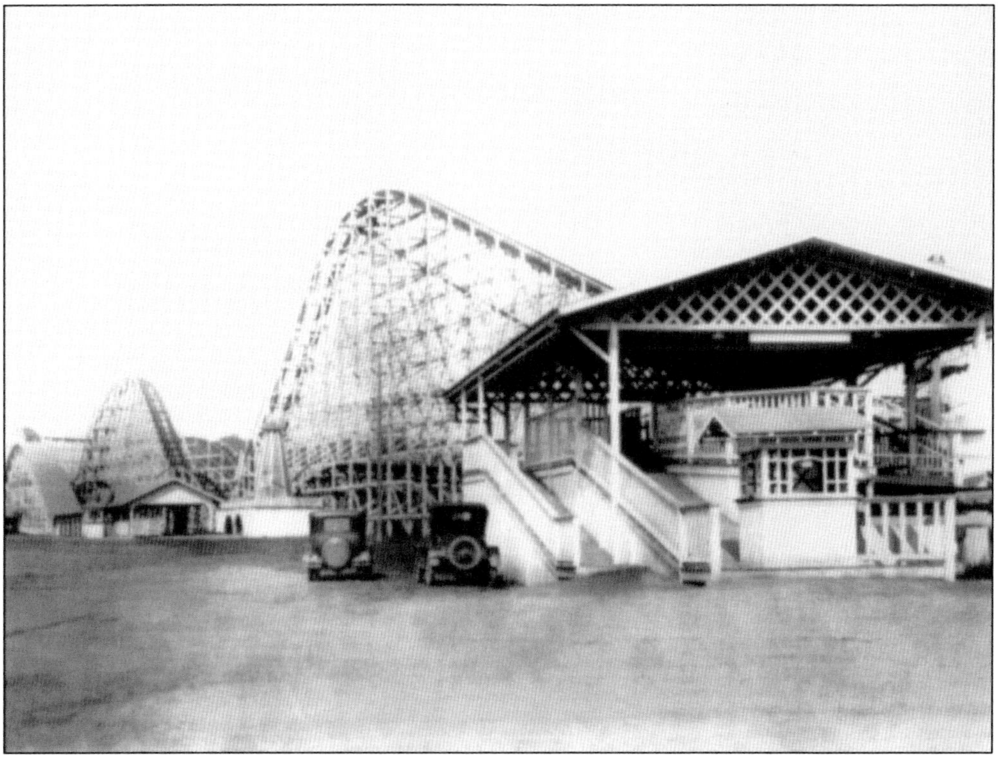

LAKESIDE ROLLER COASTER, 1925. The wooden coaster at Lakeside, built in 1925, was in operation at the park until it was destroyed by the winds of Hurricane Hazel in 1954. During its first year, the *Record American* newspaper reports that three passengers were stranded in an open car hit by bolts of lightning and soaked by a downpour of rain. An hour later, power was restored. (DC.)

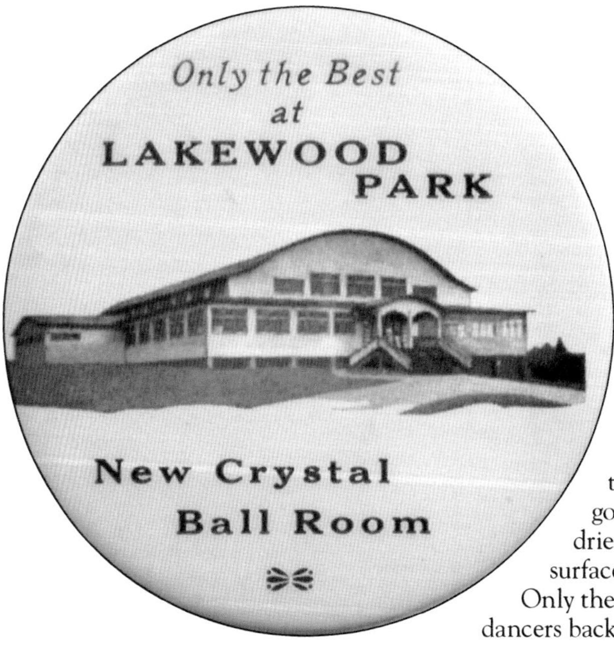

LAKEWOOD BALLROOM, 1925. Meanwhile, to keep up with the competition, Richard Guinan at Lakewood built a second ballroom. On the inside, the tall, curved wooden arches and dance floor were made of imported wood. The opening of the Crystal Ballroom was talked about for months, but all did not go well. The layer of wax on the floor dried to a sticky curdle instead of a slick surface, and the dancers were not pleased. Only the biggest-name bands would bring the dancers back. (PGG.)

DANCE MARATHON AT LAKEWOOD, 1936. Dance marathons (also called walkathons), an American phenomenon of the 1920s and 1930s, were human endurance contests in which couples danced almost nonstop for hundreds of hours (as long as a month or two), competing for prize money. Dancers, judges, announcers, and huge audiences attended. Here, local contestants autographed their picture "Dancingly Yours." They are Harry Stein of Grier City and Bobby Smith. (DC.)

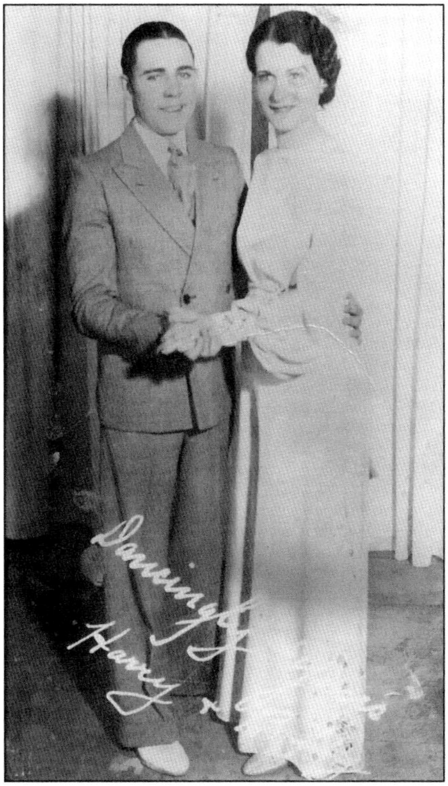

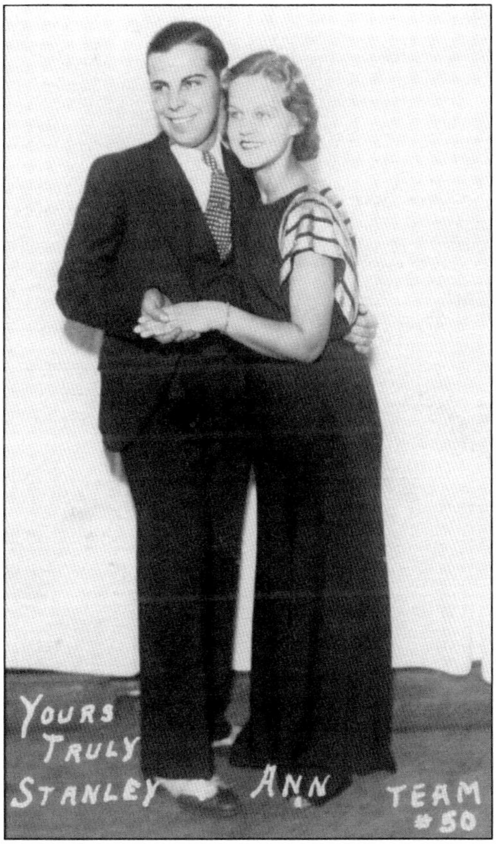

DANCE MARATHONS, 1936. In these dance endurance contests, a mix of local hopefuls and seasoned professional marathoners, danced, walked, shuffled, sprinted, and sometimes cracked under the eyes of judges and huge audiences. Here, local talent identified only as Stan and Ann, team No. 50, compete against professionals. (DC.)

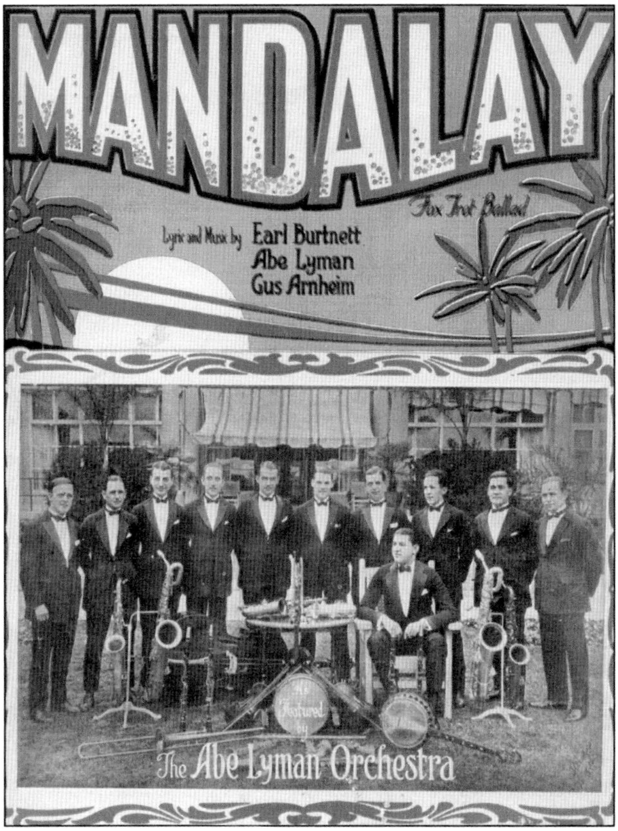

ABE LYMAN ORCHESTRA. Puck Sullivan, now 103, once asked Daniel F. Guinan if a band ever shared a loss with him. He could remember only one time, which occurred on a rainy night at the height of the Depression. Bandleader Abe Lyman approached Dan at intermission and asked, "What do you stand to lose?" Dan replied, "Roughly one thousand dollars." To which Abe replied, "Deduct five hundred dollars from my contract price. I'll share the loss." (PGG.)

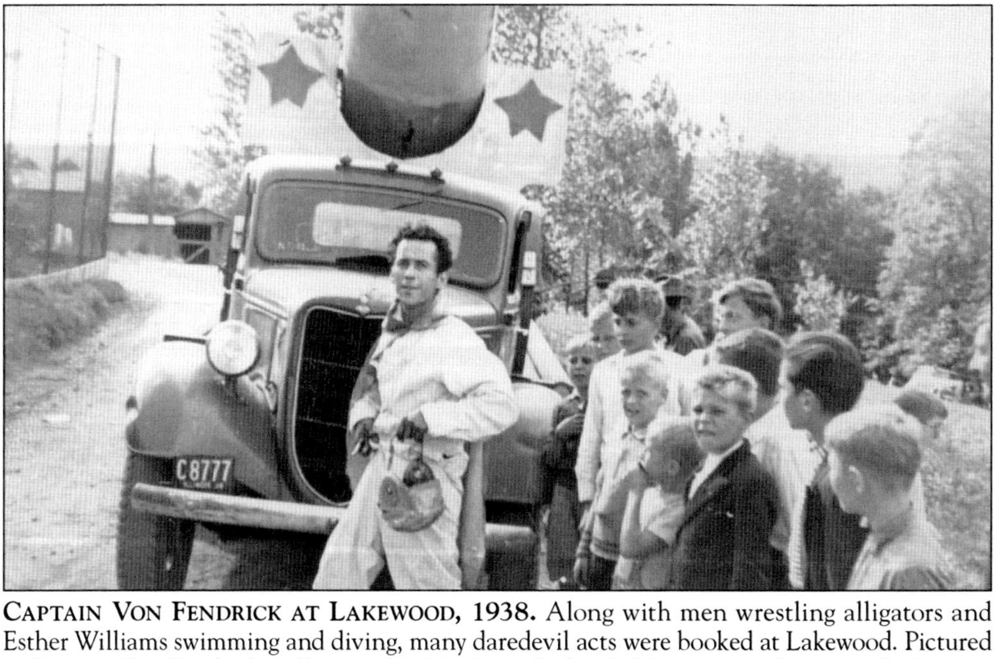

CAPTAIN VON FENDRICK AT LAKEWOOD, 1938. Along with men wrestling alligators and Esther Williams swimming and diving, many daredevil acts were booked at Lakewood. Pictured is Captain Von Fendrick walking to his Mack truck that held a cannon that propelled a man into "space." (JSK.)

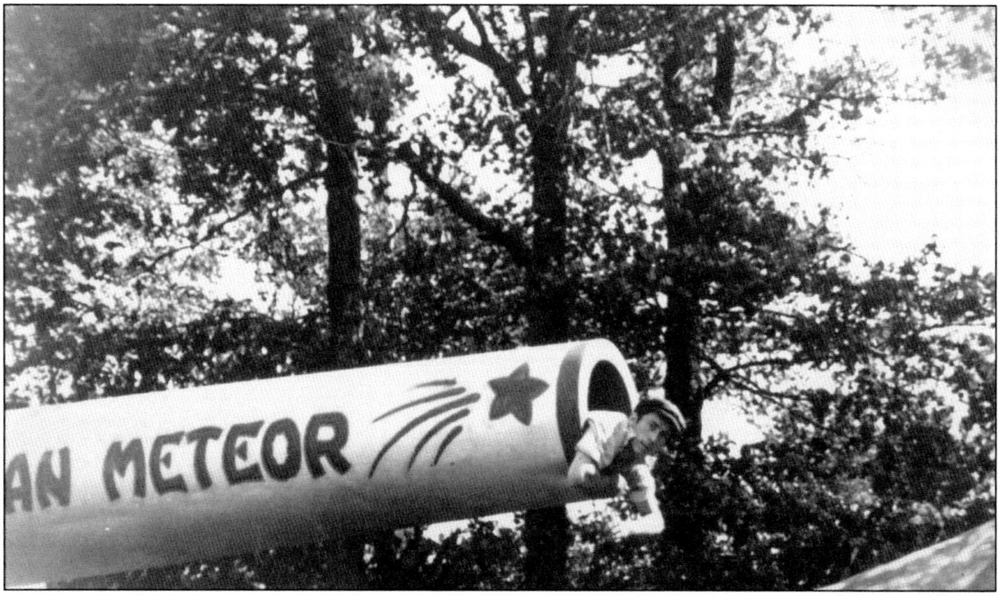

"HUMAN METEOR," 1938. Billed as Germany's Flying Ace, Von Fendrick poses in the cannon he calls the Human Meteor. Over the 100 years of circus history, dozens of acts propelled men into the air. *Billboard* reports that Von Fendrick's cannon shot him 200 feet. (JSK.)

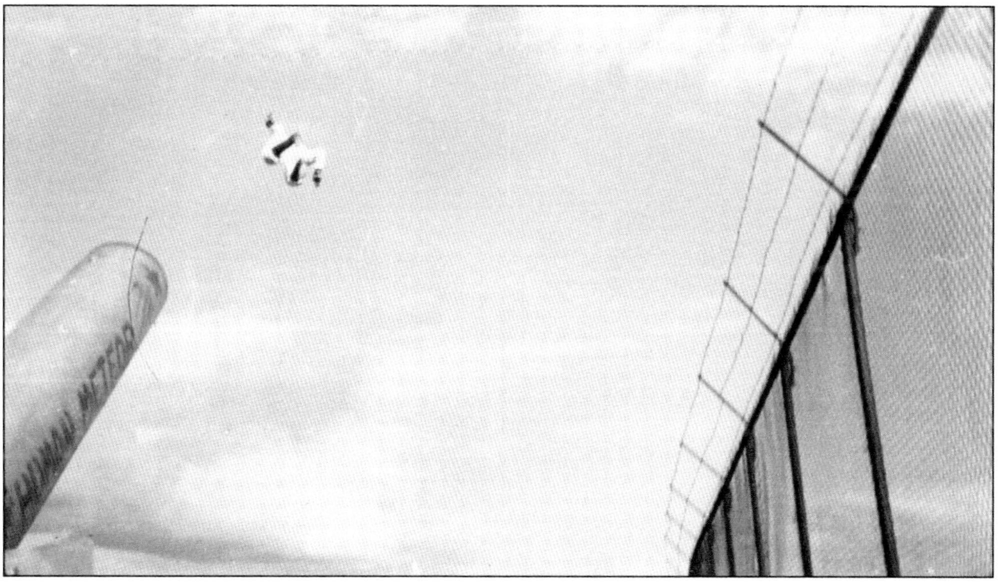

THE FLIGHT, 1938. Spectator and photographer Bill Miles captured the entire flight. The truck with cannon was parked near the tall fence around the ballroom where the flight began. Propelled straight up, the daredevil armed with only a helmet had to control his flight so he would land in the net. (JSK.)

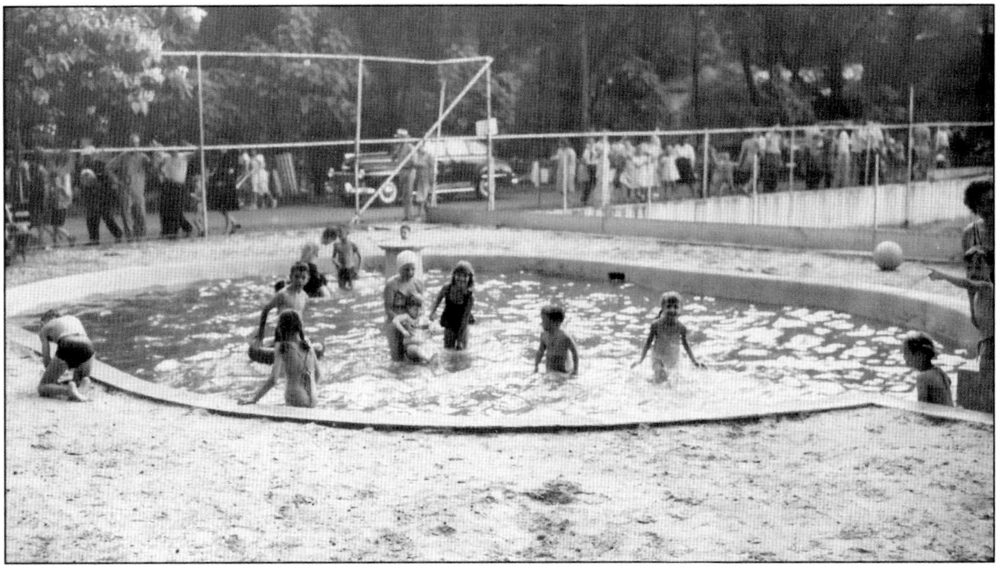

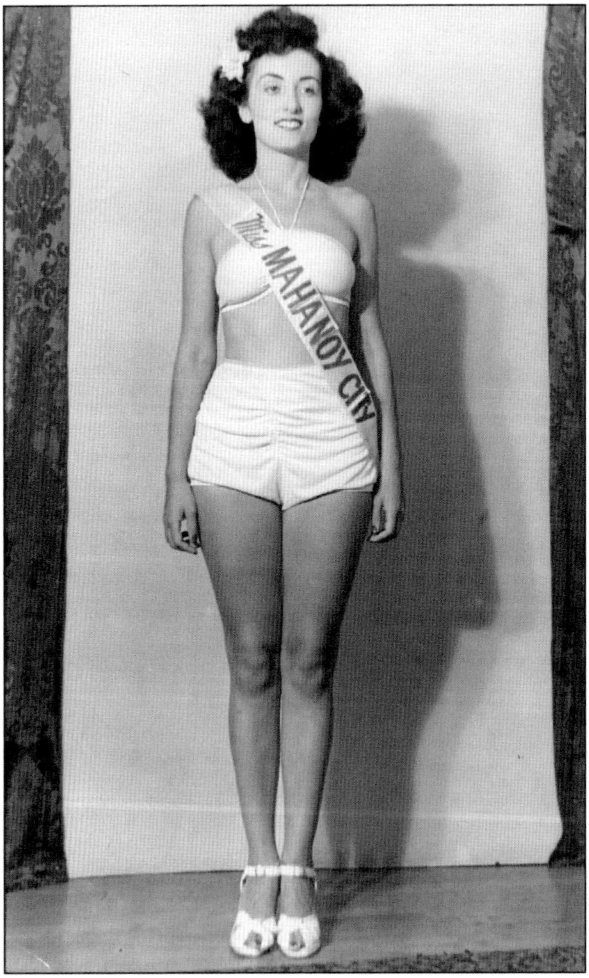

Kiddie Pool at Lakewood, 1945. The first experience many from the area had with swimming was with a kiddie pool at Lakewood. The water was usually warm from the sun and 12 inches deep, making it a perfect fit for toddlers. Swimming involved walking little hands on the bottom of the blue pool. The brave even swam under the sprinkler in the middle. (JKG.)

Miss Mahanoy City. The coal region loved nothing more than music except perhaps its beautiful women. In 1946, the Eagles Club of Mahanoy City, spearheaded by Tony Waak, held an official preliminary contest at Lakewood for the Miss America Pageant. Winner Rose Durkin (Fletcher) of Mahanoy City went on to compete in Wellsboro, Pennsylvania, where she won Best in Evening Gown but lost to a woman from Lebanon who became Miss Pennsylvania. (RDF.)

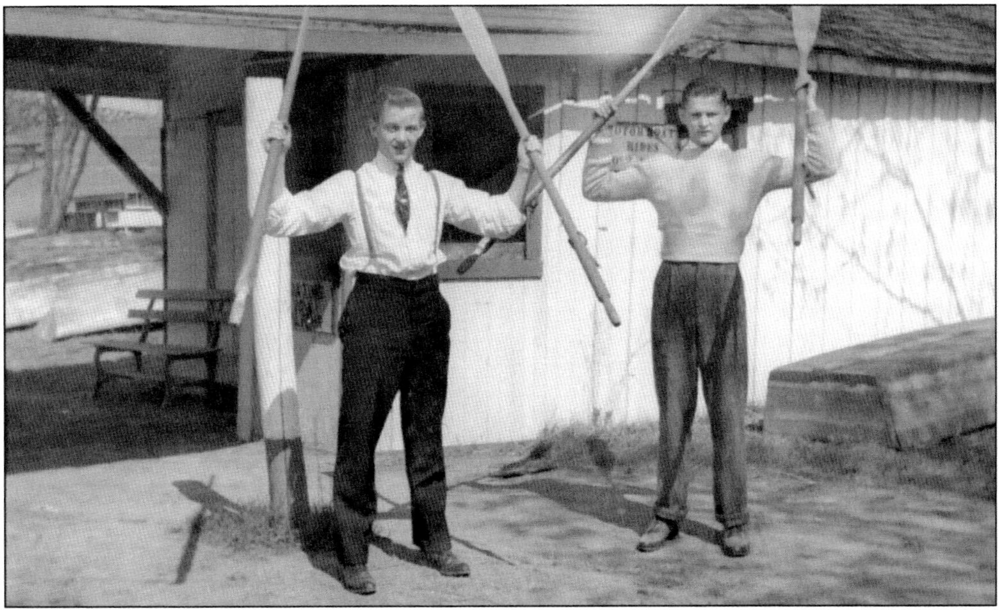

MR. MAHANOY, 1951. There was no Mr. Universe contest in the area, but there were always handsome physiques, like those belonging to the men pictured, to help paddle a rowboat in the lake. (MERP.)

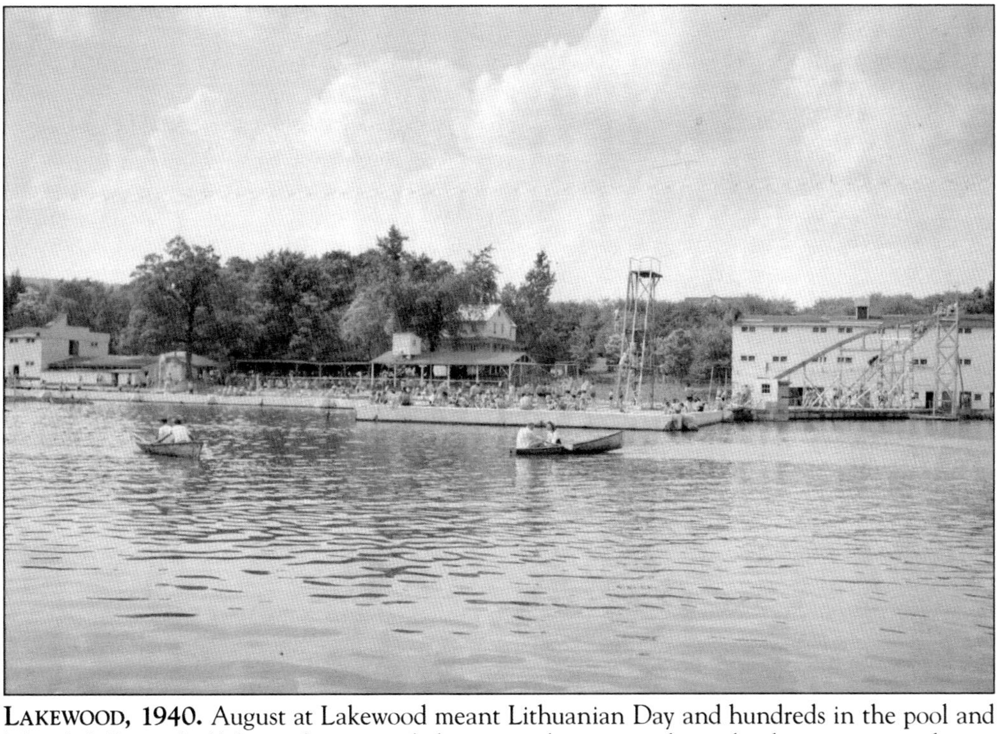

LAKEWOOD, 1940. August at Lakewood meant Lithuanian Day and hundreds in the pool and lake. A full squad of lifeguards was needed to cover the area, with one by the entrance and rings (far left), one on the permanent raft/shallow area (middle), one at the toboggan, and one in the pit and tower (foreground). In the late 1940s, the team of lifeguards included captain Jack Knoll, Jack O'Connell, Jay Hanley, and George and Paul Forster. (JKG.)

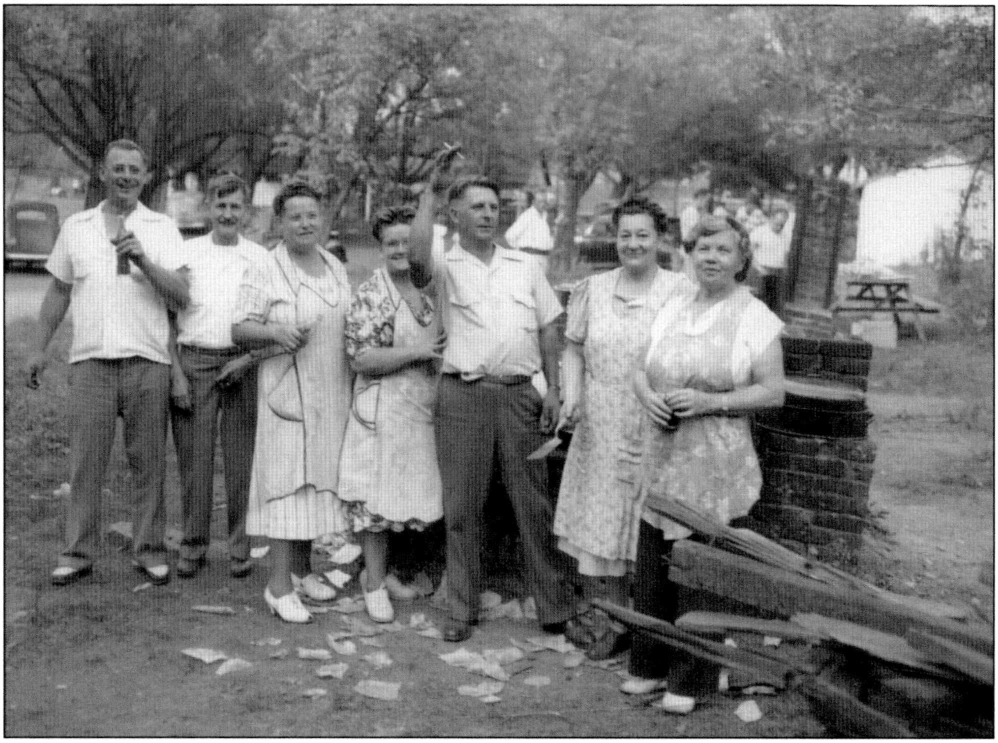

PICNIC AT LAKESIDE. Neighborhood bars had regulars, and tavern owners treated their regular customers to a picnic with plenty of food and drink. In 1948, John Ambrose (second from left) treated his customers to a picnic at Lakeside. Pictured are the men and women who prepared the feast with John. (DA.)

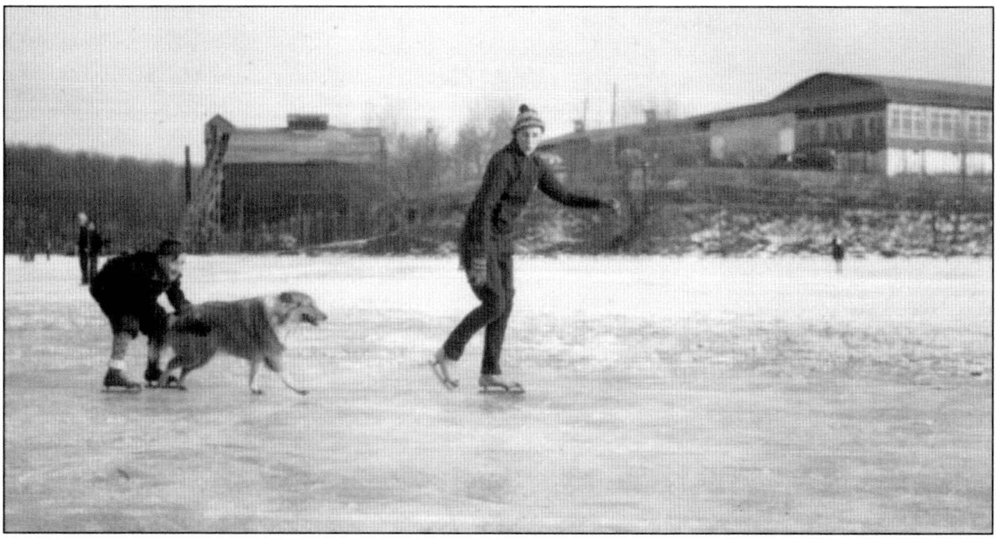

MILDRED HOLMAN WILLIAMS, 1941. Lakeside and Lakewood were not just summer recreational spots. Here, Mildred (née Holman) Williams, Mahanoy City history teacher, enjoys the frozen lake with her collie. In the distance left is the icehouse with the chute for uploading the ice. During the summer and winter, these icehouses employed several hundred men shipping the ice to the big-city markets. On the right is the back of the Lakeside Ballroom. (MHS.)

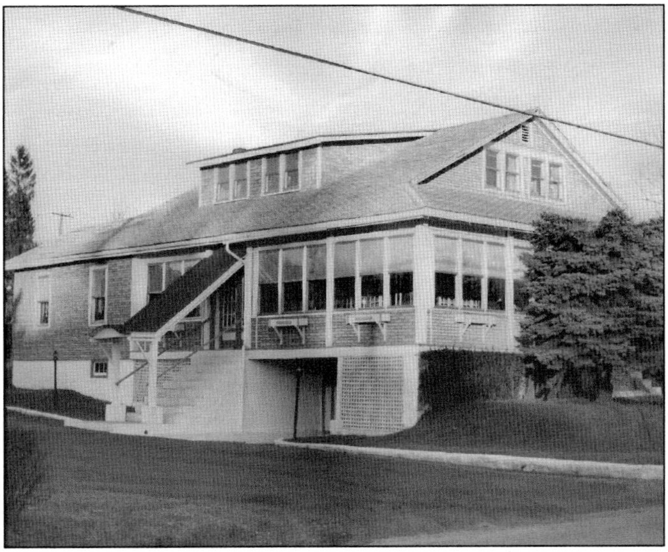

LOG CABIN, THE 1940S TO THE 1960S. This picture was taken as the Surfields prepared to sell the restaurant in 1959 and represents how it looked from the 1940s to the 1960s. Ed and Esther, founders, operated the Log Cabin until the mid-1930s, when their children Charles and Mabel Surfield resigned from their teaching jobs and took over its operation. It was Mabel who was in the kitchen when the Kenley Players came to town. (ES.)

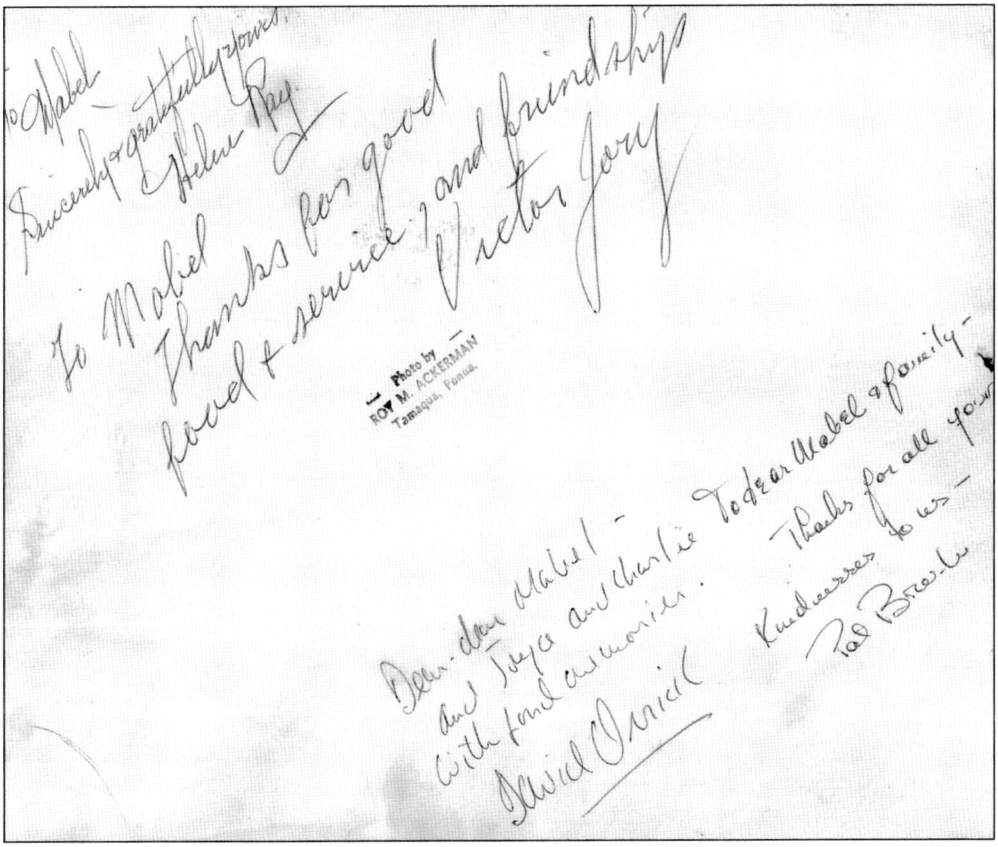

AUTOGRAPHED PHOTOGRAPH OF MABEL SURFIELD. When John Kenley brought theater to Lakewood, many of the stars stayed at Scrafford's Motel or lived bed-and-breakfast style with local families. For the paid cast, the Log Cabin became their favorite spot for nourishment and relaxation after the show. Judging from the autographs on many of the Surfields' photographs, Mabel became "mom" to many of the stars, including Victory Jory. (ES.)

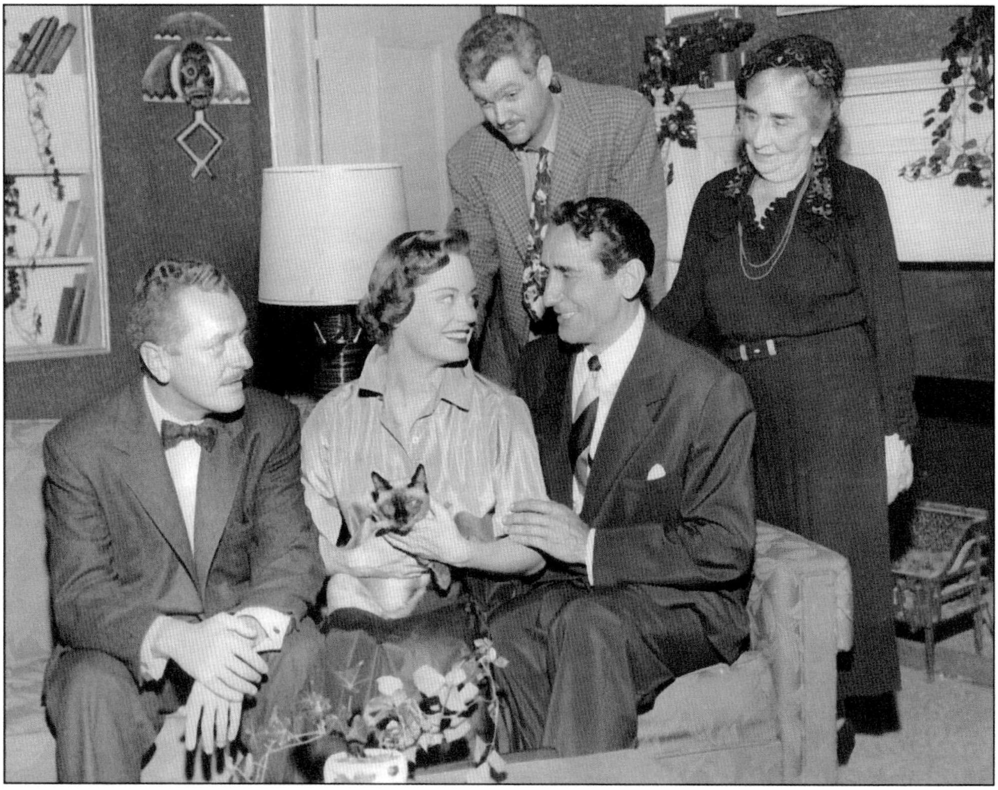

VICTOR JORY AND CAST, 1952. Victor Jory (at right on sofa) initially played romantic leads, but later was mostly cast as the villain, as in *Gone with the Wind.* Jory was with the Kenley Players in Lakewood for four shows in 1950, 1952, 1953 and 1954. This autographed publicity photograph is of the Kenley production *Bell, Book and Candle*, starring Victor Jory in 1952. Jory and his wife spent many weeks at Lakewood and became huge fans of the Log Cabin. (ES.)

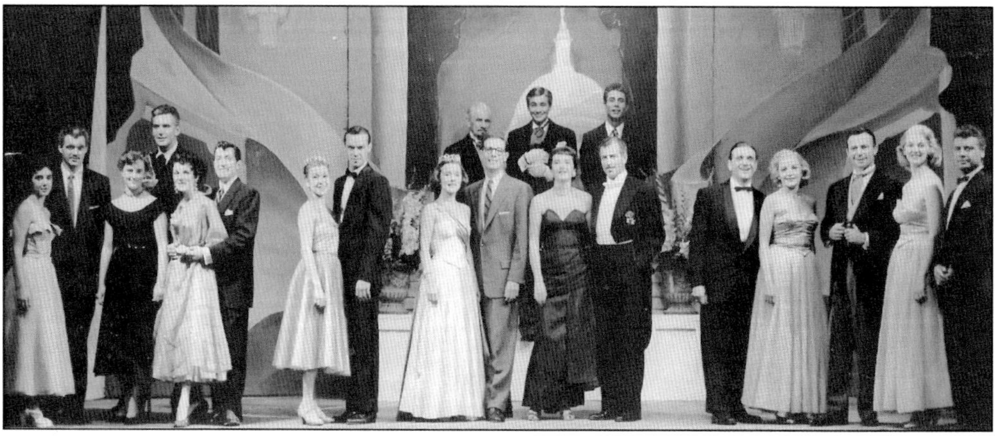

CALL ME MADAM, 1953. *Call Me Madam*, from the 1953 season, starred Jimmy Kirkwood and Pat Wilkes, in the role that Ethel Merman played on Broadway and in the movie. One of the cast members who signed the photograph, Conchita Del Rivero is better known today as Chita Rivera, the Tony-winning actress. In the first row, far left is Mary McGroarty Taylor of Mahanoy City, who ran the office and appeared in shows. This is one of the few musicals that Kenley did in Lakewood. (ES.)

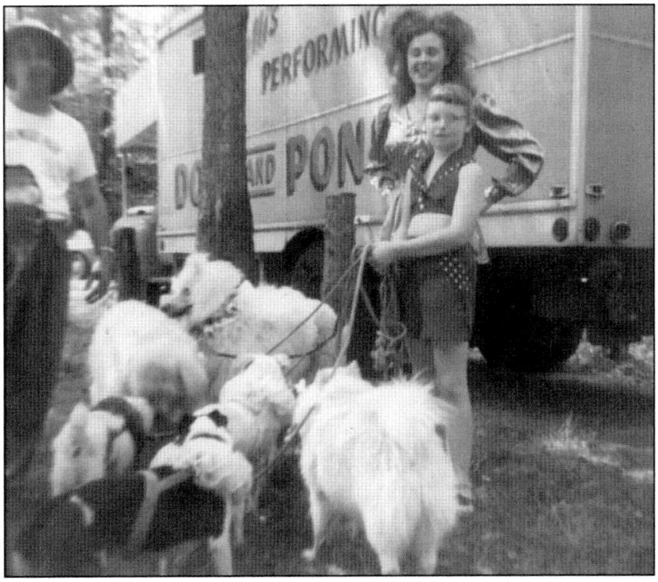

DOG AND PONY SHOW, 1955. During the end of the 19th and start of the 20th century, dog and pony shows originated as small traveling circus troupes. Here, two animals get ready to perform their tricks in Kiddieland, Lakewood. Lolly Kenvin, daughter of local stand owner Giffy Kenvin, visited with the performers before they went onstage. (MERP.)

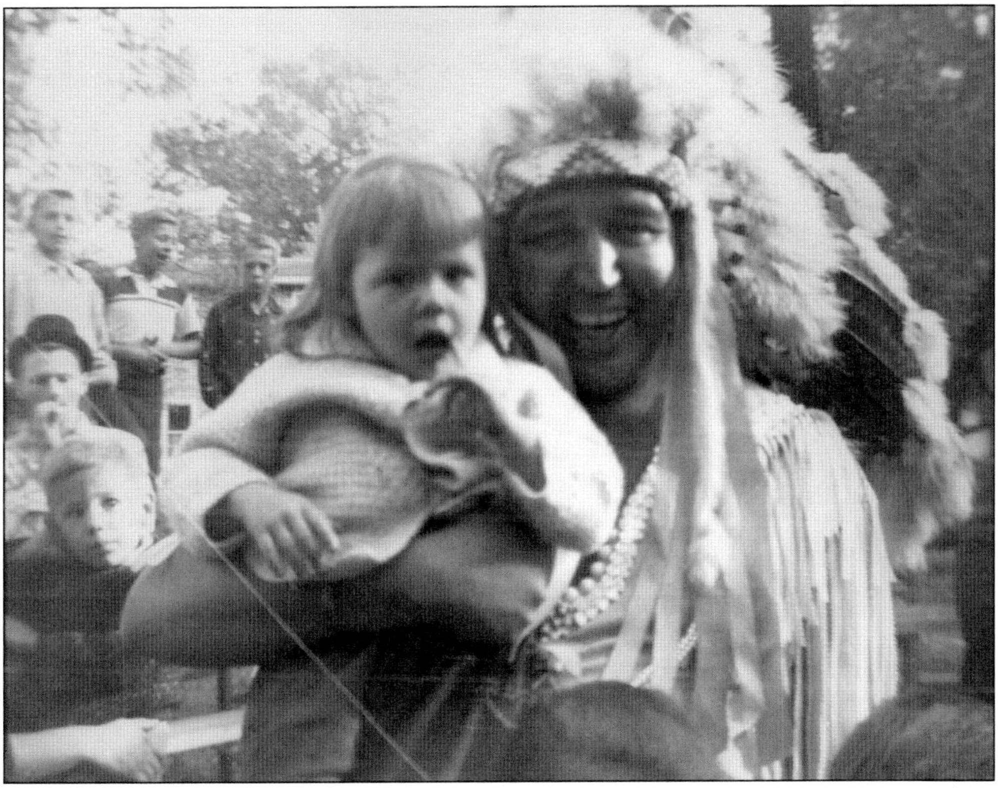

CHIEF HALFTOWN, 1956. The *Chief Halftown Show* was Philadelphia's longest-running show for kids. The show first aired on WFIL in 1951 and then on WPVI, where it ran until 1999 (48 years). The Chief, pictured here holding Mary Ellen Roberts, would appear in full Indian garb and discuss tribal customs and folklore. His classic trademark catchphrase was (phonetically) "Eeees-sta-sah-suss-a-way." Chief Halftown appeared at Lakewood at the height of his popularity. He was always described as kind, gentle, sweet, and very, very entertaining. (MERP.)

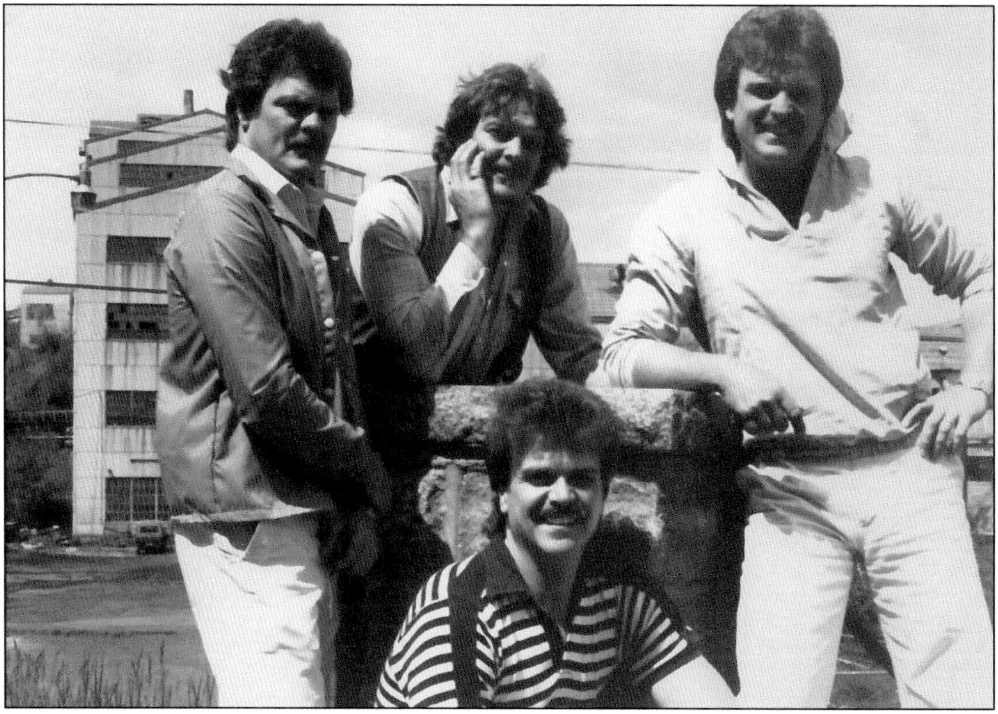

Jordan Brothers at St. Nicholas Colliery. Pictured, from left to right, are (standing) Frank, Bob, and Joe Jordan; (kneeling) brother Lewie. Their days of playing locally at Lakewood and Lakeside Parks led them to national exposure. They made three appearances on *Bandstand* and traveled with Dick Clark's Caravan of Stars. (JJ.)

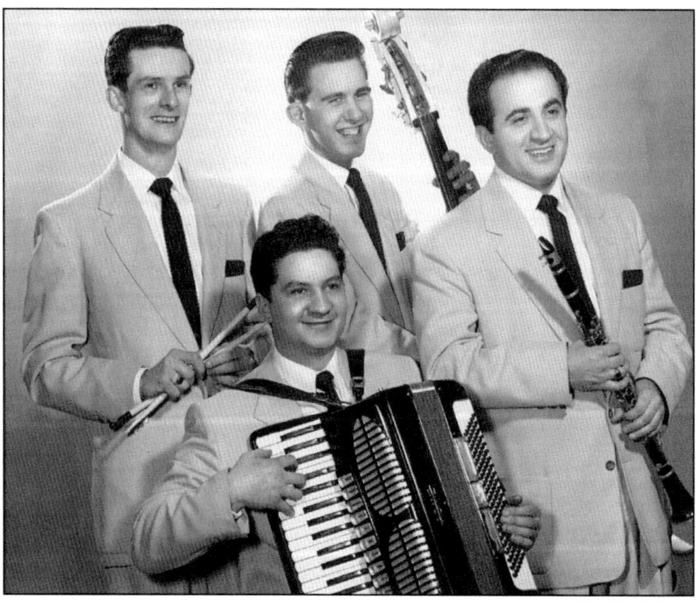

The Millionaires. Taking his training from his high school band days, Joseph "Swing" Flamini (right) played in several bands in the area, including the Minarchick Orchestra and the Millionaires. Along with Swing on clarinet and saxophone, there are, from left to right, Jack Brady on drums; Louis Jordan, uncle to the Jordan brothers, on accordion; and Jerry Hyland on bass. The Millionaires played at the Mansion Hotel for 11 years. (JSF.)

MARSHALL "DUCKY" MARTIN. Martin started his musical training as a student with Angelo Bell at Shenandoah School District. After serving in the Army and getting more training in New York City, Ducky formed his own band, The Four Storms (No. 1). Members included Mahanoy City's Bill Massolini (a music scholarship graduate of Valley Forge College) and two other musicians from the area. From the beginning, the group played professionally throughout the state and in Las Vegas. (VMM.)

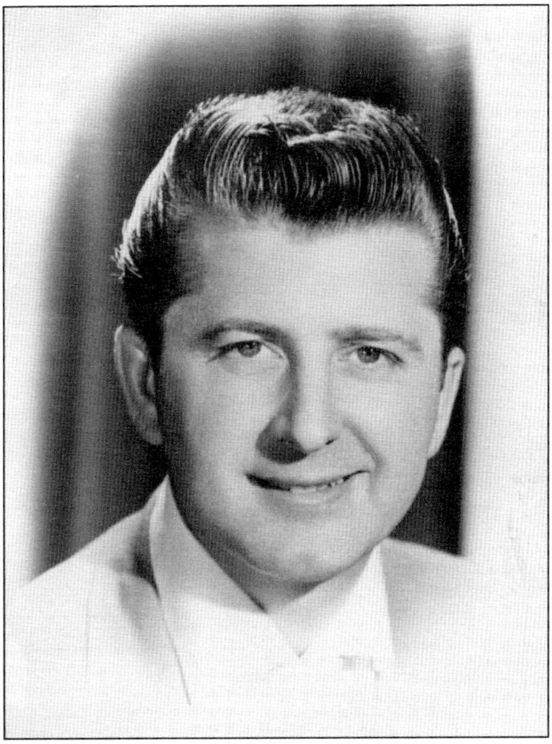

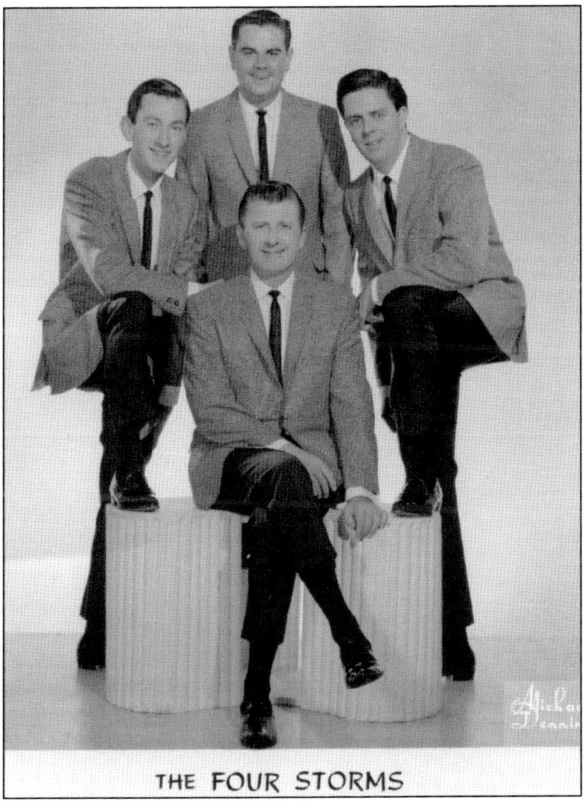

THE FOUR STORMS. In the 1960s, Ducky formed a second band, The Four Storms (No. 2), with, clockwise from left, Ronnie Goetz on bass; Gene Zakotzki, fiddle; Dave Raab, drums; and Ducky, trumpet. All the members were vocalists and musicians who backed vocalists at Lakewood Ballroom and accompanied some of the Lakewood Theater Shows, including that of Phyllis Diller. (VMM.)

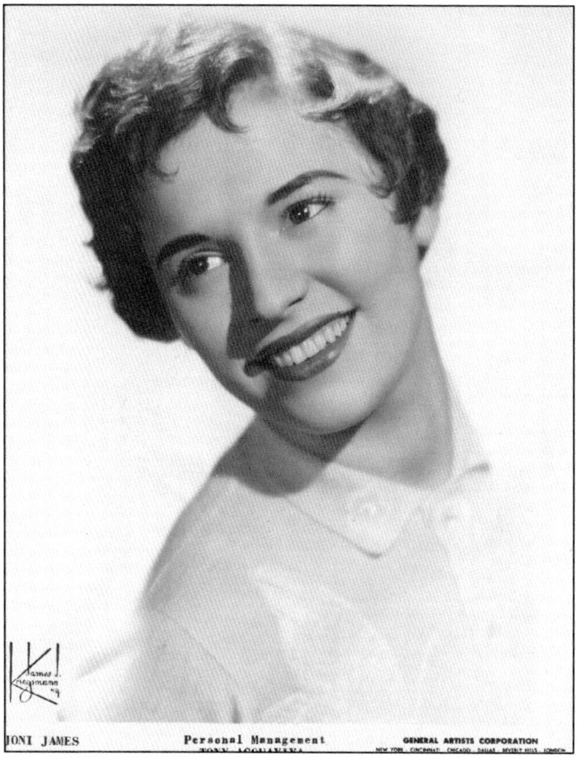

JONI JAMES AT LAKEWOOD, LABOR DAY 1960. In the big-band days, every orchestra had a featured singer, who occasionally had more star power than the band. Joni James was one of those incredible talents. On Labor Day 1960, Eleanor Fisher (Immaculate Heart High School class of 1960) and her husband, John Delaney, had their first date as Joni sang. Eleanor was impressed by the date, and she and John became two of the thousands who married after a Lakewood date. (PGG.)

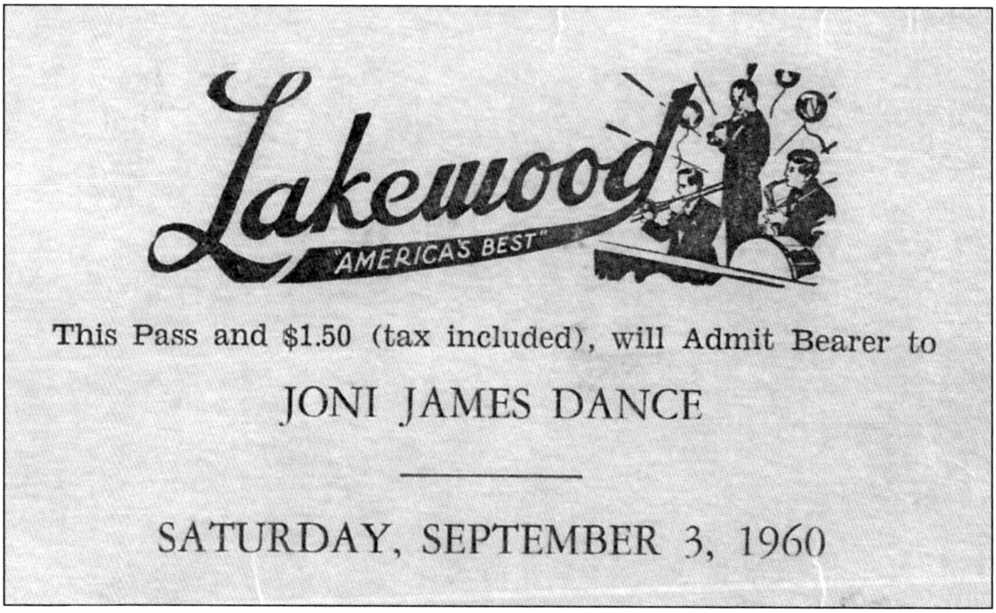

BOOSTER PASS JONI JAMES LAKEWOOD. Ed Conrad was hired for his first job as a reporter with the *Record American* days before the Joni James appearance. As he tells it, Emil Yenchik, photographer for the paper, pressured Ed into interviewing Joni. Scared stiff and starstruck, Ed completely forgot every word that she said and never wrote down notes or a story. Recently, with Joni's "comeback," Conrad read that Joni had never been interviewed during her illustrious career. Ed asks, "Correction, please." Joni talked at Lakewood. (MB.)

Six

SCHOOL DAYS, AMEN

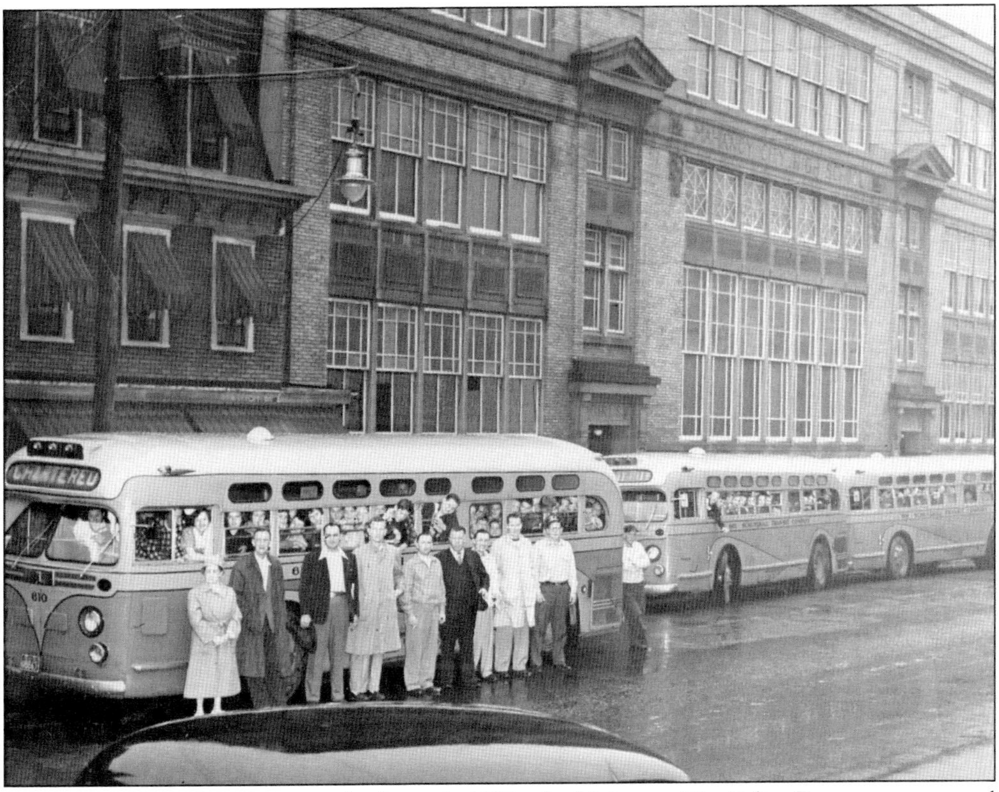

MAHANOY CITY HIGH SCHOOL. In the early 1950s, the Mahanoy City Police Department treated the school safety patrol to a trip to a Phillies baseball game. Chartered buses in this photograph are ready to leave for the game. Standing and ready to go are, from left to right, Mary Kane (school nurse), John Goepfert (physical education teacher), George Frank (police captain), Joseph Pilconis (teacher), unidentified, Joseph Boyle (school superintendent), Edward Dronginis, John Fletcher, and Robert Fletcher (bus driver). (MF.)

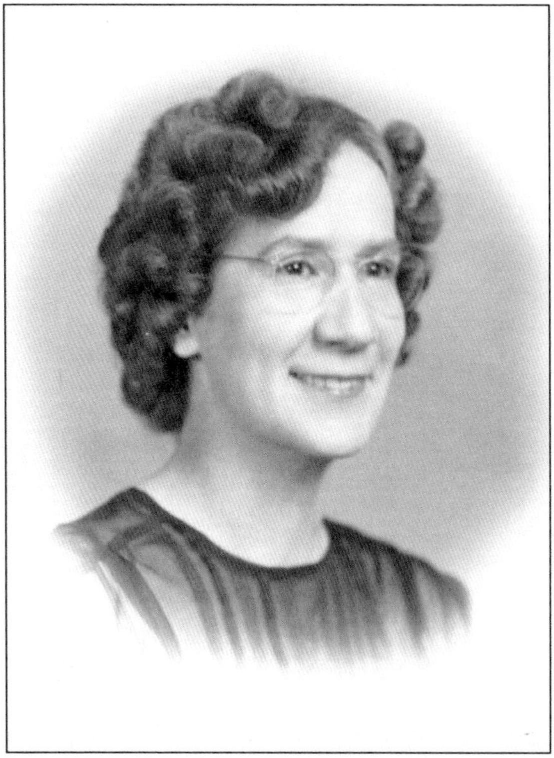

ESTELLA MAE BARNHART. Estella Mae Barnhart was born on Christmas Eve in 1904. She attended Cornell University, majoring in languages and music and graduating in 1926. After graduation, she returned to her hometown of Mahanoy City and obtained a position teaching Latin and algebra in the school district. By 1947, she was appointed music supervisor in the schools. In 1960, she was director of vocal music in the secondary schools of Mahanoy City and, throughout her career, was responsible for directing various musicals and vocal concerts. Every other year, Barnhart's students performed an operetta. Performed in 1957, the operetta pictured below is *The Gondoliers* by Gilbert and Sullivan. The cast members are, from left to right, Tom Balliett, Margaret Weikel, Edward Curvey, Francis Friel, Regina Sullivan, Karl Olson, Ruth Jane Frank, and Anthony Markosky. (Both, MHS.)

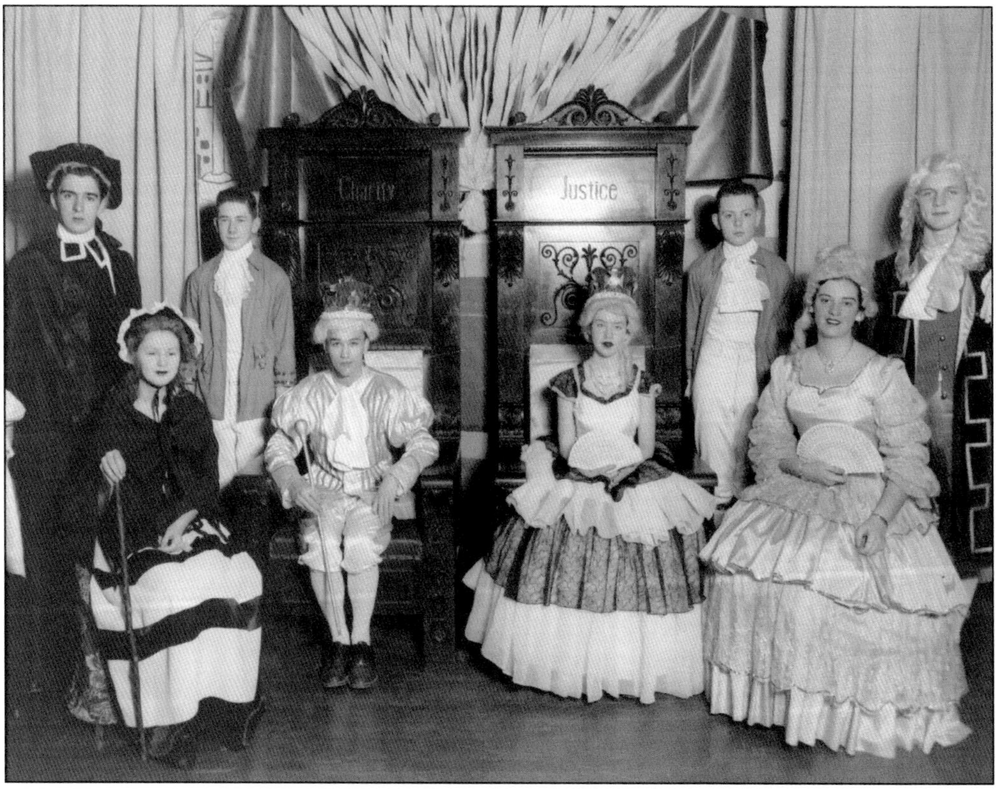

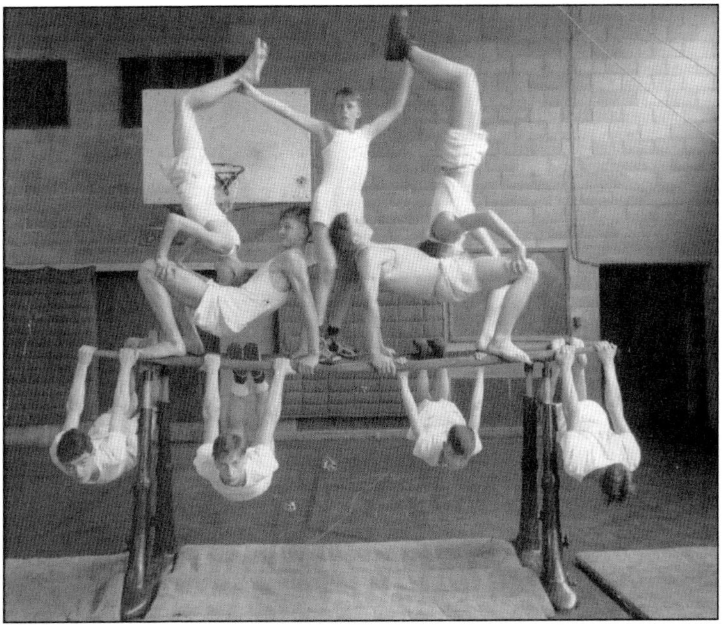

BOYS' GYM CLASS. Each year in physical education classes, both boys and girls were asked to show off their gymnastic talents and flexibility. The high school gymnasium was the backdrop for these photographs. Using the parallel bars, these boys carefully climbed and created this intricate pyramid as the young ladies in the class looked on. The photograph was then used in the high school yearbook. (MHS.)

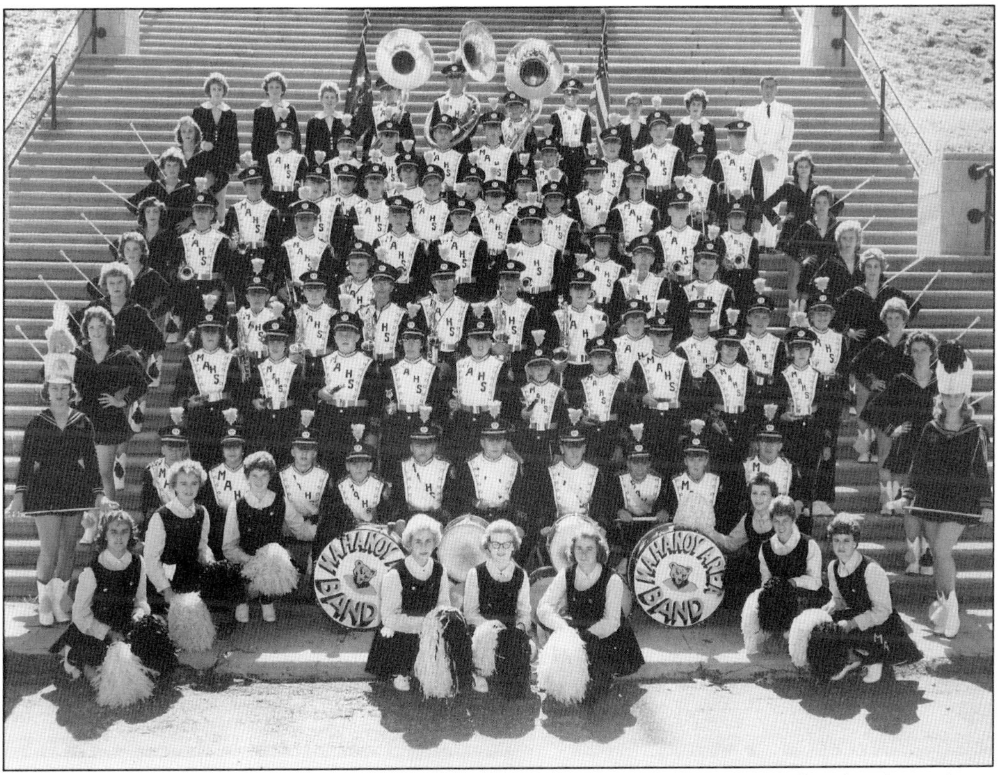

MAHANOY AREA HIGH SCHOOL MARCHING BAND. The Mahanoy Area High School marching band has always been a source of pride for the town and surrounding communities. Shown on the steps of the former Mahanoy Township School is the 1961 band under the direction of William Mitchell. The band performed in parades, at football games, and also traveled to various functions performing and making the citizens of the area proud. (DA.)

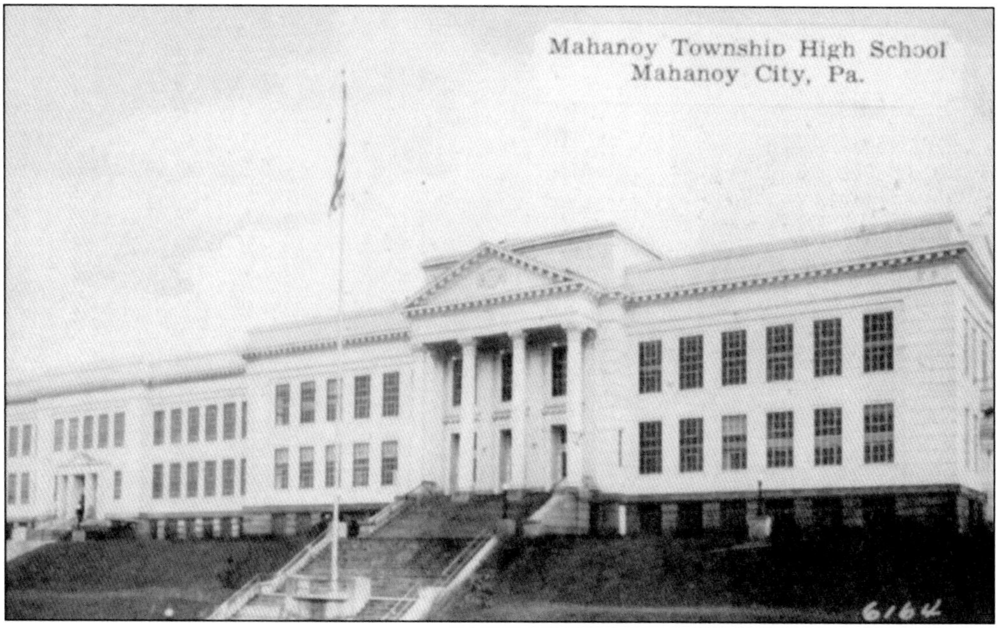

MAHANOY TOWNSHIP HIGH SCHOOL. Built in 1916, this Mahanoy Township High School building operated from 1918 to 1938. Shown in the above photograph, the school was a magnificent structure on top of the hill and housed students from the township and Mahanoy City. Students studied four curricula: college preparatory, stenographic, mathematical-scientific, and elective courses. In addition, the students learned the fine arts, including cultural art and instrumental and vocal music. Following the class night ceremony for the class of 1938, the building suffered a devastating fire and was completely destroyed, as shown in the picture below. The students and faculty moved commencement exercises to the St. Nicholas Elementary School. (Both, JSK.)

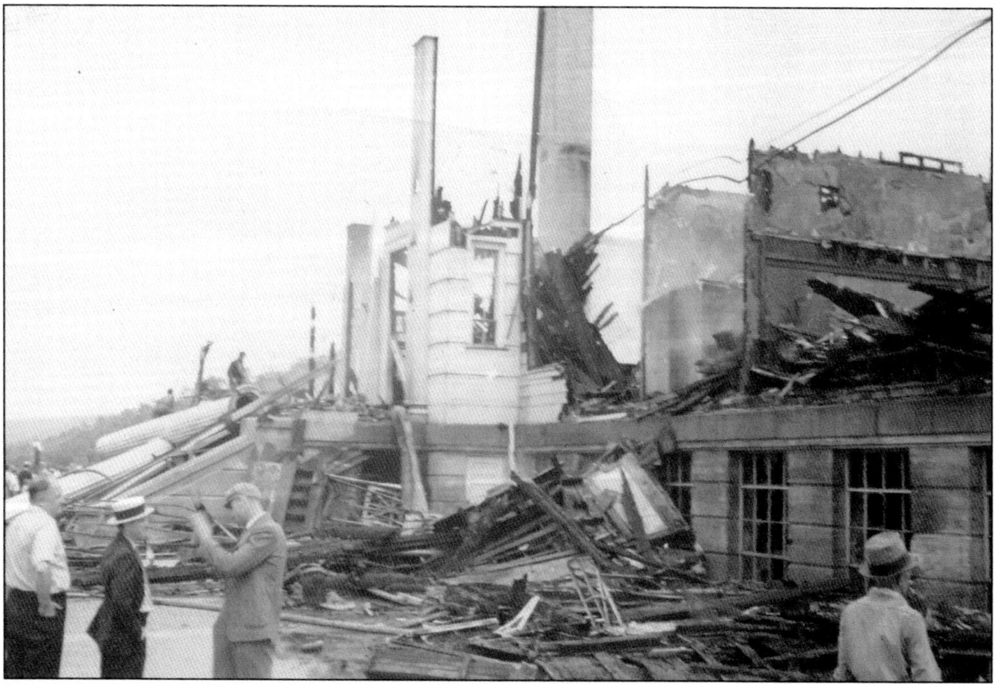

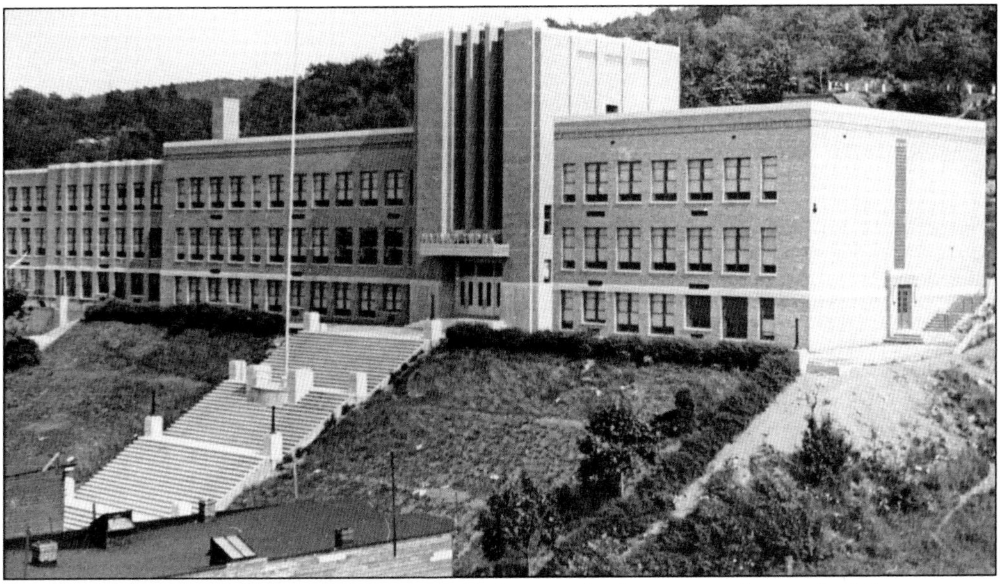

NEW MAHANOY TOWNSHIP HIGH SCHOOL. Following the devastating fire, a rebuilding program began almost immediately. Two years later, on the night of June 17, 1940, commencement took place in the auditorium of the new high school. Following the jointure in 1959, the new building housed the junior high school and, several years later, the Intermediate School of the Mahanoy Area School District. The school closed for good in 2002. (JSK.)

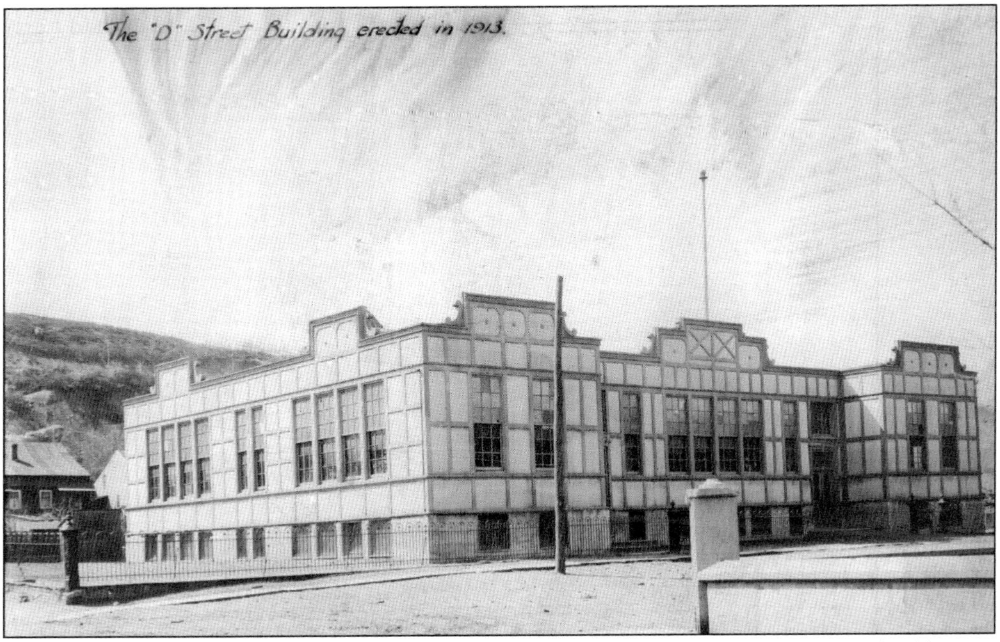

D STREET SCHOOL. Two decades after the opening of the Twelfth Street School building in December 1893, the D Street School was built on the corner of Mahanoy and D Streets. For a short time, the McCann's School of Business operated in this building. When the building was no longer used as a school, it was sold and renamed Newhart's Hall. The hall was utilized for wedding receptions and various other gatherings. This property is now the site of the West End Fire Company. (TW.)

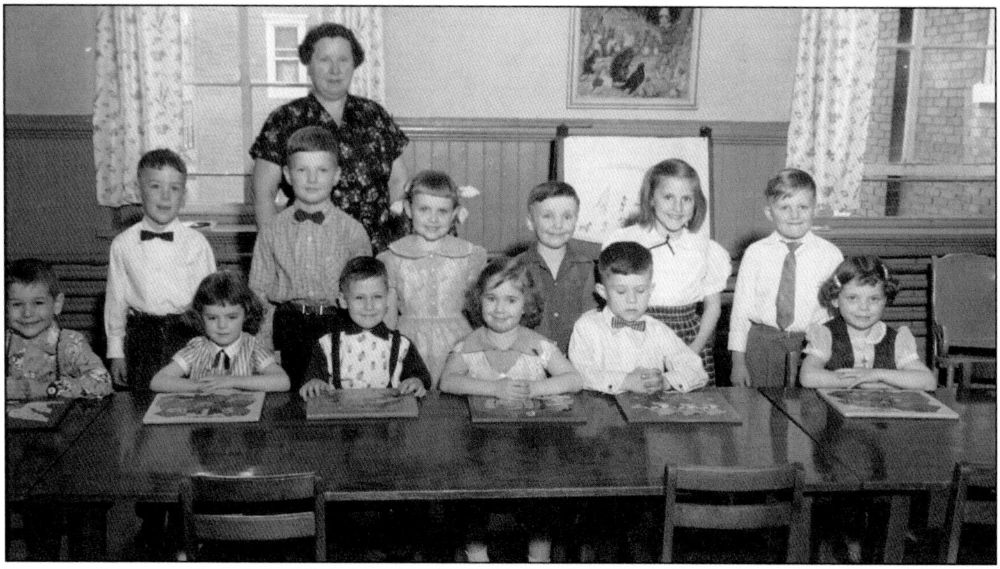

SPRUCE STREET SCHOOL. The Spruce Street School was the first school in Mahanoy City. Pictured here is the afternoon kindergarten class from 1956. The students are, from left to right, (first row) George Trusky, Anne Holland, Harry Roberts, Sharon Hause, William Killian, and Elaine Mack; (second row) John Mellon, John Chilinskas, Catherine Setcavage, Robert Sluzis, Julia Wargo, and John Sabol. The teacher is Laura Myers. (EML.)

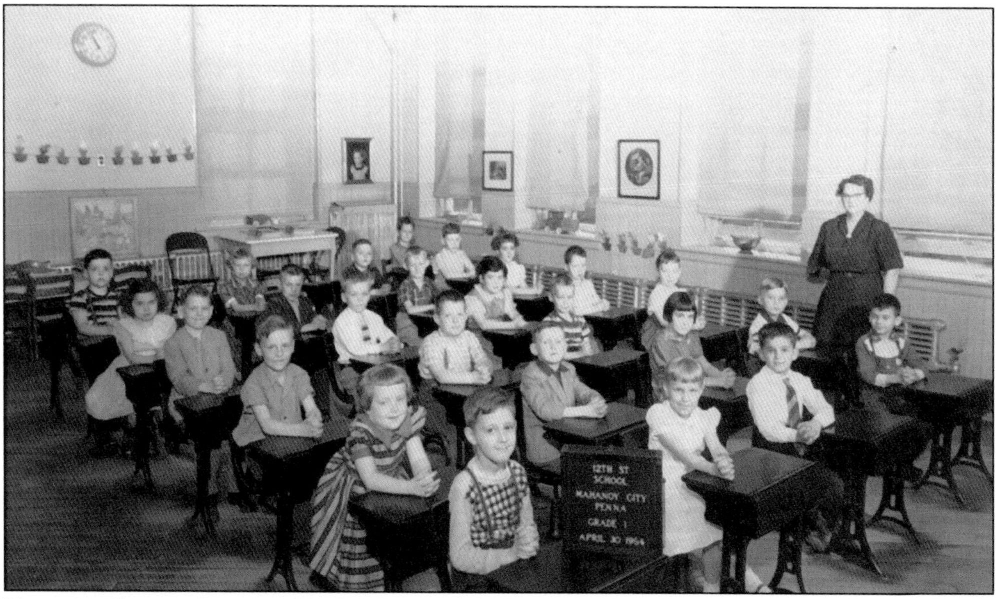

TWELFTH STREET SCHOOL. Under the watchful eyes of Eleanor Schmidt, the first-grade class of the Twelfth Street School has its photograph taken on April 30, 1954. Seated in class are, from left to right, (first row) Bernard Yudinsky, Linda Webber, Steve Harach, and Eugene Wycheck; (second row) unidentified, Thomas Freil, unidentified, and Joseph Benny; (third row) David Wall, Harry Devine, Francis McCormick, and Debra Dunsavage; (fourth row) Roy Cooper, Charles Eroh, Louise Mockaitis, and Thomas Jones; (fifth row) Susan Jenina, unidentified, Philip Gazan, and Betty Jane Koval; (sixth row) James Hiney, Rose Ann Bokus, Joseph Reilly, and Wayne Henninger; (seventh row) unidentified. (MLH.)

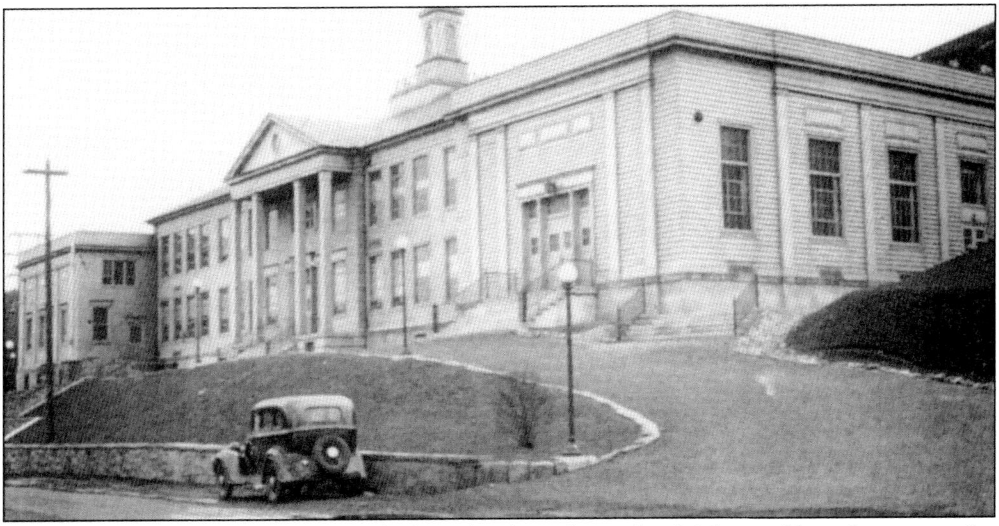

St. Nicholas School. The St. Nicholas School was located in Mahanoy Township just to the west of the St. Nicholas Breaker. The school was constructed in 1936 and opened in January 1937. Kindergarten through the seventh grade enjoyed an auditorium, gymnasium, library, cafeteria, infirmary, and music and vocal rooms, in addition to numerous classrooms. The school served children from the surrounding villages. The building was completely destroyed by fire on June 15, 1985. (MHS.)

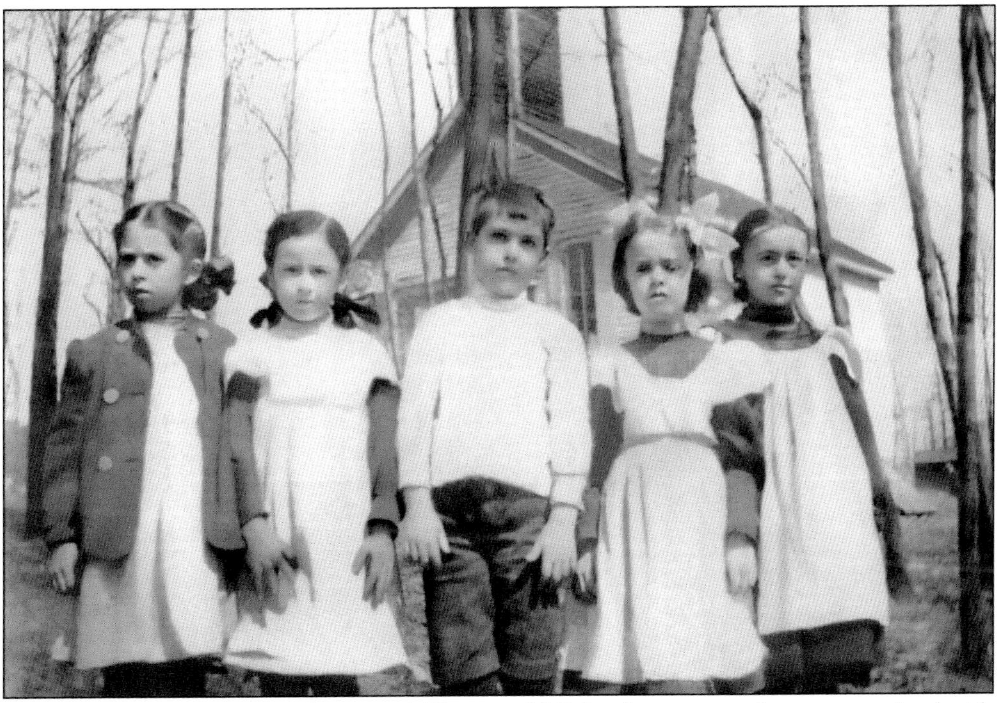

The Hosensock School. The Tunnel (Hosensock) School was a typical one-room school with limited facilities and a bell tower. It was located on Route 54, about a mile east of the Vulcan Tunnel, in Mahanoy Township. Standing are, from left to right, three unidentified children, Elizabeth McCarthy, and Catherine McCarthy. After the school closed, it was remodeled and converted to a private home. (JBW.)

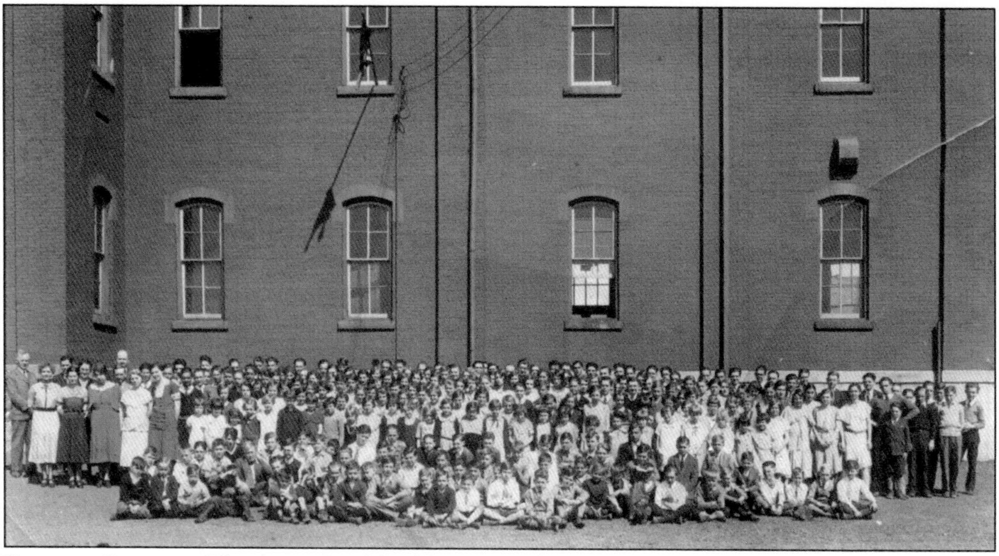

DELANO SCHOOL. The first school building in Delano was constructed in 1865 and was only 25 feet square. By 1889, there was a need for more space, and a redbrick school was built. The last graduating class at Delano High School was the class of 1950. From 1951 to 1958, students attended a temporary school or were homeschooled. In 1959, students attended the newly formed joint Mahanoy Area High School. (JSH.)

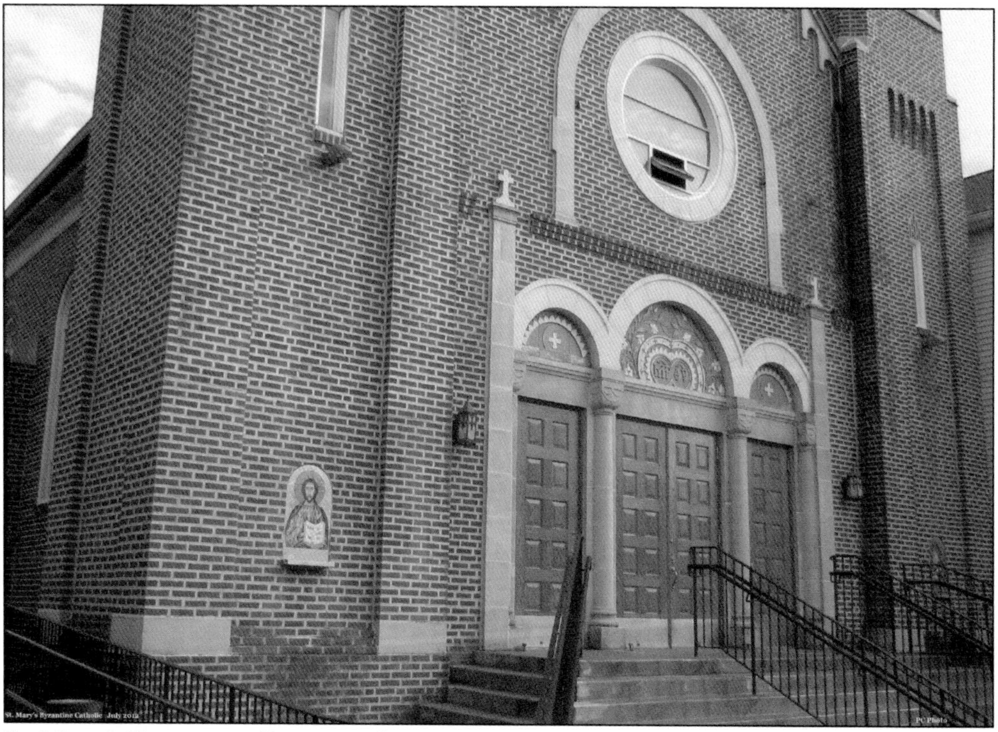

ST. MARY'S BYZANTINE CATHOLIC CHURCH. St. Mary's Church located at 620 West Pine Street was constructed in 1891. The church building was enlarged and totally remodeled in 1931. Most of the church's interior murals were painted by its artistic pastor, Rev. Anthony Kubek, the son of Rev. Emil Kubek, who served from 1904 to 1940. (PC.)

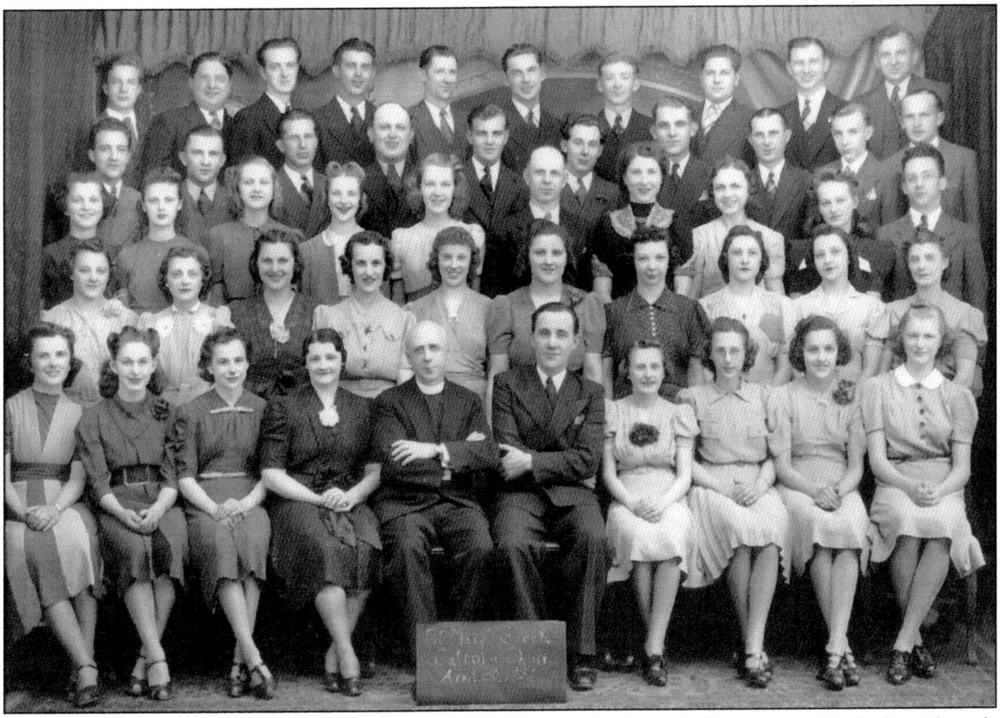

St. Mary's Byzantine Catholic Church Choir. St. Mary's Byzantine Catholic Church choir was organized in 1905. The parish is famous for its emphasis on religious church music. The ensemble pictured here is the 1939 choir under the direction of Prof. John Sekura. Rev. Anthony Kubek is also seated in the front row. A future choir director, William Coombe is standing in the fifth row, third from the left. (FS.)

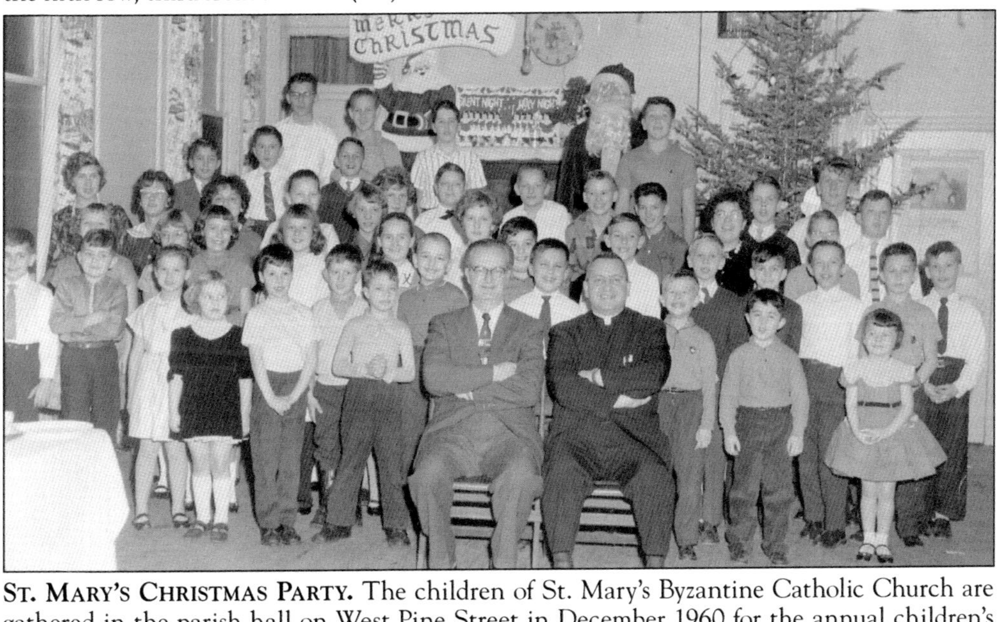

St. Mary's Christmas Party. The children of St. Mary's Byzantine Catholic Church are gathered in the parish hall on West Pine Street in December 1960 for the annual children's Christmas party. Pictured sitting along with the children and St. Nicholas are Prof. William H. Coombe, cantor and choir director, and Rev. Basil Zeleniak, pastor. (ASB.)

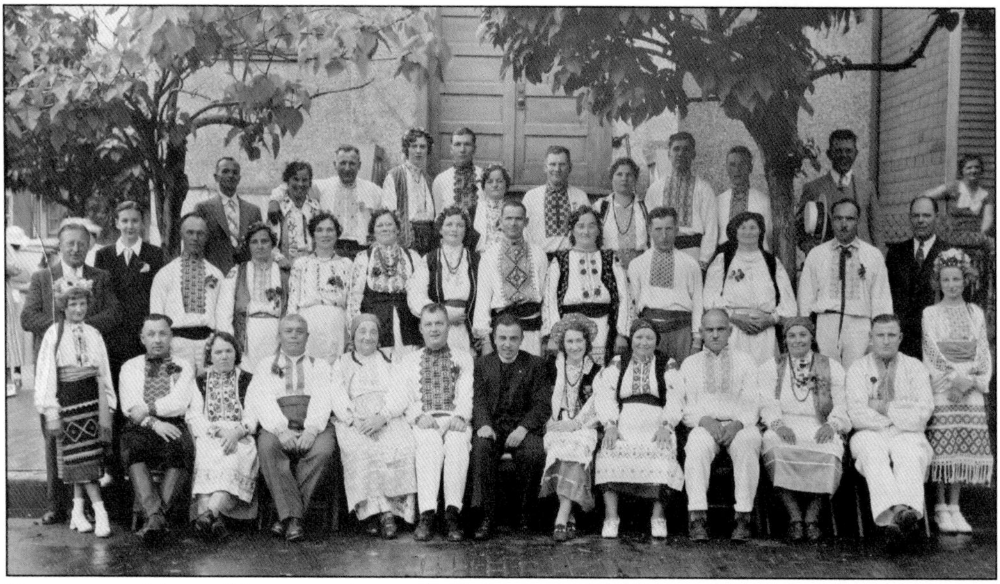

UKRAINIAN MOCK WEDDING. A popular folk custom of Ukrainian immigrants was to stage "mock wedding ceremonies" for entertainment and in some cases fundraising. This photograph shows one such parody in 1937 in front of St. Nicholas Ukrainian Catholic Church. Rev. Myroslav Boykiw, pastor in 1936–1937, officiates at this mock wedding. The participants wear traditional Ukrainian embroidered blouses, shirts, woven skirts (*plakhta*), and trousers. The headpieces are of flowers and ribbons. (AKE.)

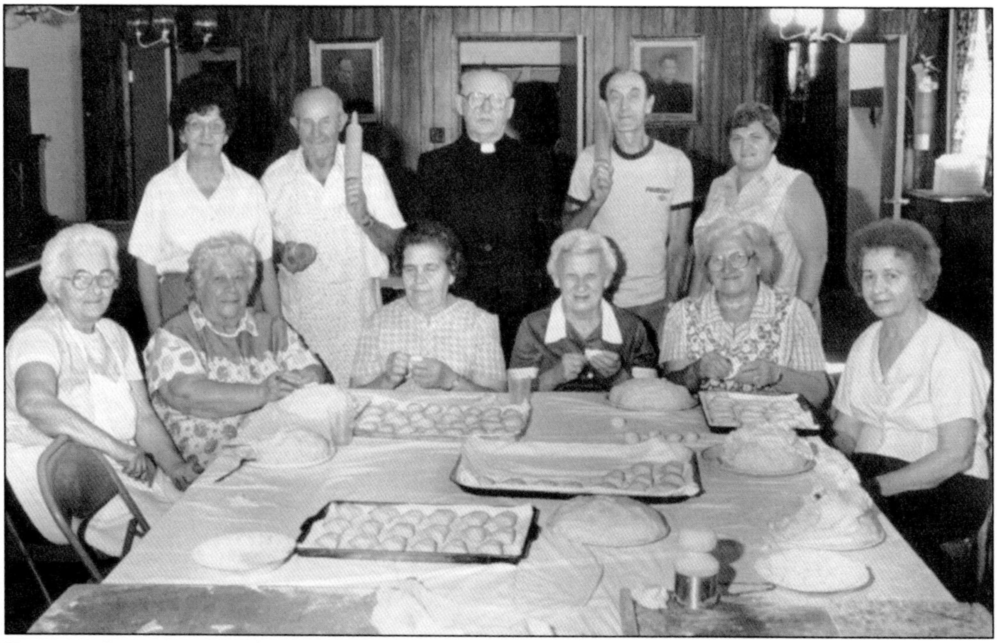

PYROHI CHEFS. A regular fundraising activity for St. Nicholas Church is pictured. Gathered together for two days of congeniality and intense work making the popular *pyrohi* are, from left to right, (first row) Jennie Reba, Anna Datchko, Julia Supar, Anna Andrusichen, Helen Korin, and Anna Kowlick; (second row) Mary Kechula, John Dudra, Rev. Michael Horashko, John Radick, and Dolores Kozie. (AKE.)

ASSUMPTION BVM. Assumption BVM (St. Mary's Slovak) Church was established in 1892 by immigrants from Slovakia, under the leadership of Rev. Francis Vlossak. Prior to the dedication of the church in 1893, Masses were said in Gorman's Hall on Linden and Market Streets. The parish grew in numbers, having 50 baptisms in its first year. In 1922, Rev. Stephen Valasek arrived and became the church's longest-serving pastor. (MEKS.)

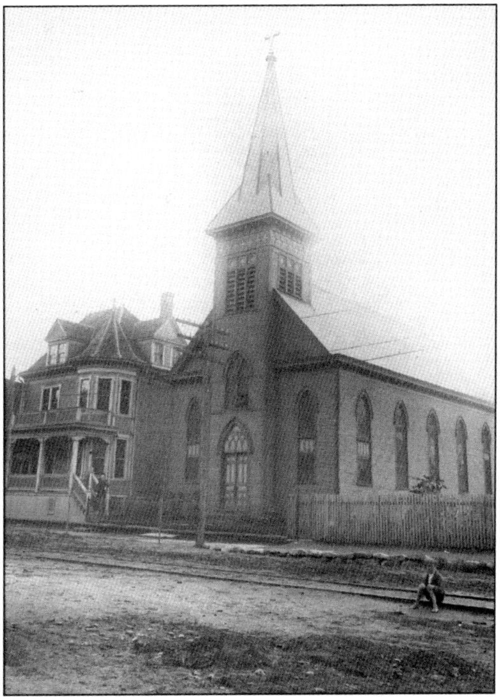

ST. MARY'S SLOVAK PARISH SCHOOL. The first graduation ceremony for students of the newly formed St. Mary's Slovak Parish School (Assumption BVM) was on June 19, 1933. The school was served by the Bernadine Sisters of St. Francis. In some years, the enrollment exceeded 250 children. Several graduates of the school followed a vocation into the priesthood. Also, student Julia Cech entered the Bernadine Order. The school closed its doors for good in 1955. (MLH.)

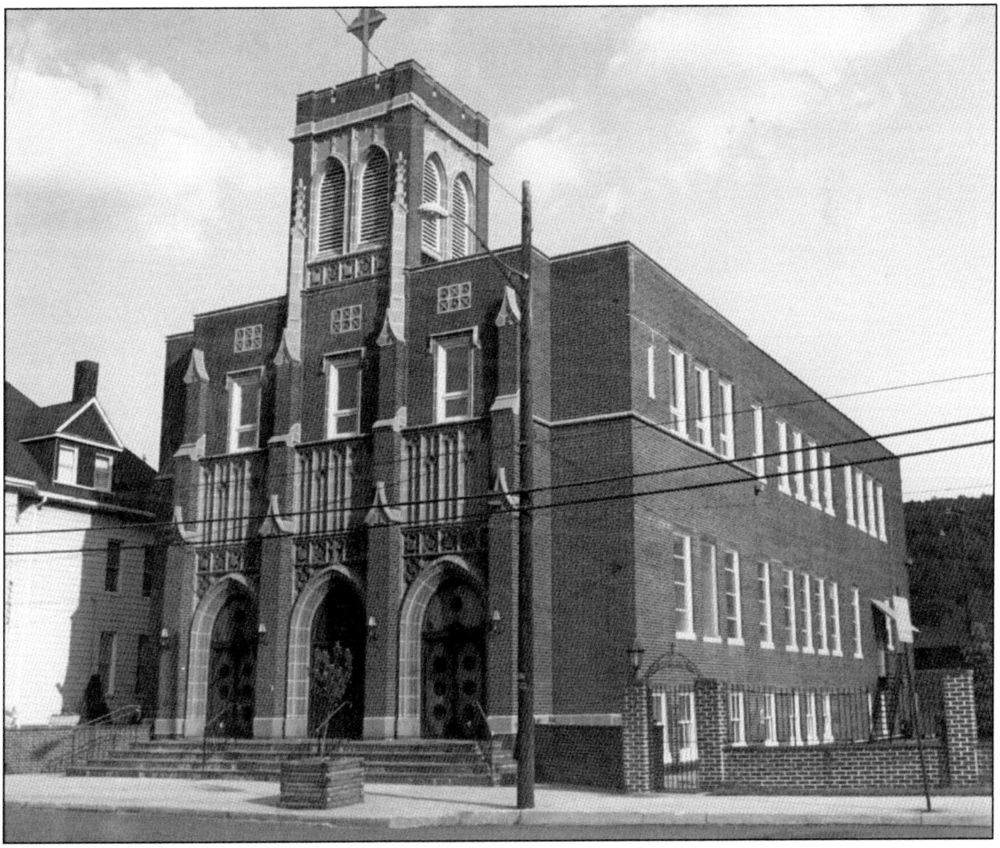

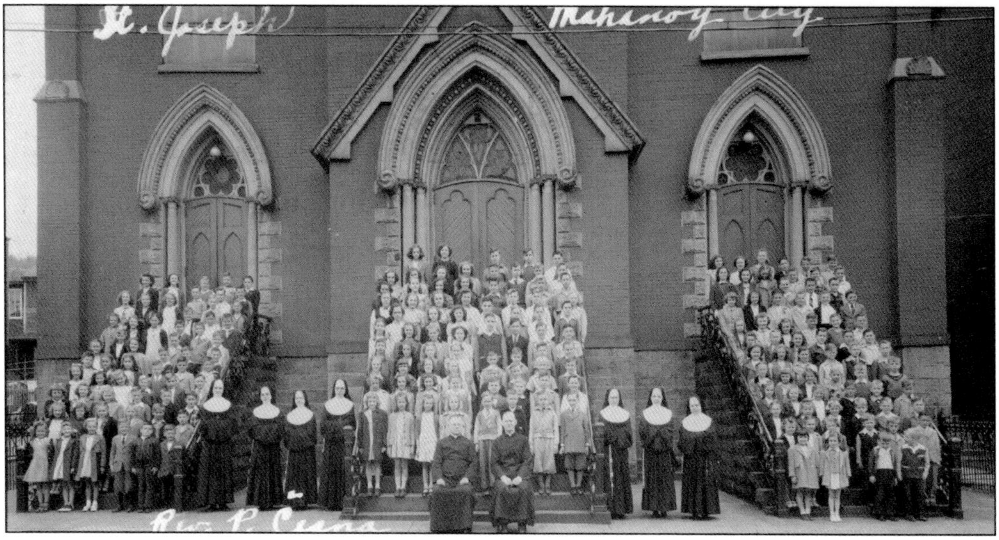

St. Joseph's Church/School. St. Joseph's Church is located at 614 West Mahanoy Street and was founded in 1888. This photograph shows its three main entrances as well as the 1945–1946 parish school student body and faculty (Sisters of Saint Francis, Providence of God). Rev. Pius Chesna served from 1921 to 1969 and is seated at left center. In 2008, the church was renamed Blessed Teresa of Calcutta. (OSF.)

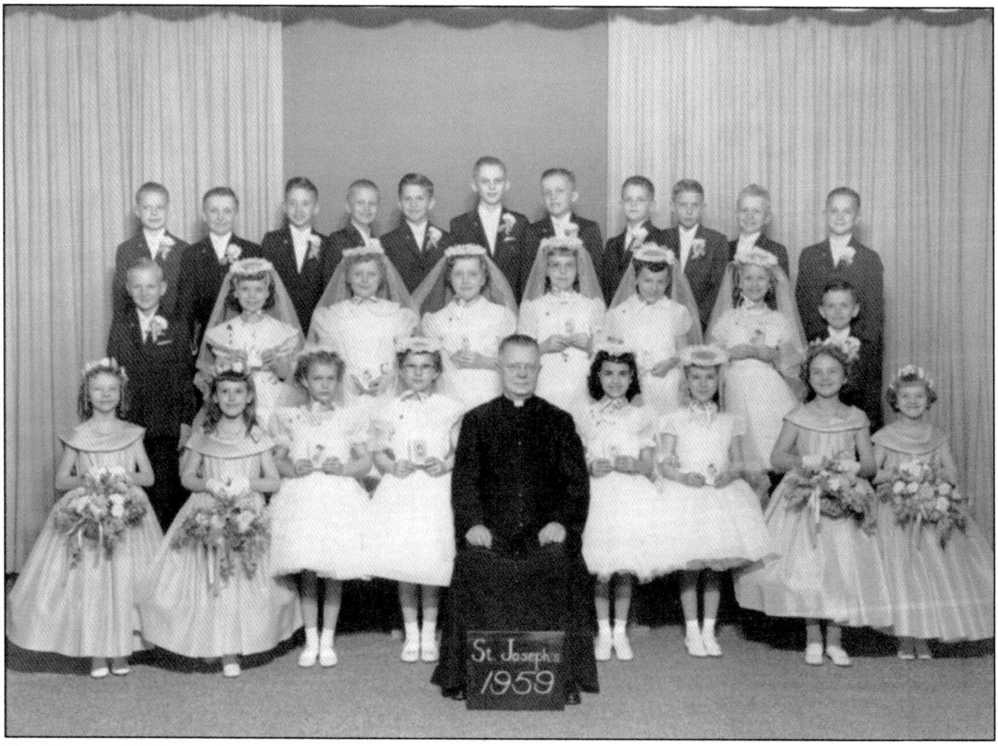

St. Joseph's First Communion. This photograph shows the 1959 First Communion class of St. Joseph's School and Rev. Pius Chesna. The boys and girls are wearing formal attire, as is traditional for this important religious event. The class received its religious instruction from Sr. Rachael Drabnis, who was absent from the photograph. (EML.)

ST. JOSEPH'S SCHOOL. St. Joseph's School was constructed in 1907 but did not open as a parish school until 1925. For 50 years, the Sisters of St. Francis, a Lithuanian order from Pittsburgh, served as faculty. The school contained eight elementary grades, stressing faith, academic achievements, and patriotism, as well as the Lithuanian language, culture, and traditions. (OSF.)

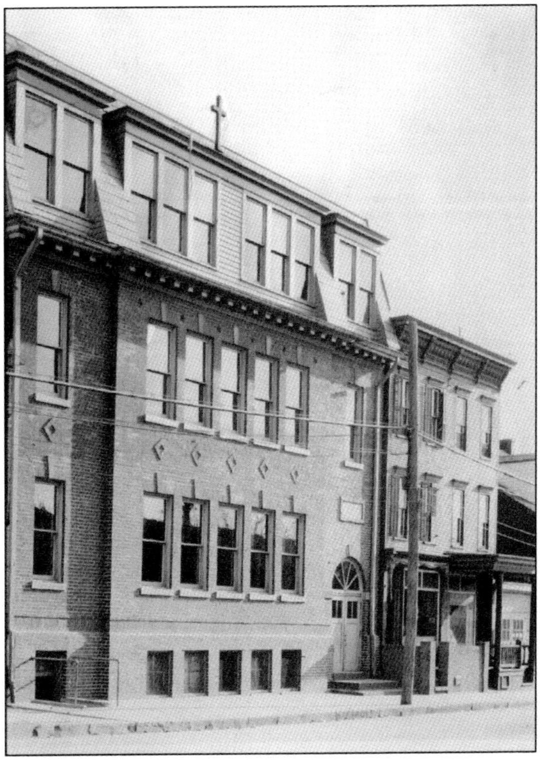

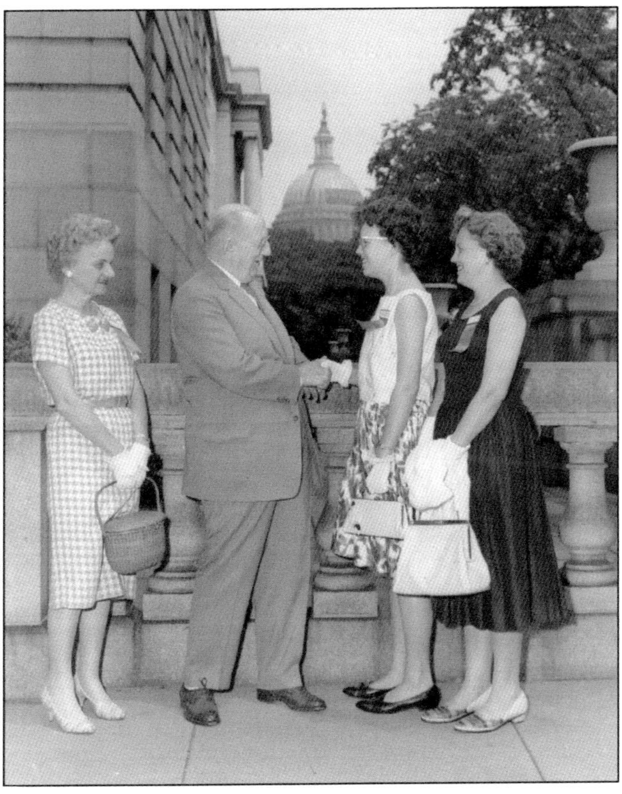

GREETINGS FROM A NEIGHBOR. In 1956, the *Pottsville Republican* newspaper sponsored the annual countywide spelling contest as part of the National Spelling Bee. Three St. Joseph's Elementary School students were county champions and went on to national competition: Anne Marie Gailuschas (1957), Marie Luschas (1960), and Ruth Roman (1963). Standing on the Capitol steps are, from left to right, Marian Sheafer (official escort from newspaper), Congressman Ivor D. Fenton, Marie Luschas, and Mary Luschas, all Mahanoy City natives. (MLO.)

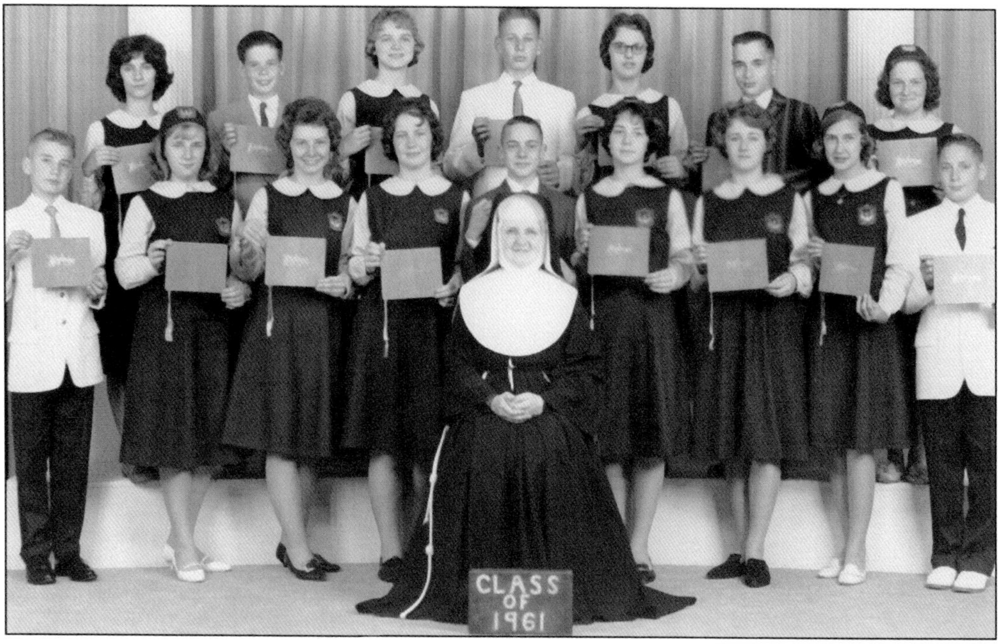

ST. FIDELIS GRADUATES. The St. Fidelis School, Mahanoy City's first parochial school, closed its doors in 1961. Pictured with the last graduating class is Sr. M. Catherine St. Anne. The students are, from left to right, (first row) Joseph Benny, Elizabeth Zilker, Kathryn Selgrath, Kathleen Luck, Paul Williams, Marjorie Fletcher, Mary Lobichusky, Mary Ellen Bias, and Richard Matz; (second row) Patricia Olimpi, John Wargo, Susan Alansky, Thomas Kondisko, Monica Gabuzda, John Klitsch, and Mary Ann Farr. (MF.)

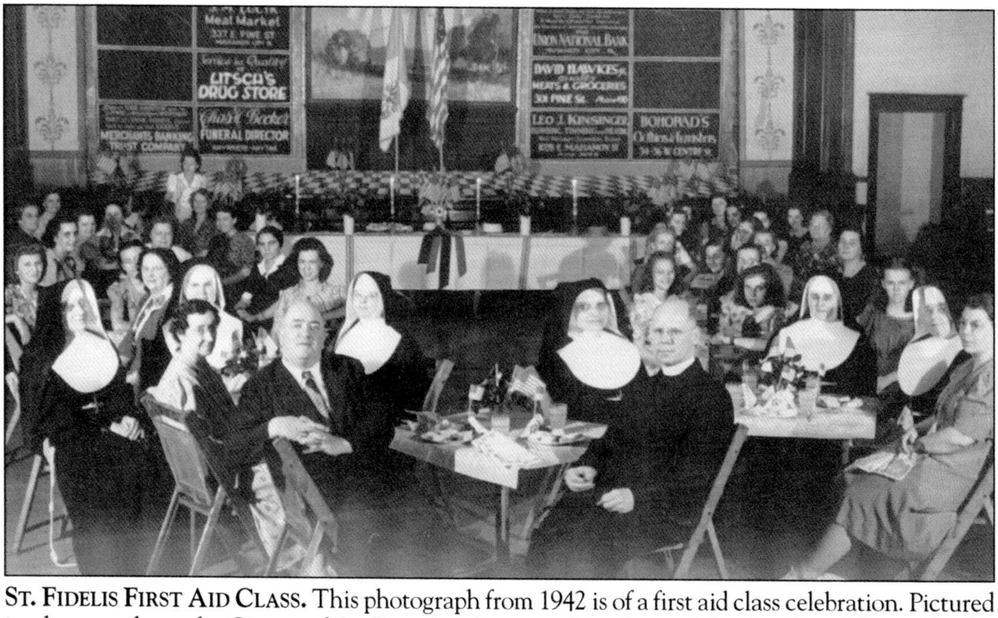

ST. FIDELIS FIRST AID CLASS. This photograph from 1942 is of a first aid class celebration. Pictured in the crowd are the Sisters of St. Francis who served in the parish school and Rev. Charles Frederick Keller, a Mahanoy City native, who was both baptized at St. Fidelis and attended six years of school there. The advertisements on the stage background show some of the businesses in town during the war years. (MHS.)

St. Casimir's Church. This photograph of St. Casimir's Church also shows the rectory to its right and the hall to its left. The Polish school stands proudly on Maple Street. The first Polish immigrants came to the community in 1873, and the first pastor was the Rev. Mathias Turnowski. On January 10, 1927, the church was destroyed by fire, and the present church was built on the same site. (MHS.)

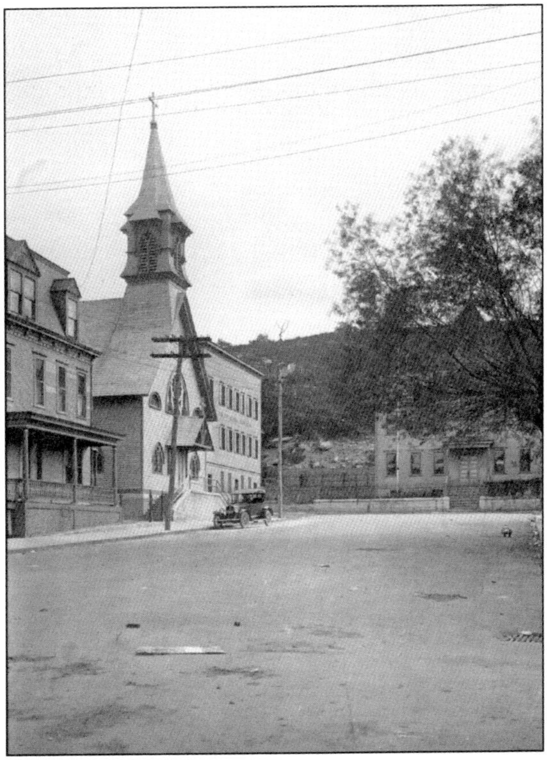

Polish Dancers. Dancing has always been a way to display ethnic background and traditions. These Polish dancers in traditional dress performed at various functions throughout the area, including Polish Day at Lakewood Park. Seen in this 1950s photograph, from left to right, are John Pasieka, three unidentified people, and Stan Matlowski. (MHS.)

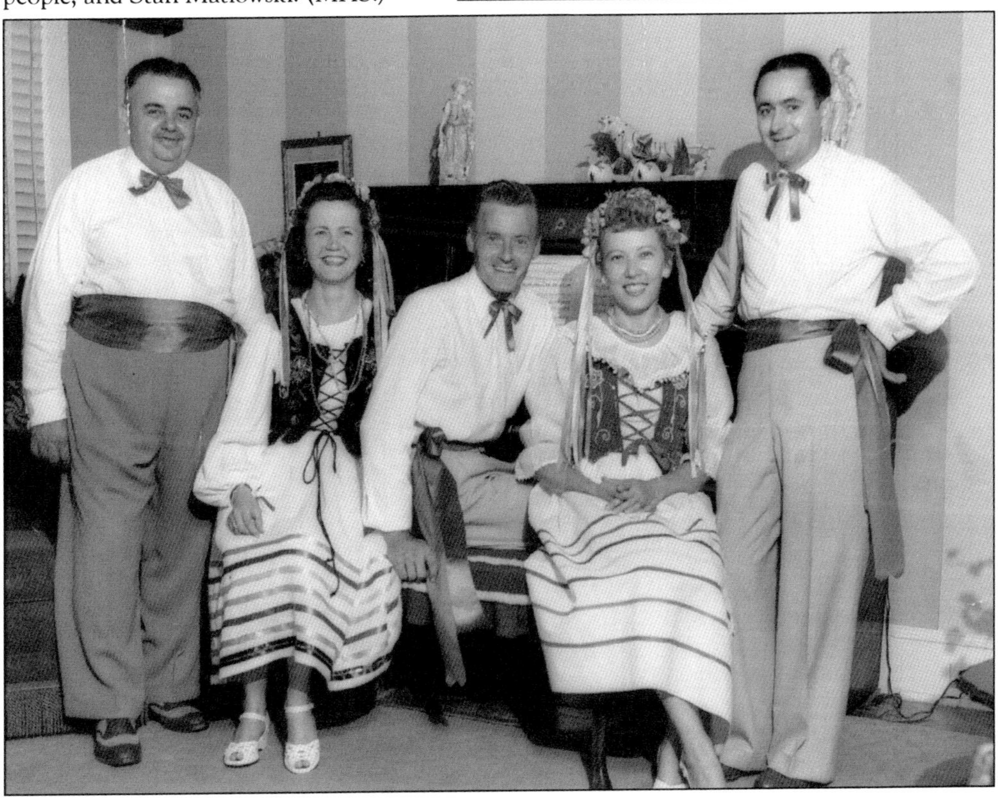

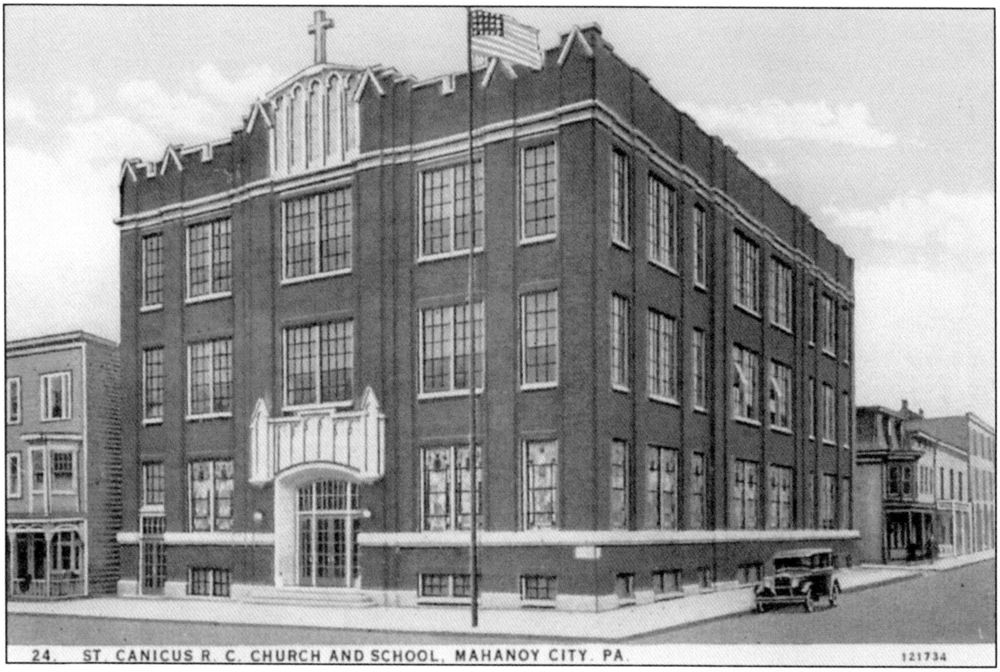

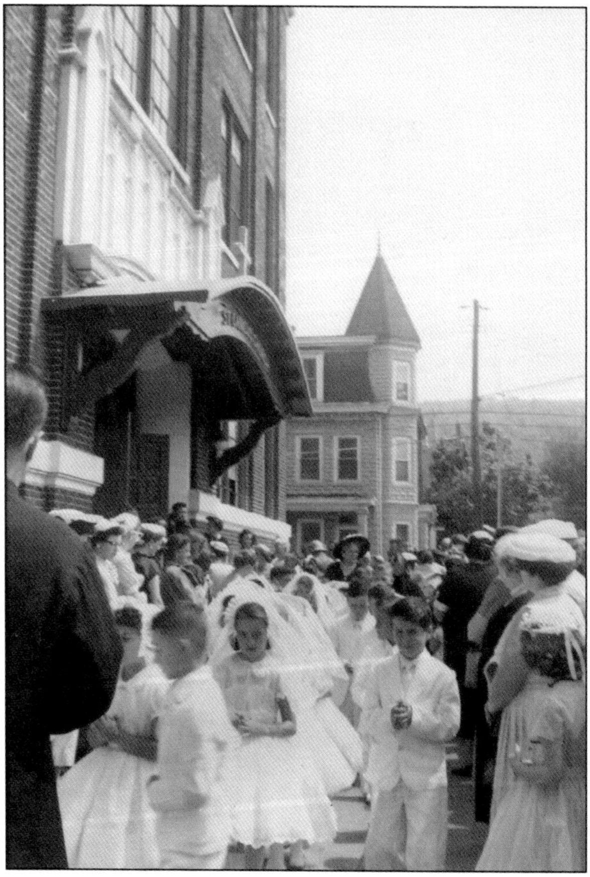

ST. CANICUS CHURCH AND SCHOOL. Throughout 1923 and 1924, St. Canicus Parish, under the leadership of its pastor Rev. A.J. Fleming, conducted a massive fundraising drive to build a new rectory, convent, school, and church. The new church was to replace the old one, which still stood across Catawissa Street and would soon be demolished. The cornerstone for the new church and school was laid on November 16, 1924. (MHS.)

FIRST COMMUNION PROCESSION. Students in the second-grade class of St. Canicus School received First Communion on a warm, sunny day in May 1957. Pictured are the first communicants under the direction of their teacher Mary Rice (at the rear in black hat), as they leave the front entrance to the church and process along Catawissa Street to the front door of St. Canicus School. (PC.)

SACRED HEART CHURCH. The history of Italian people inhabiting Mahanoy City begins in the late 1800s. In the early 1920s, a group of dedicated men under the leadership of Rev. Thomas Ottenni began the task of constructing their first church. The Catholic church was completed and dedicated by Cardinal Dennis Joseph Dougherty on July 4, 1921. Pictured here are brothers Joe (left) and John Nolter, who lived across the street. (BND.)

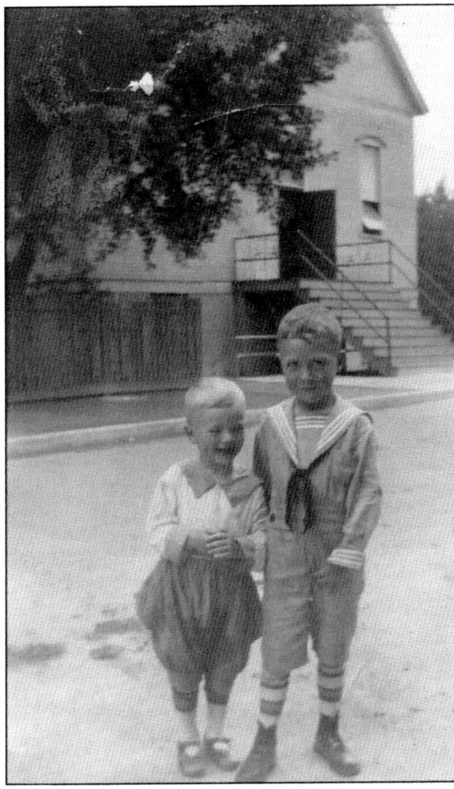

BETH ISRAEL SYNAGOGUE. Members of the Jewish community held their first service in the Beth Israel Synagogue on West Mahanoy Street in 1923. Prior to that, the small congregation held services in the house of Jacob Mayer and in Wild's Hall at 108 West Mahanoy Street. Mahanoy City's Jewish community numbered 50 families. (MHS.)

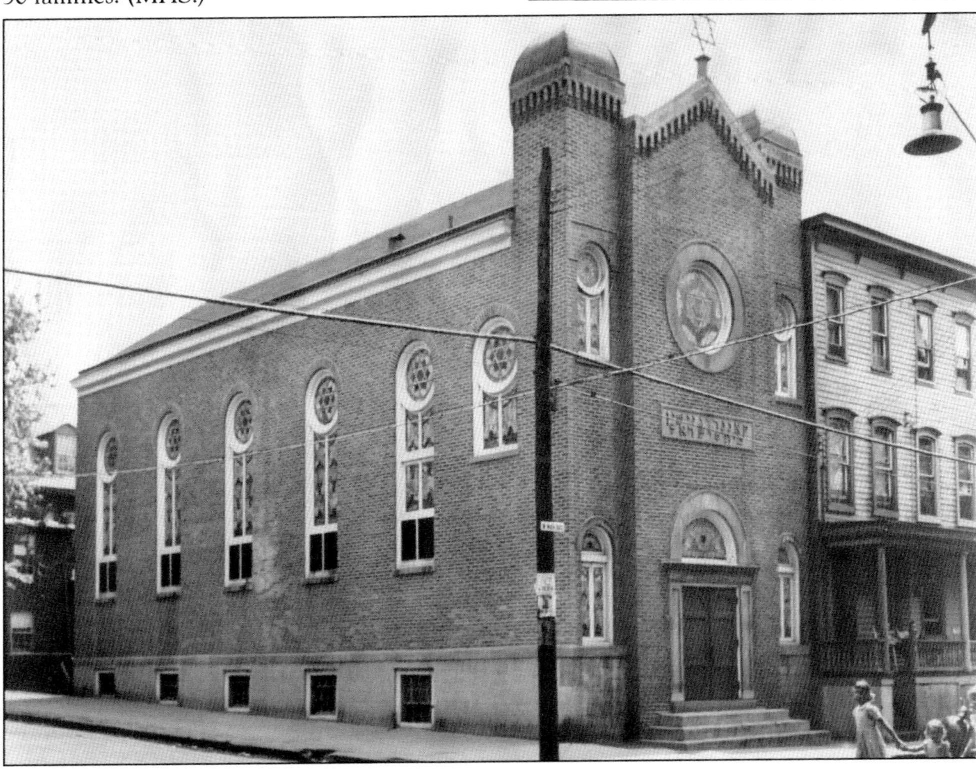

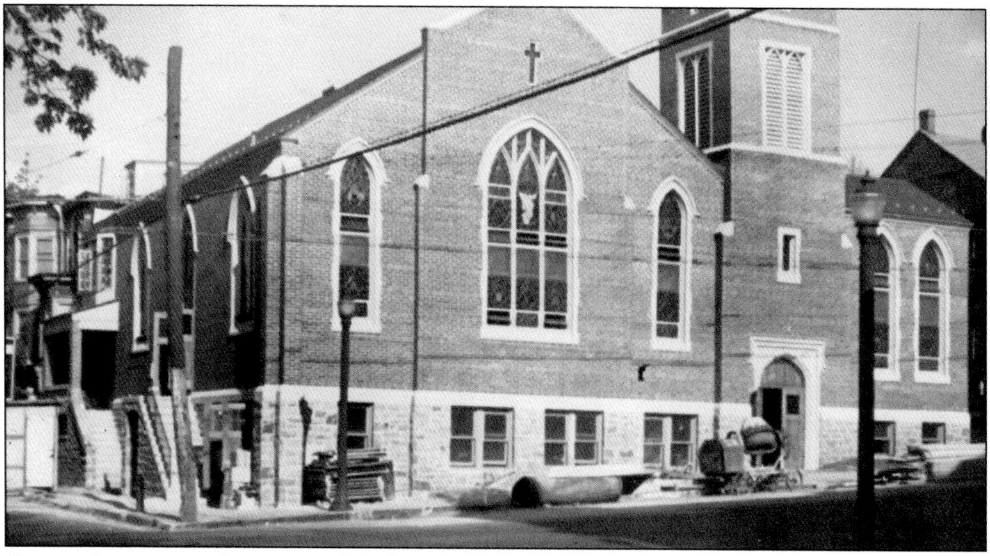

CHRIST LUTHERAN CHURCH. The Christ Lutheran Church is located at the corner of Main and Mahanoy Streets. It was one of the first churches built in Mahanoy City (1864). The church was severely damaged by fire in 1910. This photograph depicts the church during major renovations, which were completed in 1937. (JSK.)

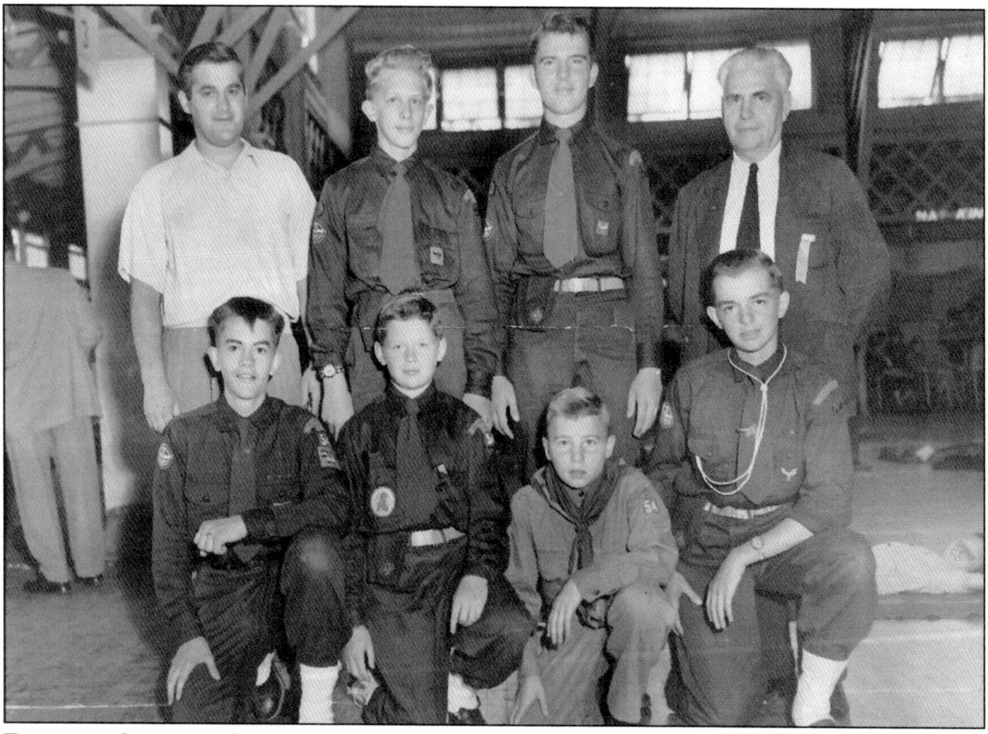

EXPLORER SCOUTS. The Explorer Scouts of Post No. 54 of Christ Lutheran Church participated and won second prize in the Regional First Aid Competition that was held at the Lakewood Ballroom in July 1950. The judges were miners' first aid squads. Pictured, from left to right, are (first row) Mark Kramer, Jack Kubert, John Mark Brown, and Russell Goodman; (second row) Arthur McCann (Scoutmaster), Peter Kapo, Robert Maurer, and Reverend Kramer. (DJK.)

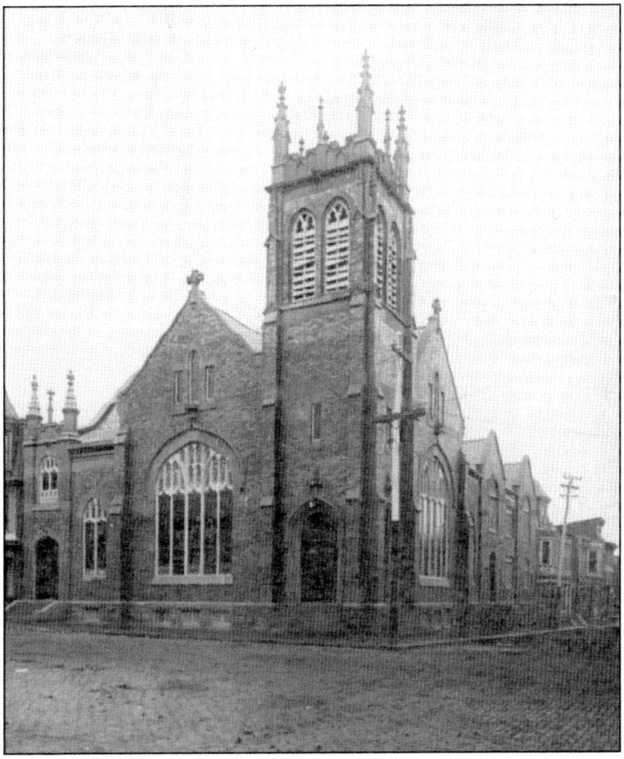

ST. PAUL'S CHURCH AND FIRE. On September 17, 1865, the first St. Paul's Reformed Church was dedicated at the south end of Main Street. In 1906, ground was purchased at Main and Pine Streets, where Thomas J. Koch, a local contractor and member of the congregation, erected a new church. Dedication of the new church took place on November 15, 1908. On January 16, 1948, at 12:35 p.m., fire was discovered in the basement. The blaze quickly spread throughout the auditorium and upper rooms of the church, and soon flames shot through the newly constructed slate roof. Throughout 1948, over $100,000 was raised by the congregation to refurbish the badly damaged town landmark. (Both, SPC.)

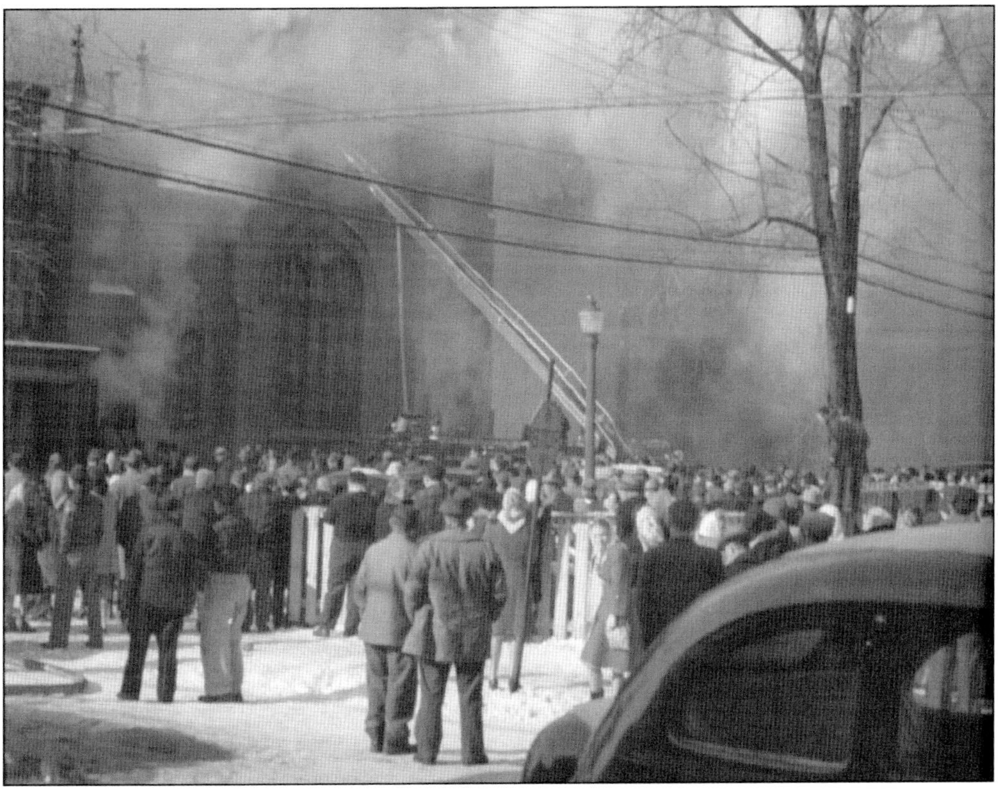

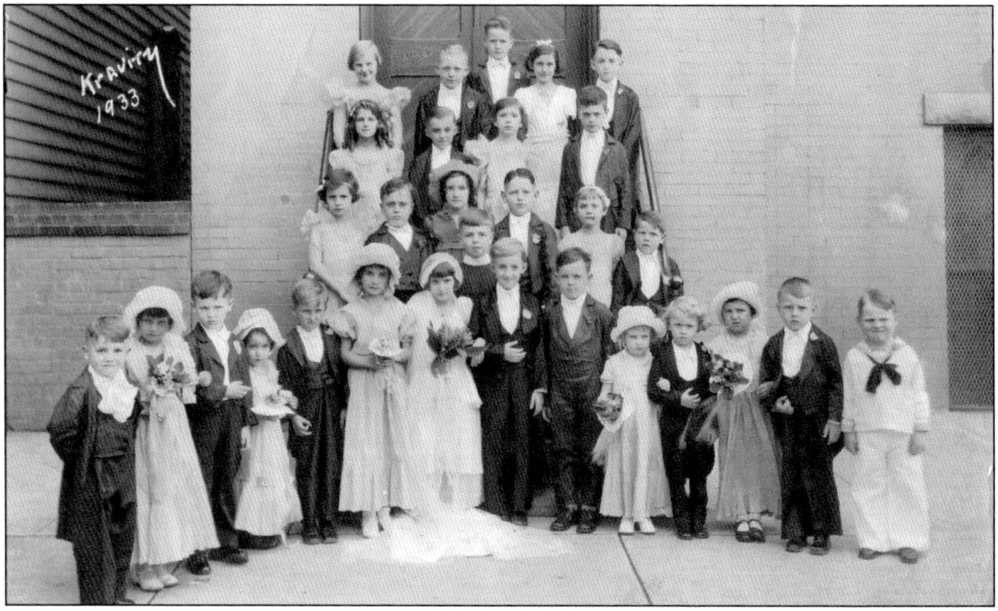

TOM THUMB WEDDING. The Tom Thumb Wedding was often used as a fundraiser for schools or churches, or just for fun. The wedding pictured was performed at the First Congregational (Bethel Welsh) Church at Seventh and Centre Streets. Theresa Fenton was the director of the wedding held in 1933. Each wedding participant was usually a child under 10 years of age and portrayed a member of the wedding party, including the minister. (MHS.)

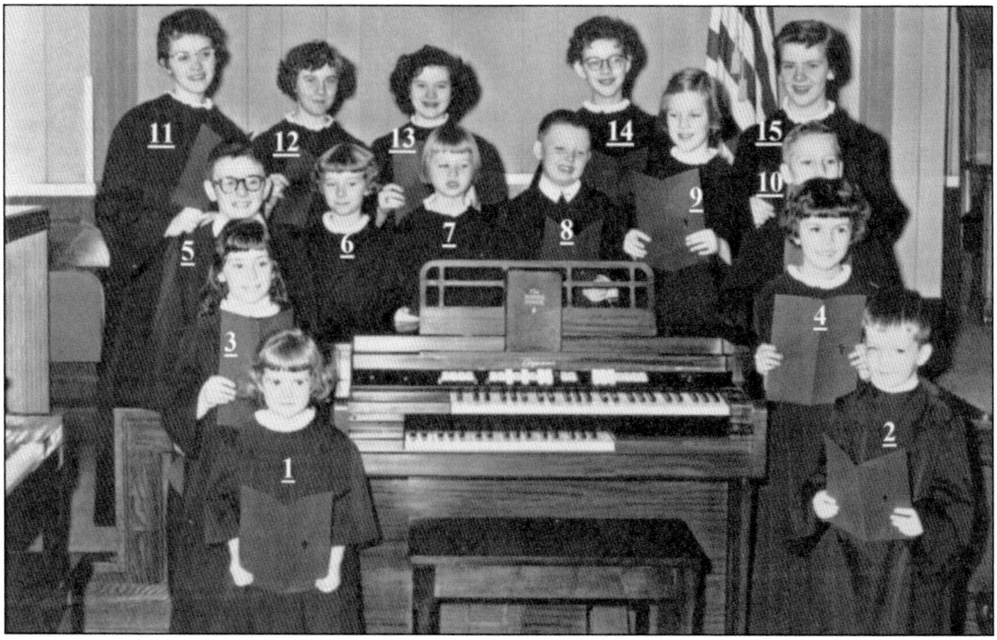

ZION BAPTIST CHOIR. In 1955, the members of the children's choir of the Zion Baptist Church at Fourth and Market Streets gather around the church organ. Pictured, in numerical order, are Beth Phillips, Albert Kieres, Ann Kathy Burnham, Joyce Llewellyn, John Wylie, Elaine Edwards, Betty Ann Kieres, Charles Dean, Donna Kieres, unidentified, Joan Llewellyn, Marylou Powell, Janet Davidson, Doris Llewellyn, and Nancy Powell. (TW.)

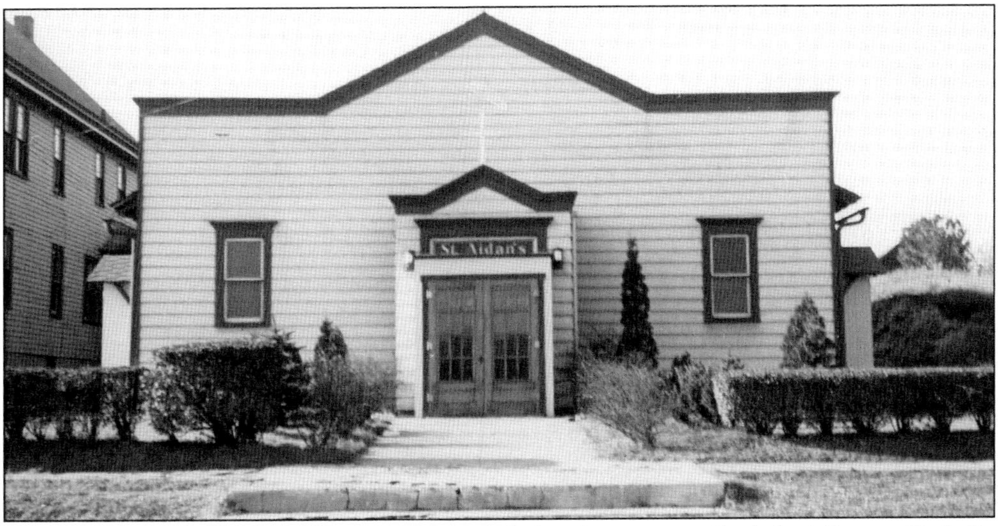

St. Aidan's. Catholics from Ellengowan attended church services at St. Aidan's Roman Catholic Church. The original church was built in 1921 and was destroyed by fire on August 13, 1933. A new church was erected and dedicated on November 17, 1934. Rev. Michael E. Munley served as pastor of St. Aidan's from 1921 to 1939. (JSK.)

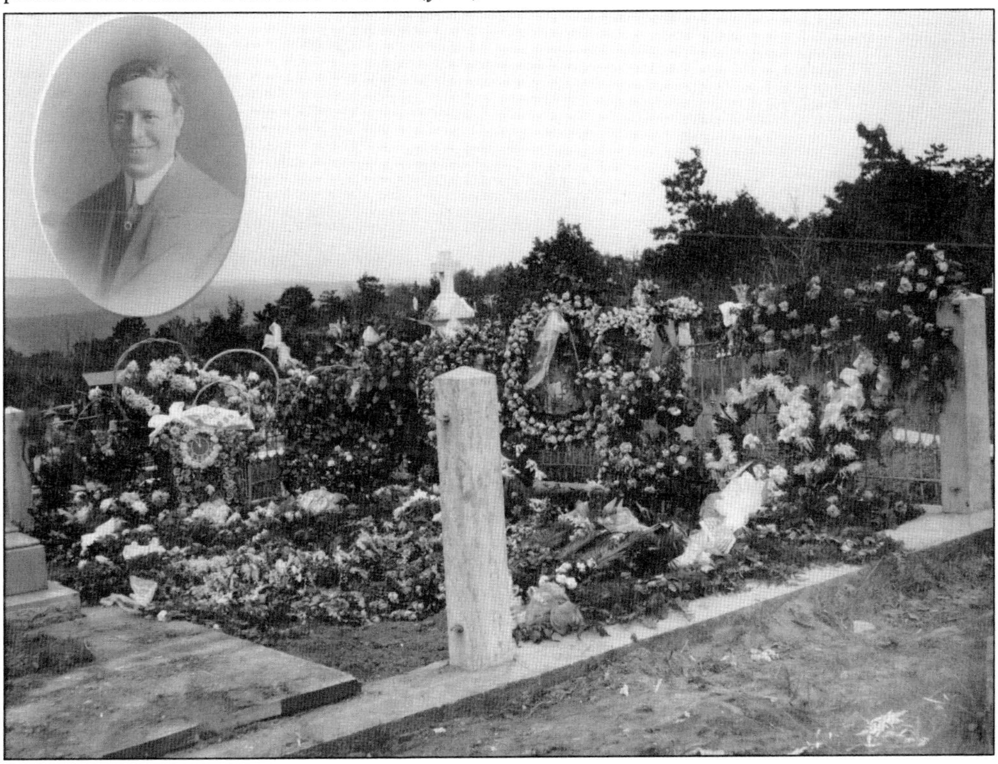

Kaier Funeral. Charles F. Kaier was born in 1879 and died at the age of 42. He, along with his sister, took over the family business following the death of their father. His death brought sadness to the town. According to his obituary, "He was liberal of purse and his kindnesses were as numerous as the sand of the shore." "Champagne Charlie," as he was affectionately known, was loved by all, and his death was mourned by the citizens of the town he so loved. (MEKS.)